Maria Johns 6.95

MUḤAMMAD

Prophet and Statesman

W. MONTGOMERY WATT

KT-415-391

OXFORD UNIVERSITY PRESS
LONDON OXFORD NEW YORK

OXFORD UNIVERSITY PRESS
Oxford London Glasgow
New York Toronto Melbourne Wellington
Nairobi Dar es Salaam Cape Town
Kuala Lumpur Singapore Jakarta Hong Kong Tokyo
Delhi Bombay Calcutta Madras Karachi

© Oxford University Press, 1961
First published by the Clarendon Press, 1961
First issued as an Oxford University Press paperback, 1964
First reprinted as a Galaxy Book, 1974
Library of Congress Catalogue Card Number: 61-2473

printing, last digit: 10

PREFACE

As stated in the Note on Sources, this book is essentially an abridgement of the account of Muḥammad in my volumes *Muḥammad at Mecca* and *Muḥammad at Medina*. Apart from the omission of a mass of detail, the chief difference is that chronological order is more closely followed. I hope this change will enable readers to gain a clearer picture of the man and his achievement.

The system of transliteration is one of the usual ones except that, to avoid unsightly ligatures, an apostrophe is placed between two consonants in certain cases to indicate that they are to be pronounced separately, e.g. Is'ḥāq. Where there is no apostrophe, the pairs *dh*, *gh*, *kh*, *sh*, *th* each represent a single sound. Between two vowels or between a vowel and a consonant the apostrophe still represents the glottal stop reckoned a consonant in Arabic.

I am indebted to Miss Shona Reid for the compilation of the index.

W. MONTGOMERY WATT

The University, Edinburgh
August 1960

CONTENTS

LIST OF MAPS

I

THE GIFTED ORPHAN

Under the blazing sun of a summer day in Syria towards the year 600 a caravan of Arab merchants with loaded camels was moving slowly southwards. They had come from Mecca, some forty days' march to the south, with Arabian frankincense, Indian spices and silks, and other luxury goods. They had sold or bartered these in the markets of Syria, presumably in Damascus ; and now, laden with other wares, they were setting out for home.

Near Bostra on the flank of the Jebel-ed-Druze they passed the cell of a Christian hermit, the monk Baḥīrā. Most of the men in the caravan had frequently passed the cell, but the monk had paid no attention to them. This day, however, he invited them to a feast. They left the youngest member of the party to keep an eye on the camels and the loads, and went to be the monk's guests. The monk was not content, however. He wanted the whole party without exception. There was in his cell a book of ancient lore, handed down to him by previous hermits who had lived there. Aided by the knowledge he had gained from this book he had become supernaturally aware that there was a personage of great importance in this caravan. He had seen a cloud and a tree protecting him from the glaring sun ; and he wanted to know whether this person had also the other signs mentioned in his book which would mark him out as a great prophet.

At the monk's insistence the Arabs agreed that the boy left with the camels should also come to the feast. The monk wanted to know all about him. He questioned the uncle in whose charge the boy was, and then he had a long talk with the boy himself. He looked at the boy's back and saw a mark between his shoulders which he recognized as the seal of prophethood. Now he was sure. As he bade them farewell, he said to the uncle, ' Go back home with your nephew, and keep an eye on him ; if the Jews see him and get to know what I know about him, they will certainly do him harm, for he is going to be a very big man'. The boy was Muḥammad.

This is only a story, of course. It is based on primitive ideas. It is the kind of story one expects to find among people who look upon all writing as akin to magic. Yet it is significant because it expresses a popular Muslim view of Muḥammad. He was a man who had been marked out from his early youth, even from before his birth, by supernatural signs and qualities.

In contrast to this are some European views of Muḥammad. The worst was in medieval times when his name, corrupted to ' Mahound ', was regarded as a name of the devil. This is not so strange as appears at first sight. We have to remember that in the first rush of expansion of the Arabs after Muḥammad's death they wrested from Christian control the lands in which Christianity had been born—Syria and Egypt. From the eighth century onwards the Muslims were attacking Christendom along its southern and south-eastern borders. Was it strange that it should say all the evil possible about this enemy and the enemy leader ? When we consider what was said and believed about the Kaiser and Hitler in recent times, not to mention Napoleon, it is not surprising that medieval Europeans thought that their enemies derived their power from the fountainhead of all evil. Things were not improved when the Western Europeans, who lived simply and roughly, saw the great luxury and refinement of the Muslim rulers of Spain.

Medieval Christian ideas about Islam were little better than war-propaganda. At their worst they were so palpably false that they damaged the Christian cause. Fighting men were encouraged to think that the Muslims were cruel and bestial savages ; and when, in the contacts of war, they found among them not a few ' very parfit gentle knights ' they tended to lose faith in their cause. So from the twelfth century onwards scholars laboured to correct the crudest errors. Yet something of the bitterness of the medieval attitude has continued in Europe till the present day, and the resources of modern scholarship have not eradicated it.

How are we then to attain to a sound view of Muḥammad's personality ? If he was neither a messenger from God nor (as a scholarly English dean called him in 1697) an old lecher, what was he ? It is not an easy question to answer. It involves not only judgements about facts, but also theological and moral judgements. Most of this book will be concerned with presenting the facts on which these ultimate judgements must be based if they are to have any claim to general acceptance.

The Rivalry of the Great Powers

The story of the monk Baḥīrā, though essentially a legend, depicts truly the kind of world in which Muḥammad lived. He was born in Mecca, and spent most of the first fifty years of his life there. The Meccans were traders, and sent caravans to Syria. Muḥammad must have joined such a caravan on at least a few occasions, and may well have travelled sometimes in the company of his uncle. Here is a fact of great significance. Mecca was a little town in the deserts or steppes near the west coast of Arabia, but it was by no means isolated from the great empires of the day. A casual reading of the sources might suggest that Islam grew out of the petty bickerings in this little town ; but a more careful study shows that the whole of Arabia had become entangled in the meshes of the politics of the great powers of the day.

One of these great powers was the Byzantine empire. When the Meccan traders took their goods to Damascus or Gaza, they had entered the Byzantine domains. This empire is also known as the Roman empire or Eastern Roman empire. It was the remnant of the Roman empire of classical times. The western part had been overrun by barbarians in the fifth century and had ceased to exist. But the eastern part, with its capital at Constantinople, had maintained itself and in the sixth century had even won back parts of the western empire from their barbarian rulers. In the year 600 the Byzantine empire included Asia Minor, Syria, Egypt and south-eastern Europe up to the Danube. It also controlled the Mediterranean islands and some parts of Italy, and had a slender hold on the coast of North Africa.

The Byzantine empire had a great rival, the Persian empire under the Sāsānid dynasty. This was ruled from the rich lands of ʻIrāq, and stretched from there to Afghanistan and the river Oxus. These were the two great powers of the day so far as Arabia was concerned. In the second half of the sixth century their rivalry led to a series of wars, with only brief intervals of peace. The climax—if we may anticipate a little—came in the later years of Muḥammad's life. The Persians defeated the Byzantines, conquered Syria and Egypt, and in 614 entered Jerusalem and took away the True Cross. The Byzantine emperor laboured patiently to retrieve the situation. Aided by dynastic quarrels in the Persian royal family, he was completely successful. In 628 the Persians had to sue for peace. They evacuated the Byzantine provinces they had occupied, and in 630 the Holy Rood was restored to Jerusalem.

This long-continued struggle of the giants had its repercussions in Arabia. The Persians had a sphere of influence in the Persian Gulf and along the south coast of Arabia. All the little principalities and sheikhdoms there had become dependent on Persia in one way or another. Often one of the local factions would be maintained in power by Persian support. From at least the fourth century the Persians had some influence in the Yemen. About 570 they sent a seaborne invading force to occupy the region, and subsequently tried to develop trade from the Yemen to 'Irāq by the overland route.

The interest of the Roman world in the trade routes of western Arabia is shown by a large expedition in 24 B.C., but this was unsuccessful, indeed disastrous. About 356 we hear of the Byzantine emperor sending a Christian bishop to the Yemen to counteract Persian influence by spreading Christianity. The Byzantines were so impressed by the importance of this part of Arabia that about 521 the emperor encouraged and approved of an Abyssinian occupation of the Yemen despite the religious and political differences between the Abyssinians and the Byzantines. The latter called their form of Christianity Orthodoxy and regarded the Abyssinians as Monophysite heretics; but they preferred friendly heretics to Persians or Persian protégés. Byzantine policy had a setback when the Abyssinians were driven out by the Persians about 570. A little later—perhaps about 590—we find the Byzantines trying to gain control of Mecca by bringing a pro-Byzantine faction to power there; but the Meccans, though more friendly to the Byzantines than to the Persians, had no desire for this kind of subordination to one of the great powers, and the would-be princeling was forced to flee.

Neither the Persians nor the Byzantines tried to control the Arabian nomads directly. With the available arms and means of communication it was a task beyond the strength even of a great empire. The method both empires employed was to support a prince on the borders between the Desert and the Sown and to see that he was strong enough to prevent the nomads from raiding the settled lands. The

Persians thus supported the princely dynasty of the Lakhmids, some of whose followers were nomads, though they themselves lived in the town of al-Ḥīrah near the Euphrates. Similarly the Byzantines, at least from 529, supported the Ghassānid princes who dominated the region east of the Jordan and of Damascus.

Besides this extension into much of Arabia of political spheres of influence there was a cultural or religious penetration. The Ghassānids had long been Christians, and towards 600 the Lakhmid king became a Christian. With the encouragement of the great powers and also apart from it Christianity had been spreading among the nomadic tribes. By Muḥammad's time there were Christians in many of the tribes, and some tribes or sections of tribes were largely Christian. Just how adequate their grasp of Christianity was, however, it is impossible to say. What is clear is that there was a connexion between religion and politics. Of the forms of Christianity Orthodoxy and Monophysitism were associated with a pro-Byzantine attitude in politics, since the Byzantine emperor was Orthodox while the Ghassānids and the Abyssinians were Monophysites. On the other hand the Nestorian (more correctly East Syrian) form of Christianity had been expelled from the Byzantine empire but had won many adherents in 'Irāq, and was therefore naturally associated with a pro-Persian policy. There was also a certain amount of Judaism in Arabia. Some of the Jews were doubtless men of Hebrew stock who had fled from persecution, but others must have been Arabs who had accepted the Jewish faith. For reasons that are not altogether obvious—perhaps it was the common opposition to pro-Byzantine Christians—the Jews were mostly pro-Persian.

The Meccan merchants may not have had a full understanding of this political environment in which they lived. Yet many of them travelled to Syria and a few to 'Irāq, and they must therefore have been aware of the main features of the situation. They were certainly aware of the rivalry of the Persians and Byzantines, and of the understanding between the latter and the Abyssinians ; and the connexions between religion and politics cannot have escaped their notice. This is an important point to keep in mind in trying to understand the career of Muḥammad.

Life in a Commercial Centre

Muḥammad is said to have been born in the Year of the Elephant. This was the year in which the Abyssinian prince or viceroy of the Yemen marched as far as Mecca with a large army which included an elephant. Scholars have hitherto been inclined to date the Year of the Elephant about 570, but recent discoveries in South Arabia suggest that the Persians overthrew the Abyssinian regime in the Yemen about this date, and the expedition may therefore have been a year or two earlier. Certainly in the Mecca in which Muḥammad grew up the merchants were adjusting themselves to the new situation brought about by the Persian occupation of the Yemen, and were apparently profiting from it.

Muḥammad's father 'Abd-Allāh had died before he was born, and Muḥammad had for guardian his grandfather 'Abd-al-Muṭṭalib, the head of the clan of Hāshim. He doubtless spent most of his early years with his mother, who belonged to another clan ; but, following the custom of many of the Meccan families, she sent him away for a year or two from insalubrious Mecca to the hard but healthy life of the desert, where he was looked after by a wet-nurse from a bedouin tribe. When Muḥammad was six his mother died, and he was directly under the care of his grandfather until he also died two years later. He then passed into the charge of his uncle Abū-Ṭālib, the new head of the clan of Hāshim.

The lot of an orphan in sixth-century Mecca was not a happy one. In the old nomadic way of life it had been understood that the head of a clan or family had a certain responsibility for the weaker members. But at Mecca in a mad scramble for more wealth every man was looking after his own interests and disregarding the responsibilities formerly recognized. Muḥammad's guardians saw that he did not starve to death, but it was difficult for them to do more for him, especially as the fortunes of the clan of Hāshim seem to have been declining at this time. An orphan, with no able-bodied man to give special attention to his interests, had a poor start in a commercial career; and that was really the only career open to him. By travelling to Syria with Abū-Ṭālib Muḥammad gained some experience, but without capital there were few opportunities of using this experience.

Not much is known of Mecca during Muḥammad's youth and early manhood. The available material is fragmentary, and it is difficult to separate the history in it from legend. Yet it gives us a picture of a city whose commerce was expanding and whose power and prestige were growing.

Shortly before 590 two events occurred with which Muḥammad was connected in a minor way. One was a series of battles, known as the Wicked War, and at one or more of these Muḥammad was present accompanying his uncles, though he is not said to have taken an active part in the fighting. This war began with a quarrel between two nomadic chiefs, one of whom was convoying a caravan from 'Irāq through the territory of the other to a great twenty-day fair held annually at 'Ukāẓ, not far from Mecca. The second felt slighted, and ambushed and killed the first. Before long the Meccans and their allies were involved on the side of the aggressor, and the group of tribes known as Hawāzin on the other. After some defeats the Meccans were victorious, and their victory meant an extension of their commercial enterprises at the expense of their rivals. They gained some measure of control over the fair of ‘Ukāẓ and even over the neighbouring town of aṭ-Ṭā’if. The latter had hitherto been a commercial rival of Mecca, and more inclined to work along with the Persians.

This success doubtless had repercussions on the relations of the various groups in Mecca. It was apparently shortly afterwards that one of the chief Meccan merchants refused to pay a debt to a trader from the Yemen who had come to Mecca. There seems to have been some question of principle involved here, though not that of commercial integrity. It was probably a deliberate attempt to stop the Yemenite merchants coming to Mecca and sharing in the trade at the Meccan end ; that is, they were to be restricted to the handling of the trade in the Yemen, while the organization of the caravans was to be entirely in the hands of the Meccans.

There was a vigorous reaction from a certain section of the Meccans. They formed an alliance of clans which we may call the League of the Virtuous, though other explanations of the name are given. Muḥammad was present at the meeting at which the League was formed, and even in later life approved of it. It aimed at upholding commercial integrity, but beyond this it was probably interested in preventing the exclusion of Yemenite merchants from the Meccan market, and the clans which formed it seem to have been those which were themselves incapable of sending caravans to the Yemen, or which had specialized in trade between Mecca and Syria.

It is unfortunate that we do not know more of the League of the Virtuous, since it seems to have played an important part in the life of Mecca, and in large part to have been directed against the men and the policies to which Muḥammad later found himself opposed. In particular his clan of Hāshim came to have a leading role in the League of the

Virtuous. Apart from religious questions the political attitude of Hāshim and the clans in alliance with it would make them tend to support Muḥammad.

Despite the divisions within Mecca revealed by this incident common commercial interests preserved a measure of unity. There was nothing comparable to the bitter fighting which rent asunder the community of Medina in the years before Muḥammad settled there in 622. The Meccans were famous for the quality of *ḥilm*, which is a combination of maturity and self-control, and contrasts with the usual hot-blooded rashness and impetuosity of the Arab. In other words they were able to smother their feelings where these would have harmed their material interests.

In this world of unscrupulous business men, how was a poor orphan, however gifted, to make his way? The one possibility was to find a rich woman to marry him, so that he could, as it were, enter into a business partnership with her. The exact position of women in Mecca at this time is obscure. In the commercial fever and social turmoil of the times, there were at least a few who had managed to win independence and property, so that they were able to trade on their own account. Divorce was frequent in Mecca, and that, together with the numerous chances of early death for the men, brought it about that a woman might have three or four husbands in succession. This must have made it easier for the talented woman to assert her independence.

Muḥammad probably set about looking for something of this sort. There is a list of women whose marriage with Muḥammad was talked about, and among these is one who was probably older than he, and whose marriage with him may have been thought of before he married at all.[1] If this

[1] This was Ḍubā'ah bint-'Āmir; cf. Ibn-Sa'd, viii. 109 f.; F. Wüstenfeld, *Mekka* (Leipzig, 1858), i. 508; etc. Her third husband had been the father of Muḥammad's opponent, Abū-Jahl.

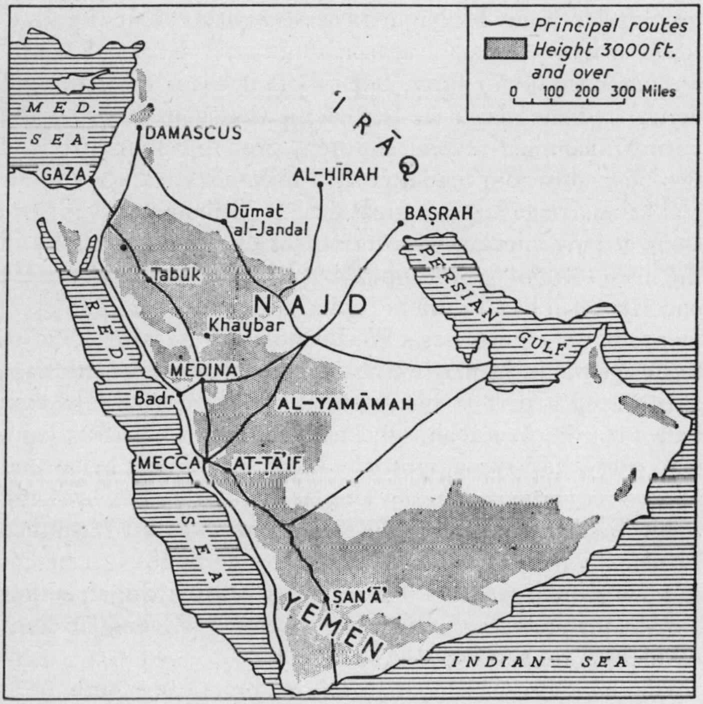

PRE-ISLAMIC ARABIA (SHOWING TRADER ROUTES)

was so, nothing came of it. Instead he married Khadījah, another woman with property and independence, who had already had two husbands. Before marrying him she tested him by sending him as her agent in a caravan to Syria. He accomplished his commission successfully, and she proposed marriage to him. Muḥammad was twenty-five at the time, so the marriage must have been about 595. Khadījah is said to have been about forty, but this is perhaps only a round figure, and she may have been somewhat younger since she bore Muḥammad several children, probably four girls and two boys, of whom the latter died in infancy.

This marriage meant a great deal to Muḥammad. For one thing it gave him an opportunity of exercising his gifts in the main form of activity open to a Meccan—commerce. He and Khadījah had sufficient capital to enable them to engage in profitable enterprises. We do not hear of him going to Syria again, but he may well have done so. But the marriage also played a part in his spiritual development. Khadījah had a cousin, Waraqah, who had become a Christian, and who is said to have supported Muḥammad in his belief that he was receiving revelations similar to those of the Jews and the Christians. It was to Khadījah too that Muḥammad turned when in moments of desolation he doubted his commission to be a prophet. His marriage with Khadījah is thus a great turning-point in his life. So long as Khadījah lived he took no other wives.

Of the fifteen years that follow practically nothing is known. Muḥammad is said to have acquired a reputation for uprightness, and to have been known as 'the trusty one'. He was able to betroth his daughters to some moderately important men, though all were somehow related to himself or to Khadījah. As partner, at least for some enterprises, he had a nephew of Khadījah's second husband.[1] Thus he had

[1] Cf. Wüstenfeld, *Mekka*, i. 471, line 2.

a modestly prosperous career. Yet he felt that his gifts were not being used to the full. He had a talent for administration that would have enabled him to handle the biggest operations then carried out in Mecca, but the great merchants excluded him from their inner circle. His own dissatisfaction made him more aware of the unsatisfactory aspects of life in Mecca. In these ' hidden years ' he must have brooded over such matters. Eventually what had been maturing in the inner depths was brought to light.

II

THE CALL TO PROPHETHOOD

'Rise and Warn'

It is axiomatic that the new religious movement of Islam must somehow or other have risen out of the conditions in Mecca in Muḥammad's time. A new religion cannot come into being without a sufficient motive. In the experience of Muḥammad and his early followers there must have been some need which was satisfied by the practices and doctrines of the embryonic religion. What precisely the unsatisfactory conditions or the needs were is a point on which opposite views may be held. Before discussing it let us see what were the events surrounding the call to prophethood and what was the earliest message of the Qur'ān.

Muḥammad's concern for the troubles of Mecca at this period made him seek solitude. On one of the barren rocky hills in the neighbourhood there was a cave where he sometimes went for several nights at a time to be alone and to pray and meditate. During these solitary vigils he began to have strange experiences. First of all there were vivid dreams or visions. Two in particular stood out as being of special significance. We know something of their content, for they are described in the Qur'ān (53. 1–18 ; cf. 81. 15–25). In the first vision there appeared to him a glorious Being standing erect high up in the sky near the horizon ; then this strong and mighty One moved down towards him until he was only two bow-shots or less from him, and communicated to him a revelation, that is, some passage of the Qur'ān. The second vision was of the same glorious Being, but this time he was beside a lote-tree near a garden and the lote-tree was covered in some strange and wonderful way.

This must be an authentic account of Muḥammad's fundamental experiences. This was how the matter appeared to him when he looked back. It was his supreme justification for thinking that he was 'the messenger of God'. The visions are mentioned in the Qur'ān to confirm the assertion that the passages which Muḥammad is making public and which he claims to be revelations from God, indeed have objective validity, and are not delusions or deliberate inventions. They must also have meant much to Muḥammad himself. When things were not going well with him and he took a pessimistic view of the future, he remembered these visions and renewed his faith in his divine commission.

To begin with he thought that the glorious Being was God Himself. Later he may have thought that it was a superior kind of angel called the Spirit. Finally he identified it with the angel Gabriel. The change of interpretation is probably due to Muḥammad's having become aware of the Jewish teaching that God cannot be seen. The precise interpretation of the visions, however, does not matter; what is important is the support these gave to Muḥammad's belief in himself as a man who had been given a special commission by God.

Stories are also told of how Muḥammad, in moods of despair, would go walking over the rocky hills and think of flinging himself down from a precipitous crag, and how he would then see an angel who reminded him, 'Thou art the Messenger of God'. If there is some truth in these stories, then Muḥammad must have distinguished such appearances from the two visions. The visions were the primary experience in which a divine act made him aware of his prophethood, but the other experiences were at most secondary, perhaps supernaturally caused, but still only rememberings of the primary experience.

In trying to understand the career of Muḥammad this primary experience must never be forgotten. Muḥammad had his moments of gloom, as was not surprising in view of the apparently insuperable obstacles which confronted him. Yet he never altogether lost the conviction that he had been called by God and given a special work to do in his day and generation. This conviction sustained him in the face of opposition, mockery, calumny and persecution ; and when success came to him, it did not turn his head, but only deepened his belief that God who had called him was also working for him in historical events.

Involved in the conception of Muḥammad's special mission was the receiving of ' revelations ' or messages from God. One such message was included in the first vision. For over twenty years, until the end of his life, Muḥammad continued to receive such revelations at frequent intervals. He and his followers memorized them, and they were repeated in the ritual worship or prayer which he introduced. Most of them were probably written down during Muḥammad's lifetime, but writing materials were scarce in Mecca and Medina, and one of the traditional accounts is that after Muḥammad's death one of his secretaries found passages of it written on pieces of paper, stones, palm-leaves, shoulder-blades, ribs and bits of leather. This sounds like an attempt to exaggerate the simplicity of life in Muḥammad's day, and need not be taken too seriously. It seems likely that to a great extent the sūrahs or chapters of the Qur'ān were given their present form by Muḥammad himself ; but the final ' collection ' of all the passages of revelation and the assignment of their present order in the Qur'ān took place shortly after 650 or about twenty years after Muḥammad's death.

The Qur'ān, as we now have it in our hands, either in the original Arabic or in an English translation, is thus the body of the revelations received by Muḥammad. In form God is the speaker, addressing Muḥammad or the Muslims or people in general, and frequently using the ' We ' of majesty.

The earlier passages often contain commands to Muḥammad. For Muslim tradition the Qur'ān is thus the Word or Speech of God, and Muhammad himself must also have regarded it in this way. Moreover he must have been perfectly sincere in this belief. He must have been convinced that he was able to distinguish between his own thoughts and the messages that came to him from 'outside himself'. To carry on in the face of persecution and hostility would have been impossible for him unless he was fully persuaded that God had sent him; and the receiving of revelations was included in his divine mission. Had he known that these revelations were his own ideas, the whole basis would have been cut away from his religious movement.

To say that Muhammad was sincere does not imply that he was correct in his beliefs. A man may be sincere but mistaken. The modern Westerner has no difficulty in showing how Muḥammad may have been mistaken. What seems to a man to come from 'outside himself' may actually come from his unconscious. This, of course, is not a final solution of the problem. It explains the form of Muḥammad's experiences, as it does that of the experiences of the Old Testament prophets who proclaimed, 'Thus saith the Lord, . . .'; but it does not explain the content of these experiences. This is a more complex question, about which I shall say something in the concluding chapter. Without settling it, however, it is possible to take the Qur'ān as a body of ideas and to study the significance of these ideas in their social and historical context.

Muḥammad's belief that the revelations came to him from God would not prevent him rearranging the material and otherwise emending it by omission or addition. There are references in the Qur'ān to God making him forget some passages, and a close study of the text makes it almost certain that words and phrases were added. Such additions, of course, would not be of Muḥammad's composition. Presumably he had some way of ' listening ' for revelations where he thought they were needed, and would only emend the text if he received an emending revelation. Islamic orthodoxy has always recognized that some passages of the Qur'ān containing rules for the Muslims were abrogated by later passages, so that the original rules ceased to be binding. The story of the ' satanic verses ' (in the next chapter) is an instance of the emendation of what had been publicly proclaimed as a revelation.

In the first of the two visions Muḥammad had received a revelation from the glorious Being, but this was not the normal manner in which he received revelations. In many cases it is probable that he simply found the words in his heart (that is, his mind) in some mysterious way, without his imagining that he heard anything. This seems to be what was originally meant by ' revelation ' (*waḥy*). A Qur'ānic passage (42.50), which refers to this, also mentions God speaking to a man ' from behind a veil '. If this applies to Muhammad's own experience, it would imply that he imaginatively heard something without imaginatively seeing anything ; but perhaps the primary reference is to Moses at the burning bush (cf. Qur'ān, 20.9 ff.). The same passage also speaks of God sending a messenger to a man. This could be a description of the first vision as Muhammad latterly interpreted it ; but it has commonly been held by Muslims that many revelations were brought to Muhammad by the angel Gabriel, and it may be that in his closing years the receiving of a revelation was normally accompanied by an imaginative picture of the angel.

On some occasions at least there were physical accompaniments. He would be gripped by a feeling of pain, and in his ears there would be a noise like the reverberation of a bell. Even on a very cold day the bystanders would see great pearls of sweat on his forehead as the revelation descended upon him. Such accounts led some Western critics to suggest that he had epilepsy, but there are no real grounds for such a view. Epilepsy leads to physical and mental degeneration, and there are no signs of that in Muḥammad; on the contrary he was clearly in full possession of his faculties to the very end of his life. These physical accompaniments of religious experiences are of interest to the religious psychologist, but they can never either prove or disprove the truth of the content of the experiences. This is a matter for theology, and will be discussed in the conclusion.

It is worth noticing that, even from the Muslim point of view, according to which the Qur'ān is entirely from God and is unaffected by passing through Muḥammad's consciousness, the Qur'ān is evidence for the outlook of Muḥammad and the Muslims. This is for two reasons. One is that Muhammad accepted the Qur'ān as true. Even if he did not originate the Qur'ānic ideas, they were the ideas that dominated and moulded his thoughts. So it is not inconsistent to speak of these ideas as Muhammad's and yet at the same time to hold that he was sincere in regarding them as coming from outside himself. The second reason is that the Qur'ān was addressed to Arabs of the early seventh century, and must therefore be expressed not merely in the Arabic language, but in the thought-forms of the Arabs, except in so far as it was making criticisms. Thus it should be possible, by studying what is implied in the Qur'ān, to learn something of the intellectual environment of Muhammad and the earliest Muslims.

The passage which is usually accounted the first of the whole Qur'ān to be revealed may be rendered as follows:

> Recite,
> In the Name of thy Lord, who created—
> Created man from a blood-clot.

Recite,
For thy Lord is bountiful,
Who taught by the Pen,
Taught man what he knew not. (96. 1–5)

In this, as in most of the other early passages, the lines are short and rhythmic, closing with rhyme or assonance. (The 'blood-clot' is a reference to the embryo in the womb.)

With this may be compared another passage which is sometimes held to have been the first to be revealed.

O immantled one,
Rise and warn;
Thy Lord magnify,
Thy raiment purify,
The Wrath flee.
Give not to gain more,
For thy Lord endure. (74.1–7)

Later scholars tried to reconcile these two accounts by saying that the former was the first revelation of all, while the second was the first after a long gap. This seems to be no more than a conjecture, however. Circumstances had altered so much by the end of Muḥammad's life that people had forgotten what the first beginnings of Islam were like. It may be that some other passages of the Qur'ān were earlier than either of these two. Perhaps some of the earliest have been omitted from the Qur'ān as we have it.

What may be said is that the two passages quoted have a logical importance and a logical priority. The word translated 'recite' (*iqra'*) is from the same root as 'Qur'ān', and the latter could be rendered as 'recitation'. It apparently comes, however, from the Syriac word *qeryāna*, and that was applied to the scripture lesson which was 'read' or 'recited' by Christians in public worship. Thus the command to 'recite' seems to imply that public worship is to be instituted along the lines of that of the Syriac-speaking Christians, and that instead of their lessons from the Bible this revelation is to be 'recited'. When other revelations came they were also recited, and the word 'Qur'ān' was applied both to the separate revelations and also to the whole collection. Thus the revelation generally accepted as first certainly has a logical priority.

The other revelation quoted is also important because it contains the phrase 'rise and warn'. In the early years Muḥammad defined his prophetic function in its social aspect as being that of a 'warner'. He was to warn the Meccans that they must ultimately face God the Judge on the Last Day. In insisting on this point he was disclaiming any desire to have a position of importance in the political or economic life of Mecca. The command to 'rise and warn' thus logically marks the beginning of his public activity, since warning implies that there are people who have to be warned.

For a man in remote seventh-century Mecca thus to believe that he was called by God to be a prophet was something stupendous. It is not surprising that Muḥammad is reported to have been assailed by fears and doubts. There is evidence for this in the Qur'ān as well as in the narratives of his life, though it is not certain at what period he received the Qur'ānic assurances that God had not forsaken him.

Part of his fear was probably the old Semitic fear of the divine as of something dangerous, of which there are examples in the Old Testament. He may have put on a mantle to protect himself, and this may be the reason for his being described as 'immantled'. It is also possible, however, that the mantle may have been put on to induce revelations. Another form of fear would be fear of madness, that is, according to the Arab ideas of the time, of being possessed by spirits or jinn. Many of the people of Mecca explained his revelations in this way, and he must sometimes have wondered whether they were right.

The chief source of his doubt and bewilderment, however, must have been the stupendous character of the claim to prophethood. Many of the revelations of the later Meccan period, when there was vehement opposition to him in Mecca, explain how this opposition does not disprove his prophetic vocation, since previous prophets regularly met with opposition. In the early days, soon after the first revelation, he is said to have been encouraged to believe in his vocation by his wife Khadījah and, more particularly, by her cousin Waraqah. The latter had become a Christian and was reputed to be familiar with the Bible. At this time the average Christian Arab probably had no direct knowledge of the scriptures. Thus the statements about Waraqah may be true, and yet his knowledge may have been slight. Nevertheless, the testimony of a Christian that the revelations to Muhammad were similar to those formerly received by Moses must have greatly strengthened his belief in his vocation. Such testimony is almost logically necessary.

However obscure and doubtful many of the details are, it is an indisputable fact of history that early in the seventh century Muhammad began preaching in Mecca and claiming to be a prophet. The year 610 may be taken as a rough date for the first revelation, and the year 613 as the beginning of his preaching to the people of Mecca in general.

The Earliest Message of the Qur'ān

For our understanding of Muhammad's career it is important to know what was contained in his preaching in the earliest days. Unfortunately this is not such a simple matter as it might appear, since the Qur'ān is not arranged in chronological order. Various European scholars have tried to determine, at least roughly, the dates of the various chapters or sūrahs and of the separate passages within each sūrah, but there has been much disagreement, especially about the earliest of all. The two most important and widely accepted of these attempts are those of Theodor Nöldeke and Richard Bell, which may be dated 1860 and 1937–39 respectively. As a fairly objective method of discovering the earliest message of the Qur'ān we may look at the contents of those passages which both Nöldeke and Bell regard as early.

A further refinement is possible, however. Already in these early passages there is mention of opposition. Now it would seem to be necessary that before a preacher can stir up opposition he must have been saying something to which his hearers objected. What he preached before the opposition appeared must therefore be the earliest message of all, since it was this message, or part of it, which produced the opposition. If, then, we are to determine, as objectively as possible, the earliest message of the Qur'ān, we shall restrict ourselves to considering passages which fulfill two conditions: (a) they are regarded as early by both Nöldeke and Bell; (b) opposition to Muḥammad is not mentioned or implied in them. The passages which fulfil these two conditions would appear to be the following (according to the older European numbering of Gustav Flügel): 96. 1–8; 74. 1–10; 106; 90. 1–11; 93; 86. 1–10; 80. 1–32 (omitting 23 ?); 87. 1–9, 14 f; 84. 1–12; 88. 17–20; 51. 1–6; 52, parts; 55. The main themes of these passages can be classified under five heads.

(1) *God's goodness and power.* The most prominent theme in the early passages is that of God's goodness and power. This is seen in many natural phenomena, and especially in the formation of human beings. The passage commonly held to be the first revealed speaks of man's creation or formation from a blood-clot or embryo, and there are several other

references to the conception, birth and growth of human beings.

> Of what thing did God create (man) ?
> Of a drop of seed
> He created and proportioned him,
> Then made easy his way (from the womb),
> Then caused him to die and be buried,
> Then, when He pleases, will raise him. (80. 17–22)

> Praise the name of thy Lord, the Most High,
> Who created and fashioned,
> Who proportioned and guided. (87. 1–3)

It is also in all the works of nature, however, that God's power is to be seen.

> Will they not consider the camels, how they are created,
> The heaven, how it is raised,
> The mountains, how they are fixed,
> The earth, how it is spread ? (88.17–20)

Above all His goodness is seen in the provision He makes for the sustenance of His creation.

> We showered the water in showers,
> Then fissured the earth in fissures,
> And cause to grow in it grain,
> And grapes and clover,
> And olives and palms,
> And orchards dense,
> And fruits and pasturage. (80.25–31)

God's goodness is also seen in particular cases. Thus the Quraysh, the people of Mecca, are called on to worship God because ' He provisioned them against famine, And secured them against fear ' (106. 3 f.). Muḥammad himself, presumably in a moment of gloom, is reminded of God's special goodness to him.

Thy Lord has not abandoned thee nor hated.
Better for thee the last than the first.
Thy Lord shall truly give thee and thou shalt be satisfied.
Did He not find thee an orphan and house thee ?
Did He not find thee erring and guide thee ?
Did he not find thee needy and enrich thee ? (93. 3–8)

In all this the darker side of life is not neglected. God causes man to die and be buried. He turns the green herbage of the Arabian spring into the blackened drift left behind by the torrent in the wadi (87. 5). Yet this transitoriness of created existence serves to point the contrast with the permanence of the Creator.

All those upon (earth) pass away;
Eternal is the face of thy Lord in glory and honour.
(55. 26 f.)

It is contrary to our preconceived ideas of Islam that this theme of God's goodness and power should be so prominent in the early passages. The preconceptions rest on the later developments of Islamic dogma, when the fact that God is unique was emphasized and idols were declared to be nothing. In other words Muḥammad's original message was not a criticism of paganism. It appears to be directed to people who already had a vague belief in God, and to aim at making this belief of theirs more precise by calling attention to particular events and natural processes in which God's agency was to be seen.

The vague monotheism accepted by thoughtful Meccans of the day, and presumably at first by Muḥammad, allowed them to regard the Lord of the Ka'bah (the shrine of Mecca) as identical with God. This is shown by the passage in the Qur'ān which calls on the Meccans to ' worship the Lord of this House ' (106. 3). The identification of the Lord of the Ka'bah with God is taken for granted. There is no emphasis on the point, and no special justification was felt to be required. In other words, the Meccans, under Judaeo-Christian influence, must have been moving towards monotheism. This movement may have been facilitated by the fact that the word for 'God' in Arabic is simply 'the god' (*al-lāh* or *al-ilāh*). Greek is similar; *ho theos* may be 'the god' of a particular polytheistic shrine, such as Delphic Apollo, but in the New Testament it is 'God'. Similarly in Arabic there would be an easy transition from 'the god' of the Ka'bah to 'God' the creator of all things.

The monotheism in the thought-world of Mecca was vague, however, in the sense that it was not sharply contrasted with polytheism. This is illustrated by the story of the 'satanic verses'. Muhammad, wearied by the opposition he was encountering in Mecca, was longing for a revelation which would remove the difficulties felt by the leading Meccans. In this mood he received a revelation containing two (or three) verses which permitted intercession to the deities at some of the shrines round Mecca. He subsequently realized that these verses could not have come to him from God and must have been suggested by Satan. At first, however, he was ready to accept them; and this shows that at this stage his monotheism did not exclude some form of prayer to subordinate supernatural beings, who were perhaps regarded as a kind of angel.

What, then, is the point of the Qur'ān's insistence on God's goodness and power? Against whom is it directed? It is directed against the materialism of the Meccan merchants who thought that, because of their wealth and influence, they were little gods, disposing of Meccan commerce and politics as they pleased. But that belongs rather to the third theme.

(2) *The return to God for judgement.* There has been much discussion among European scholars about the part played

by fear of the Last Day (or Day of Judgement) in the origin of Islam. Some have held that such a fear was the main motive which made Muhammad into a prophet and the founder of a religion. Others have tried to deny this, and to assert that the fear of the Last Day was not present in the earliest revelations, but appeared in Muhammad's later years in Mecca. It is sometimes also held that before he spoke of the Last Day, he preached a temporal calamity which would befall unbelievers.

The various matters are all present in the Qur'ān. The dispute is mainly about dating. If the above selection of early passages is sound, then the following assertions may be made. There are to begin with no lurid descriptions of the terrors of the Day of Judgement such as occur in later Meccan passages, and therefore the motive of fear cannot have been so prominent as has sometimes been maintained. In the earliest passages there is no mention of a temporal calamity to punish the unbelievers. Logically, too, this must be secondary, for the unbelievers who are to be punished in this way are people who have received a message from a prophet and have rejected it.

On the other hand, from the very earliest times a belief in the Last Day was present in some form. The words 'rise and warn' (74. 2) imply that Muḥammad is to tell the Meccans about something bad or unpleasant, and this can hardly be anything but the Last Day. Three verses later there are words which are almost certainly to be translated 'the Wrath flee'; the Arabic word *rujz* seems to represent the Syriac *rugza*, 'wrath', which was used in translations of the New Testament in the phrase 'the wrath to come'.[1] In verses attached to the first revelation it is stated that 'to thy Lord is the return' (96. 8). The Judgement is also implied by God's raising of man after his death and burial

[1] Montgomery Watt in *Journal of Semitic Studies*, ii, (1957), 360–65.

(80. 22), and by the verse, 'over every soul is indeed a watcher' (86. 4)

The fullest description of the Last Day in the early passages is that in 84. 1–12.

When the heaven shall be rent
And obey its Lord and be right,
When the earth shall be levelled
And spew those in it and be void
And obey its Lord and be right,
O man, thou art toiling heavily to thy Lord and meeting Him.
Who gets his book in his right
Shall be reckoned with easily
And return to his folk rejoicing ;
Who gets his book behind his back
Shall invoke destruction
And feed a furnace.[1]

The conclusion from all this is that the conception of a resurrection to judgement, followed by reward or punishment, is present from the very beginning, but that fear of punishment does not seem to have been the main driving motive behind the Islamic religion.

(3) *Man's response—gratitude and worship.* Because God is good as well as powerful it is fitting, indeed incumbent, that man should be grateful to Him and worship Him. Gratitude is here the inner recognition that man is dependent on God for his creation and preservation, and that it is better to live than not to live ; worship is the formal expression of this dependence.

The opposite attitude is expressed in various ways. It

[1] The rending of the heavens, and the earth's giving up of those buried in it, are signs of the Last Day. The precise meaning of the words translated 'be right' is obscure. When men meet God for judgement, the righteous are distinguished from the wicked by the way they receive the 'book' with the record of their deeds. The wicked man wishes he would perish utterly rather than burn in Hell.

is noteworthy that the Arabic word for ' unbeliever ', *kāfir*, before it became a technical term among Muslims, could have the meaning of ' ungrateful '. That suggests that the Muslims felt that it was those who were ungrateful towards God who rejected His messenger. A common expression is a word which may be translated ' presumption '. In Arabic it evokes a picture of a torrent, swollen by recent rain, rising high above its usual level, and it then comes to be applied to a man who goes beyond the normal bounds and becomes insolent. In the Qur'ān the underlying thought seems to be of a man who presses on regardless of obstacles, regardless of moral and religious considerations, and full of confidence in his own powers.

Another word that is used in the Qur'ān to express the false attitude towards God means roughly ' pride in wealth ', but it is difficult to bring out its full connotation in English. The basic meaning is ' free from want ', but out of this are developed the distinct ideas of wealth and independence. We think of the hard life of the nomads in the desert, where lack of wealth was lack of camels, which made it necessary sooner or later to ask a wealthier group for help, and so to become dependent on them. In the religious context of the Qur'ān the word comes to mean not only the actual possession of wealth, but also the spiritual attitude which the possession of wealth fostered among the Meccan merchants. Because of their financial strength the leaders among them felt themselves independent of any higher power, and in control of the affairs of the peninsula.

Thus both ' presumption ' and ' pride in wealth ' are bound up with a glorification of the power of the creature, and imply a disregard or denial of the Creator and the absence of a sense of creatureliness. In contrast to this the Qur'ān calls on men to acknowledge their dependence on God by performing acts of worship. It is to Him that their prosperity is due, and it is therefore fitting that they should serve Him.

From the first, though the details are obscure, worship was a distinctive feature of Muḥammad's community. He himself engaged in devotional exercises before the first revelation, and for a time he and his followers observed the practice of night-prayer. It is probable, too, that they sometimes performed their acts of worship in public. After opposition had appeared, public worship was one of the points it attacked, for the Qur'ān (96. 9 f.) has a reference to a Muslim being prevented from worshipping; the man is spoken of as a 'slave', but this may mean either an actual slave or a slave in the sense of a servant of God. In the story of the 'satanic verses', likewise, all the leading men of Mecca are said to have joined with the Muslims in their worship.

In trying to understand this demand that men should worship God, there are two points to be kept in mind. One is that for the people of the Middle East worship is not simply an inner experience. It may contain such an element, but it is first and foremost a public affirmation of the stand one takes. To get something analogous in our lives we must think of things like sporting the party colours on election day. A staunch supporter of the red rosettes could not possibly wear a blue one. It is unthinkable; it would be treachery. When we are dealing with the Middle East we must remember that public religious observances are acts of this kind.

The other point is concerned with the nature of Muslim worship. The Arabic *ṣalāt* is usually rendered 'prayer', and it is best to adhere to this, though 'worship' might be more appropriate. In the standard form of prayer, as it has been practised through the centuries, the main elements are physical acts of standing erect, bowing and prostrating oneself, though there is also an opening exclamation, 'God is very great', and a repetition of the Fātiḥah (the opening chapter of the Qur'ān, which has some of the functions of the Paternoster among Christians). The climax of the prayer is the prostration in which the worshipper kneels on the ground and touches it with his forehead. In this way he acknowledges the might and majesty of God and his own dependence on Him as a slave. This prostration was presumably included in the prayer from the first, and in that case reinforces what has been said about the significance of the demand that men should worship God.

(4) *Man's response to God—generosity.* Belief in God's power and goodness leads not only to gratitude and worship but also to a certain attitude or way of life in practical affairs. In the early passages which we are studying there is little about this, apart from an injunction to Muḥammad himself which was doubtless regarded as applying also to his followers.

> As for the orphan, oppress not,
> As for the beggar, refuse not,
> As for thy Lord's mercy, expatiate. (93. 9–11)

If we cast our net a little wider, however, the result is interesting. The following examples are taken from the sūrahs of Nöldeke's first period which are described as 'early Meccan' or 'Meccan' by Bell. There is mention of opposition in some of them, and so they are probably a little later than the passages in the list above. Nevertheless they show the emphasis at a fairly early period.

What comes out clearly is the importance of the attitude to wealth. One early passage runs:

> Woe to every slanderer, scoffer,
> Who gathers wealth and counts it,
> Thinking wealth will make him immortal. (104. 1 f.)

Another contrasts two ways of life :

As for the giver and God-fearer
Who believes the best,
We shall aid him to ease ;
As for the niggardly and wealth-proud
Who disbelieves the best,
We shall aid him to trouble ;
Nought avails his wealth when he goes down. (92. 5–11)

In another passage (68. 17–33) there is the 'parable of a blighted garden', the story of a group of men who resolved to reap their garden on a certain day without permitting the poor to have any share in it ; when they came to it in the morning they found that the crop had disappeared, and they bemoaned their 'presumption'.

In contrast to this parable there is direct criticism of the faults of the Meccans :

You respect not the orphan,
Urge not to feed the destitute,
Devour the heritage greedily,
Love wealth ardently. (89. 18–21)

It is also asserted that these faults lead to eternal punishment. The man who is condemned on the Last Day is thus described :

He was not believing in God Almighty,
Nor urging to feed the destitute ;
Today he has no friend here. (69. 33–35)

In another passage it is said that hell-fire

Calls him who backs out and withdraws
And amasses and hoards. (70. 17 f.)

Of the pious, on the other hand, it is said :

Little of the night would they slumber,
Betimes would they ask pardon ;
Of their goods was a share for beggar and outcast.
(51. 17–19)

Now this is almost all there is about man's conduct towards his fellow-men not merely in the earliest passages, but also in those not quite so early. Man is not to amass wealth for himself and to become overweening because of his wealth, but is to use his wealth to feed the destitute and is to deal honourably with orphans and other weak persons and not oppress them. These are, of course, good and sound injunctions, but what is surprising and puzzling is that this is the only aspect of conduct that is mentioned (apart from worship of God and belief in Him). There is nothing about respect for life, property, parents and marriage or the avoiding of false witness. These essentials of civilized life are taken for granted. At the moment we simply notice this curious fact, and reserve it for subsequent discussion.

(5) *Muhammad's own vocation.* The theme of Muhammad's own special work in the contemporary situation occurs in the early passages, but is not emphasized. There is the command, already mentioned, to ' rise and warn ' (74. 2) ; and a similar one to ' remind, if the Reminder profits ' (87. 9). To begin with, however, the message was more important than the messenger. The essential thing was the relation of the community or the individual to God. This implied someone to convey the message to the person or persons involved, but the messenger had no function beyond that of conveying the message.

Later, however, the function of the messenger was seen to be more than this. When the Meccans came to be divided into those who opposed him and those who accepted the message, he inevitably became the leader of the latter group. Through his vocation as prophet this little religious movement became linked up with previous religious movements, which had also had their prophets. When he went to Medina, it was his position as a prophet, that is, a leader whose leadership was grounded in religion and not in kinship, that gave the warring factions there the prospect of obtaining peace through his impartiality. All this was in the future ; yet it was implicit from the first in these words ' rise and warn '.

* * *

Before anything is said about the significance of these five themes, it will be helpful to look at the accounts of the growth of the new religious movement up to the time when the first opposition appeared.

The First Muslims

It is universally agreed that the first person to accept Muḥammad's revelations as coming from God and to become a Muslim was his wife Khadījah. This is thoroughly in keeping with the conception of their relationship derived from the more authentic stories. She was an older person than her husband, had some knowledge of public affairs and was friendly with her Christian cousin Waraqah. She was presumably also serious-minded and concerned about the contemporary troubles of Mecca. She would therefore be ready to comfort and support Muḥammad (as she is said to have done) when he began to have his strange experiences ; and her friendship with her cousin would predispose her to accept the experiences as what they purported to be—revelations from God.

There has been a dispute from early times about the identity of the first male Muslim. Some maintained he was 'Alī, Muḥammad's cousin and the son of his uncle Abū-Ṭālib, whom he had taken to live in his house at a time of famine when Abū-Tālib was having difficulty in feeding all his children. This claim may well be true, but it is not of great importance, since at the time 'Alī was admittedly only a boy of nine or ten. Another claimant to the position was also an inmate of Muḥammad's household. This was Zayd ibn-Ḥārithah, a youth of Arab descent, who had been brought to Mecca as a slave and had come into the hands of Khadījah and Muḥammad. They set him free and he was reckoned as their son ; but this was probably due to the automatic working of traditional ideas and not to some formal act of adoption, such as we have nowadays. A great affection sprang up between Muḥammad and Zayd, all the greater no doubt when Muḥammad lost his own sons by Khadījah. The older man clearly trusted the younger, and the younger showed considerable promise—much more so than 'Ali. He would be about thirty when the first revelations came and would therefore be in a position to appreciate them. It is thus probable that he was the first adult male to profess Islam.

The third claimant, even if he was not actually the first male Muslim, was the most significant of the early converts. He was Abū-Bakr, a man only two years younger than Muḥammad, and probably his friend for many years. Like most of the leading Meccans he made a living by commerce, but the fact that his fortune, even before he began to spend it in ransoming Muslim slaves, was only 40,000 dirhams[1] shows that his business was on a small scale. His services to Islam, however, were very great indeed. He is said to have introduced to Muḥammad a group of five men who became the mainstay of the young Islamic state in Muḥammad's closing years and after. Even if this report is in part a reflection of the later importance of these men, it is still probable that they became Muslims at a comparatively early date and that Abū-Bakr was responsible for this. Certainly before Muḥammad left Mecca for Medina Abū-Bakr had

[1] A dirham (from the Greek *drachma*) was the standard silver coin, worth about 10*d.* at pre-1914 values. The standard gold coin was the dīnār (from the Latin *denarius*). Its relation to the dirham varied, but it was usually equivalent to ten or twelve.

established himself as his chief lieutenant and adviser ; and this position he maintained to Muhammad's death, so that he was the obvious choice for successor.

These conversions, whatever their order, occurred in the period of three years between the first revelation and the beginning of the public preaching, of which the approximate dates are 610 to 613. A list has been preserved, containing about fifty names, of those who were early converted to Islam—and by this is probably meant before the public preaching and in the first few months of it. Some biographical details have been preserved about these men and women, and from this material it is possible to form an idea of the kind of men who were attracted to Islam. They fall into three groups.

Firstly, there were a number of young men from the most influential families of the most influential clans. These were closely related to the men who actually wielded power in Mecca and were foremost in opposing Muhammad. At the battle of Badr in 624 between the Muslims and the pagan Meccans there were instances of brothers, or father and son, or uncle and nephew, being on opposite sides. The most notable representative of this class was Khālid ibn-Sa'īd of the clan of Umayyah (or 'Abd-Shams) ; his father Sa'īd, also known as Abū-Uhayhah, was in his later years one of the two or three strongest and richest men in Mecca. For reasons that are not altogether clear Khālid ibn-Sa'īd did not play an important part in the later development of Islam.

Secondly, there were men from other families and clans, still mostly young. This group is not sharply distinguished from the first, but, as we move down the scale to the weaker clans and families, we find among the Muslims men of greater influence within clan and family. At least one man of over sixty made the Hijrah to Medina with Muhammad, but this was exceptional. The majority were under thirty when they became Muslims, and only one or two were over thirty-five.

Thirdly, there were a number of men who were really outside the clan system. Some were foreigners, of Byzantine or Abyssinian origin, who might originally have come to Mecca as slaves. At least one was sufficiently wealthy to attract the cupidity of the pagan Meccans. Usually these men were nominally under clan protection, but the clan was either unwilling or unable to protect them. There were also a number of Arabs from outside Mecca attached to clans as 'confederates'. This sometimes meant that they were dependent on a strong member of a strong clan for protection, and were therefore in an inferior position. But it did not necessarily imply inferiority, since in Muḥammad's time the head of his mother's clan was technically a confederate. On the whole it was only in exceptional cases that the confederates were without adequate clan protection. Mostly they were in the position of members of the weaker families of a clan, and would therefore belong to the second group.

This analysis of the social position of the early Muslims goes far to confirm the statement in an early source that they consisted of 'young men and weak persons'. In confirming the statement, however, it also makes it more precise. In particular it shows that the meaning of 'weak' is 'without good clan protection' and that the bulk of Muḥammad's followers were not 'weak persons' in this sense but 'young men'. It is therefore misleading to say that his followers consisted of the 'plebeians' or 'members of the lower social strata', as is sometimes asserted.

The distinction between patricians and plebeians does not fit Meccan society, or at least that section of it with which we are chiefly concerned. There is a distinction between 'Quraysh of the centre' and 'Quraysh of the outskirts', but nearly all the people who are mentioned in the sources belong to ‘Quraysh of the centre’, whether they are friends or enemies of Muhammad. There were no clear distinctions between noble and ignoble ancestry that could be regarded as parallel to the distinction between Muslim and pagan. All the clans reckoned as ‘Quraysh of the centre’ had a common ancestry.

Such differences as there were between the Meccan clans in Muhammad's time seem to have depended on their relative strength, and that in turn depended largely on their wealth and commercial prosperity. In the half century or so before 610 there had been some ups and downs in the fortunes of the various clans. The premature death of a wise leader or a promising youth might bring about a steep decline in the fortunes of a clan. Then there were the political developments of the period which might affect a man's undertakings in unforeseen ways and produce either disaster or spectacular success. Certain groupings can be traced among the Meccan clans, but these seem to be based mainly on common commercial interests, or on common commercial rivalries. Even the old alliances, like the League of the Virtuous, probably had a basis in common material interests, and, though there was a measure of loyalty to an old alliance, there are several instances of clans changing from one group to another or forming new groups.

By the time Muhammad had begun to preach, the growing commercial prosperity of Mecca may be said to have produced a new topmost stratum of society, namely, the leading, richest and most powerful merchants. These were at the same time the heads of the strongest clans or had great influence within them, and they also seem to have been securing a monopolistic grip on the most lucrative forms of trade. There were rival parties within this stratum, sometimes following the lines of the old clan alliances, and sometimes overstepping them. This stratum was almost solidly opposed to Muhammad.

The simplest way of describing the main body of Muhammad's followers is to say that they were the strata of society immediately below this topmost stratum. Since the majority of the Meccans did not follow him, it may be inferred that they either were deeply involved in the commercial operations of the topmost stratum or else in some other way were its hangers-on. Those who followed Muḥammad would be those with a certain measure of independence from the topmost stratum. The younger brothers and cousins of the chief merchants must have been wealthy young men, while the men from other clans, like Abū-Bakr, were probably struggling to retain such independence as still remained to them. There may even have been a similar purpose in some of the 'weak persons', since they could presumably have obtained full protection by submission to one of the leading merchants. Thus we see that, while the nascent Islamic movement was a movement of 'young men', it was by no means a movement of 'down-and-outs'.

The Influence of Judaism and Christianity

The earliest passages of the Qur'ān show that it stands within the tradition of Judaeo-Christian monotheism with its conceptions of God the Creator, of resurrection and judgement, and of revelation. In later passages the dependence on the Biblical tradition becomes even more marked, for they contain much material from the Old and New Testaments. This introduces some complications into our task of trying to understand why Muhammad began to preach as he did round about the year 610.

First of all, we have to consider the form in which Judaeo-Christian influences may have affected Muhammad. The possibility of his having read the Bible or other Jewish or Christian books may be ruled out. Orthodox Islam holds that Muhammad was unable to read and write; but this assertion is suspect to the modern Western scholar because it is made in order to support the belief that his production of the Qur'ān is miraculous—something no illiterate person could ever have done by himself. On the contrary, it is known that many Meccans were able to read and write, and there is therefore a presumption that an efficient merchant, as Muhammad was, knew something of these arts. The form of the Biblical material in the Qur'ān, however, makes it certain that Muhammad had never read the Bible ; and it is unlikely that he had ever read any other books. Such knowledge, then, as he had of Judaeo-Christian conceptions must have come to him orally.

Here there are various possibilities. He might have met Jews or Christians, and talked about religious matters with them. There were Christian Arabs on the borders of Syria. Christian Arabs or Abyssinians from the Yeman may have come to Mecca to trade or as slaves. Some of the nomadic tribes or clans were Christian, but may still have come to the annual trade fair at Mecca. There were also important Jewish groups settled at Medina and other places. Thus opportunities for conversations certainly existed. Indeed Muhammad is reported to have had some talks with Waraqah, Khadījah's Christian cousin ; and during his lifetime his enemies tried to point to some of his contacts as the source of his revelations.

It is possible that after Muhammad had publicly come forward as a prophet and had claimed to be preaching the same message in essentials as Moses and Jesus, he took advantage of such opportunities as he had in order to increase his factual knowledge of the contents of the Bible by questioning Jews and Christians (though he always maintained that the wording of the Qur'ānic references to Biblical stories came to him by revelation). In the early passages, however, there is nothing to suggest dependence on a single oral source.

Rather it is implied that there is already among the more intellectual Meccans some familiarity with Biblical conceptions. In other words the whole mental environment appears to be permeated by these conceptions. A little before the time of Muhammad there are said to have been some Arabs who set out to discover the true religion, which was assumed to be some form of monotheism ; and the early passages of the Qur'ān assume that the Lord of the Ka'bah, worshipped as such, is identical with God, the creator of all things.

All this tends to show that in certain circles in Mecca men already accepted a vague monotheism. The Qur'ān does not begin by attacking polytheism. The monotheism was vague, however, because there was no specific form of worship attached to it and because it involved no specific renunciation of polytheism. The Qur'ānic account (105) of the deliverance of Mecca from the Abyssinian expedition with the elephant, which interprets it as due to God's intervention, may not be an original Qur'ānic interpretation but may reflect an interpretation current among the more enlightened of the religiously minded Meccans.

The conclusion of this matter is that Muḥammad received his knowledge of Biblical conceptions in general (as distinct from the details of some of the stories) from the intellectual environment of Mecca and not from reading or from the communication of specific individuals. Islam thus in a sense belongs to the Judaeo-Christian tradition because it sprang up in a milieu that was permeated by Biblical ideas.

The question of interest for us thus becomes : Why were certain Biblical ideas of so great interest and importance for Muhammad and the Muslims, and why were others neglected ? This question, however, cannot be answered until some standpoint is adopted with regard to cultural borrowings ; and this is a field of study which is only beginning to be cultivated.

A useful point at which to begin outlining the position here adopted is afforded by Sir Hamilton Gibb's formulation of three 'laws' which govern the influence of one culture upon another.[1] These are:

> (1) . . . cultural influences (. . . genuinely assimilated elements) are always preceded by an already existing activity in the related fields, and . . . it is this existing activity which creates the factor of attraction without which no creative assimilation can take place.
>
> (2) The borrowed elements conduce to the expanding vitality of the borrowing culture only so far as they draw their nourishment from the activities which led to the borrowing in the first place.
>
> (3) A living culture disregards or rejects all elements in other cultures which conflict with its own fundamental values, emotional attitudes, or aesthetic criteria.

One of the interesting things about these three laws is that they make it clear that—to speak in terms of the particular case—the Islamic religion cannot have been produced simply by these extraneous Judaeo-Christian influences, but that there must have been some previous activity in Arab life to which these influences were relevant. What signs are there of a previously existing activity of such a kind that it would explain both the adoption of Biblical ideas and the development of a new religion?

It might be suggested that this previous activity was the attempt to find a satisfying religion. There are the stories about the men who were trying to find the pure worship of God. In all this, however, religion is thought of mainly as personal piety, coupled with certain standards of uprightness

[1] 'The influence of Islamic Culture on Medieval Europe' *Bulletin of the John Rylands Library*, xxxviii. 82–98, esp. 85–87.

in one's private life. Now this is a conception of religion which is widespread at the present time, but impartial study of the past shows that it is exceptional; and the sociologist might go so far as to say that it is due to the peculiar circumstances in which professing Christians have found themselves in the last century or so. Indeed many professing Christians are beginning to share the view that the recent past is exceptional. In most societies, both primitive and advanced, religion is intimately connected with most aspects of social life.

In the particular case of Islam there are further reasons for thinking that the previously existing activity was not the search for a purely personal piety. Why was there the insistence on practising generosity and avoiding niggardliness? This may be regarded as personal morality, but in commending it to other people a man is showing a concern for social welfare. Moreover, the Qur'ān shows concern for orphans and other persons liable to be oppressed by the wealthy. This goes beyond merely personal piety. Similarly, if the Muslims had merely wanted to worship in their own way, it is hard to see why they were persecuted so fiercely. If it is replied they were persecuted because they attacked polytheism and so threatened the economic prosperity of Mecca, this may be countered by saying that the attack on polytheism presupposes a concern for something more than one's own salvation. Finally, why, after going to Medina, did the Meccan Muslims not live quiet secluded upright lives, worshipping God as they pleased? Why did they take the lead in attacking pagan Meccan caravans specially? Thus to say that the previously existing activity was the attempt to discover a satisfying form of personal piety and conduct does not account for all the facts.

The most likely view is that the previous activity was the attempt to find remedies for the social malaise of Mecca. It is not obvious, however, how the religious ideas of the early passages of the Qur'ān correspond to the social conditions of the time. Indeed any discussion of the relation of religious ideas to social conditions raises thorny problems. The following is a brief statement of the general position underlying the present interpretation of the origins of Islam.

(1) The setting of social life is provided by material factors. These include the geography of the country in which the society lives, the techniques known to it, and its relations to neighbouring societies. In a sense these are all economic factors, though the wider term 'material' seems preferable. It is more important to notice that there is a certain inevitability about them. If the society next to yours has a better kind of cereal and a better way of growing it, so that it can feed a larger population more adequately, then (assuming similar geographical conditions) your society will be defeated and perhaps exterminated by this other society unless you adopt their technique and get seed from them. The change of grain and technique is in one sense a matter of choice, but in another sense your society has no alternative, since it cannot contemplate extermination.

(2) In any material environment some social systems will be more suitable than others. In the Arabian steppes in pre-Islamic times the simple family of one man, one woman and several children would not have been a viable unit. To meet the hardships and accidents of such a life there had to be a larger unit, which may be called a clan or tribe. So long as the material environment remained stable the actual tribal system of Arabia, with the associated ideas and code of conduct, worked very well. Perhaps some other system, or some modification of this system, would have worked just as well; but most other systems that we can think of would not have worked so well. This adaptation of a social system to the material environment comes about through a process of trial and error, in which the most suitable social forms survive

while the less suitable die out or are abandoned. Before any form can be tried out it must have occurred to someone that it might be an improvement. Thus the material environment does not necessarily determine the social system. Yet, because in the sense explained above the material environment is inevitable and given, it has a part to play in determining the social system in that it is the measure of the suitability or survival-value of any social system.

(3) Where there is a change in the material environment, which may be as a result of the discovery of a new technique or of altered relations to neighbouring societies, the existing social system will normally cease to be wholly suitable. Social malaise will appear, and people will feel dissatisfied. A process of trial and error will begin in order to discover a social system more suited to the new material environment. What is tried out is always a modification, greater or less, of the existing system.

(4) In a stable society, where the social system is satisfactorily adjusted to the material environment, there is a corresponding set of religious and other ideas. The acceptance of these ideas produces in the members of the society certain conscious attitudes towards the society and its environment, and without these conscious attitudes the life of the society would be much less satisfactory. At many points it is unnecessary for the members of the society to be conscious of what they are doing, but it is usually essential, for example, that they should believe that the life of their society as a whole is meaningful and significant.

(5) Ideas, especially religious ones, have an important part to play in the adjustment of a social system to a change in the material environment. As stated above, the immediate result of material change is social maladjustment, and this involves dissatisfaction and discontent in the members of the society. These, however, are negative, in that they are move-

ments away from something. They do not become effective movements until they have a positively conceived goal, and this, if it is to be consciously accepted by many members of the society, must be expressed in ideas.

(6) The conscious attitudes on which the life of a society is based have deep, and so partly unconscious, roots. Because of this they are firmly held, and it is usually impracticable to eradicate them. To produce new attitudes, equally firmly held, would take several generations. Men therefore try to modify rather than uproot the basic attitudes in making adjustments in a social system. They do so by making slight modifications in the accepted set of ideas and by analysing the new situation in terms of these ideas. This leads to the propounding of a goal which is in accordance with the analysis. Thus, where there is adjustment to a new material situation, religious ideas not merely provide a positive goal but also harness traditional attitudes in the pursuit of this goal. In this way religious ideas provide a focus for a social movement. Without ideas there would not be a movement at all in the strict sense, but only social discontent without a single clear direction.

This, then, in brief outline, is the general position from which I am interpreting the origin of Islam and trying to explain the position in it of Biblical ideas. Scholars have argued about the relative strength of Jewish and Christian influences, but from the present standpoint it is not so important to try to answer this question as to identify the activities among the Arabs into which the Biblical ideas fitted.

The Social Relevance of the New Religious Ideas

In the Mecca in which Muḥammad began to preach an important material change had been taking place. It had begun half a century or more earlier, but its momentum had been gathering during recent years. This change was the growth of trade to such an extent that Mecca had become the centre of far-reaching and complicated mercantile operations.

From ancient times there had been a shrine and sanctuary at Mecca. To this the nomads from many parts of Arabia had come at a particular time each year to make pilgrimage. The months near the date of the pilgrimage were sacred months, and the district round Mecca was sacred territory. In the sacred territory and during the sacred month or months blood-feuds were in abeyance. This made it possible for the nomads to take part in the pilgrimage without danger of being attacked. At the same time it was an opportunity for them to meet traders and to exchange their wares for the products of the settled agricultural lands. In such circumstances, the ownership or custody of the sanctuary could become a source of much profit, as the Meccans early realized.

No agriculture was possible at Mecca because of its rocky character, and it is unlikely that the inhabitants at the time of Muhammad's birth were able to gain their entire livelihood from trade. They must therefore have continued to some extent to live as nomads. The Arabian nomads or bedouin can live almost entirely from their herds of camels. After the winter and spring rains (which can be most erratic) they go to parts of the desert or steppe where a lush vegetation springs up for a month or two. In the sandier parts no wells can be dug, but human beings can obtain all the liquid they need from the camels' milk. When this temporary vegetation disappears the nomads move to other regions where there are wells and a perennial scrub. We hear of a number of wells at Mecca.

The main food of such nomads is camel-milk. Only occasionally do they kill and eat a camel. Those who do not penetrate so far into the waterless steppe also have sheep and goats, but they tend to be militarily weaker than those who rely entirely on camels. In addition the nomads prey on one another and on any settled lands near them, and get fees for protecting settled communities from other nomads and for giving safe convoy to traders' caravans. With these fees and the proceeds of the sale of camels and camel products they are able to buy some cereals and other commodities from agricultural regions.

It is possible that Muḥammad's great-great-great-grandfather (the ancestor of all the leading clans in Mecca) was the first to establish an all-the-year-round settlement at the sanctuary. Through their control of the sanctuary and their share in the trade at the pilgrimage, his descendants prospered, and the settlement grew into a town. For reasons that are not altogether clear their commercial enterprises expanded greatly during the second half of the sixth century, until by about 600 the Meccans had in their hands most of the trade through western Arabia. Besides local products like the frankincense of South Arabia they carried goods from India and Abyssinia to the Mediterranean. They organized regular caravans southwards to the Yemen and northwards to Damascus or Gaza. They also became involved in business enterprises, such as mining, in various areas. Many of the inhabitants of Mecca must now have been gaining their livelihood solely or largely by trade.

Here then was an important material change—from a pastoral, nomadic economy to a mercantile one. The Meccans had retained the attitudes and social institutions appropriate to the life of the nomad in the desert, such as blood-feuds and clan solidarity. Even if they had not been pure nomads for some time, they had remained sufficiently close to the desert to have preserved much of its outlook. The essential situation out of which Islam emerged was the contrast and conflict between the Meccans' nomadic outlook and attitudes and the new material (or economic) environment in which they found themselves.

At the level of social institutions this was seen in the breakdown of the tribe or clan and of the solidarity associated with it. In the hard conditions of the desert men had to join with one another in order to survive. They did so on the basis of kinship in units which may be called tribes or clans. Solidarity, or loyalty to one's kin, was of the utmost importance. If you saw your kinsman in danger, you went to his help without asking whether he was right or wrong.

In Mecca this tribal solidarity was being replaced by individualism. There may have been some beginnings of individualism among the nomads, but at Mecca the trend to individualism was mainly due to the growth of commerce. The great merchants put business interests before everything else, and would join with business associates against their fellow-clansmen. Muḥammad suffered from this in his last year or two at Mecca, because his uncle Abū-Lahab had friends among the great merchants who induced him to turn against his nephew. In a sense a new type of unit was being formed by common business interests, but to this unit few of the older social attitudes were attached, and it was incapable of solving the problems of Meccan society.

The breakdown of the tribe or clan led to the oppression of weaker members of the community such as widows and orphans. The successful merchant thought only of increasing his own power and influence. His wealth might originally have come to him as chief of a clan, but he was no longer prepared to carry out the chief's traditional duty of looking after the poorer members of the clan. This is one of the points which the Qur'ān attacks. The merchants had a slight excuse in that this was a new situation which was not provided for in the traditional social system of the desert. There the chief received a quarter of the booty taken on raids to enable him to perform such a function. But the merchant's fortune was gained largely by his own shrewdness, not derived from raids. The traditional moral code could not be said to oblige him to help the poor.

With this breakdown of the tribe or kinship-group went a breakdown of the public opinion which had helped to enforce the nomadic moral code. Public opinion had been fostered and guided by the poets. Strange as this seems to us, these had fulfilled a function not dissimilar to that of the more responsible press in recent times. They had sung of the honour of their tribe and the dishonour of its enemies, and the satire of a well-known poet was greatly feared. But they had been dependent on patrons, such as the chief of the tribe; and now the most likely patrons were the great merchants. The poet was thus unlikely, even if the application of the traditional moral code had been clear, to criticize his patrons or potential patrons. In other words, wealth gave men some control even over public opinion.

With this breakdown of morality and failure of public opinion was connected a deterioration in the religious life of the Meccans. Half a century before Muḥammad that had already been something of a mixture. There were numerous old cults in Arabia connected with various shrines, of which the shrine at Mecca was one of the more important. Many of the old practices were retained, especially where taboos of time and place made trade easier by suspending blood-feuds. Yet on the whole these cults seem to have had a peripheral place in the lives of the Arabs. The story is told of a chief who went to a god and drew lots with arrows to discover a propitious day to set out to avenge his father; after receiving several discouraging answers he seized the arrows, broke them, and flung them at the idol with the words, 'If it had been your father who had been killed, you wouldn't have answered, No'. Even if this chief was a Christian, the story may be taken as typical of the pagan attitude—some residual practice, but little belief.

The religion by which the Arabs really lived may be called tribal humanism. According to this the meaning of life consists in the manifestation of human excellences, that is, all the qualities that go to make up the Arab ideal of manliness or fortitude. The bearer of these excellences is the tribe rather than the individual. If they are seen in the life of an individual, that is because he is a member of a tribe which is characterized by them. The thought that is uppermost in the mind of the individual is that of the honour of the tribe. Life is meaningful for him when it is honourable, and anything involving dishonour and disgrace is to be avoided at all costs.

This religion of tribal humanism had no cult forms in the strict sense, but the practice of reciting poetry had a function similar to that of a religious cult. One of the chief tasks of the poet was to recount the glorious deeds of his fellow-tribesmen (not excluding himself) in which the excellences of the tribe were manifested. At times he would turn and criticize other tribes and show the dishonour attaching to them. These were known respectively as 'boasting' and 'satire', and both contributed to strengthening the tribesman's belief in the meaningfulness of life as a member of his tribe. It was primarily this tribal humanism which constituted the religion by which men lived.

In the Mecca of Muḥammad's prime, however, men had ceased to think much of honour. Honour was bound up with the traditional morality of the desert, and much of that had become irrelevant in Mecca. Instead they thought of increasing their own wealth and power. It was in super-eminent wealth that they found the meaning of life. Wealth gave a man power. To increase one's wealth and power became the great aim in life, not only for the few very rich men in Mecca, but also for the great majority of the population who aped them from a distance. Those who had some success in achieving this aim became filled with a ' pride in wealth ' that soon merged into ' presumption ' or an exaggerated conception of the capacity of man. This appears to have been the religious position at Mecca when Muḥammad began to preach.

If we now turn to the earlier passages of the Qur'ān which were studied above, we see that the points made there are relevant to the contemporary situation. When these points are looked at in the light of the situation, it is at once seen that the Qur'ān places the chief emphasis on the religious aspect of the troubles of Mecca. It calls on men to acknowledge the power and goodness of God their Creator and to worship Him. Thereby they will be denying the omnipotence and omnicompetence of the wealthy man. The Qur'ān thus provides a corrective—a more satisfying alternative—to the ' presumption ' and ' pride in wealth ' which it regards as the root of the materialistic humanism underlying the social malaise of the times.

Another way of stating this would be to say that the Qur'ān looks upon a man's life as meaningful when it is upright. The supreme aim in life is not to live honourably or to increase one's wealth and power, but to live uprightly so as to attain to the joys of Paradise. The man who pursues wealth unscrupulously, whom the Qur'ān characterizes as ' niggardly ', will forfeit Paradise. In making niggardliness a serious sin, the Qur'ān is showing the incompatibility between the worship of God and the worship of wealth and power.

This basic religious idea leads to some practical conclusions. Men are to be generous with their wealth, especially towards orphans and destitute persons. They are not to oppress the weaker members of their families and clans. By injunctions of this kind the Qur'ān is recalling men to some of the virtues of nomadic life which social changes, such as the breakdown of the kinship-group and the growth of individualism, were causing them to neglect. Moreover this recall to virtue is given a powerful sanction in the doctrine of the Last Day when God will reward or punish men according to their deeds. It is made clear that this is something which happens to the individual; his kinsmen are unable to help him or to influence God's judgement. Fear of punishment and hope of reward is thus a sanction which is effective in an individualistic society. The attempt is being made to revive some of the virtues of the desert in this new urban society.

The emphasis on generosity and consideration for the weak, and the absence of any special mention of respect for life, property and marriage—those fundamentals of all social life—is in keeping with the Meccan situation as it has been described. The malaise arose from the unscrupulous pursuit of wealth, and the Qur'ān tries to curb this. That explains its concentration on what appear to be supererogatory duties. The more fundamental matters—the prevention of murder, theft and adultery, especially the first of these—were still adequately dealt with by traditional custom, and in particular the blood-feud. The avenging of death or injury was still felt to be a binding obligation on the kinship-group, though the strict *lex talionis* of an eye for an eye and a life for a life was often modified by the growing practice of accepting a hundred camels as the equivalent of the life of an adult male.

The early passages of the Qur'ān cannot be said to have any clear conception of a new social unit. Men are treated as individuals, but as individuals within a unit; and it is assumed that this unit is a tribe or like a tribe. It is to a tribe or similar unit that a prophet is sent. Yet even this very simple idea contains the germs of future developments. It connects the social unit with religion. Later, when many of the Meccans rejected Muḥammad, a distinction had to be drawn between those members of the tribe who accepted Muḥammad and those who did not. In this way there was formed the idea of the community of those who accepted the prophet, and this community had its basis in religion and not in kinship. When the Qur'ān was first revealed, however, that development lay far in the future.

After this study of the relation of the Qur'ān to its social context, the three laws of cultural influence may be looked at again. The first asserted the necessity of a previously existing activity, and this activity may be best described as working for the social well-being of Mecca as a whole. Muḥammad had a concern about this before he began to receive revelations, and it continued throughout his life. Something of the same concern was also found in many members of his community after his death, and it was doubtless this concern, and the intellectual and practical activities which proceeded from it, which nourished the Biblical conceptions and enabled them to contribute to the expanding vitality of Islamic culture. This is in accordance with the second law of cultural influence.

The third law of cultural influence—the avoidance by a living culture of elements conflicting with ' its own fundamental values, emotional attitudes or aesthetic criteria '—is illustrated in the limited range of Biblical conceptions found in the Qur'ān. There is nothing of the teaching of the writing prophets of the Old Testament, and practically nothing of the teaching of the New Testament. Such Biblical elements are relevant to a society with many centuries of settled life behind it. Meccan and Medinan society had only recently exchanged nomadism for a settled life, and it is not surprising that they most fully appreciated those parts of the Bible which reflect the experience of the Israelites in the period shortly after they had made a similar change.

Islam thus stands within the Biblical or Judaeo-Christian tradition, or, to use a phrase which avoids any suggestion of inferiority, within the Abrahamic tradition. Yet it is no mere pale reflection of the older religions. It arises from the fusion of Biblical elements with an independent movement of the human spirit arising from local conditions. All these aspects must be retained in explaining the birth of Islam.

III

OPPOSITION AND REJECTION

In the house of al-Arqam

In later times Muslims would boast that an ancestor had become a Muslim ' while Muḥammad was in the house of al-Arqam '. This was their way of referring to a period near the beginning of Muḥammad's career as a preacher. There was an earlier period, but only a handful of the elite could claim to be descended from men who embraced Islam ' before Muḥammad entered the house of al-Arqam '.

While the sources, with the exception of the earliest of all, are agreed in recognizing the importance of this period, almost everything else about it is in obscurity and uncertainty. Muḥammad may have gone to this house before he began his public preaching, or he may not have gone to it until after his public preaching had roused opposition. His reason for going to it depends on the date assigned. The sources mention reasons, but these are presumably no more than the conjectures, more or less intelligent, of the writers. Not only in this matter, but in all the points that will be dealt with in this chapter, there is this obscurity and uncertainty. It would be tedious to mention all the possibilities. The present account will neglect all but the chief probabilities, and, in the attempt to make a coherent story, will give these a more dogmatic form than is strictly justified. With this warning to the reader let us proceed.

Al-Arqam was a young man of from twenty to twenty-five. He belonged to the clan of Makhzūm, the clan of some of the wealthiest and most powerful men in Mecca. He must have been wealthy himself, since he owned a large house near the centre of Mecca. Little is known with certainty about his father, who may have been dead. Certainly al-Arqam was able to act with greater freedom than many other young Meccans of his age.

It was perhaps in 614 that Muḥammad made al-Arqam's house the centre of his preaching activities. He is said to have had thirty-nine followers at the time. He did not live in the house, but spent most of the day there. His followers came to him in it, and were taught the Qur'ān and otherwise instructed. Together the Muslims performed their distinctive acts of worship, which culminated in the prostration, the touching of the ground with one's forehead in acknowledgement of the might and majesty of God. It was also possible for enquirers to come to Muḥammad in this house and talk about their difficulties and about all the troubles of the people of Mecca.

It is not clear whether there was any vigorous opposition to Muḥammad when he first went to this house. Possibly such opposition as there was amounted to no more than verbal criticisms. In other words, if there was opposition, it was not yet absolute opposition. There was still the chance that a reconciliation might be brought about.

During the period while the house of al-Arqam was Muḥammad's centre there did develop bitter opposition to his movement, led by some of the most powerful of the Meccan merchants. One of the bitterest was a man of his own age, Abū-Jahl of the clan of Makhzūm. Happening to meet Muḥammad one day, Abū-Jahl taunted and insulted him most offensively, but Muḥammad made no reply. The incident was observed by a freedwoman who reported it to Muḥammad's uncle Ḥamzah as he returned from hunting, and he at once went to find Abū-Jahl in the Ka'bah and struck him with his bow. Ḥamzah had hitherto been a pagan, but he now openly professed Islam. 'Will you insult my nephew now that I am a follower of his religion?' he asked. Some of Abū-Jahl's kinsmen made to help him, but, perhaps because he respected the great physical strength of Ḥamzah, he admitted that he had gone too far in insulting Muḥammad, and the incident was closed. Ḥamzah, however, was a notable accession to the strength of the Muslims.

What made a man like Abū-Jahl so furious with Muḥammad? It has sometimes been suggested that the Meccan merchants were afraid that the new religion would lead to a disregard of the sacredness of Mecca and so to the reduction or destruction of its trade. There are strong reasons, however, for rejecting this view. The Qur'ān, by speaking of God as 'the Lord of this House' (the Ka'bah), accepts the Meccan sanctuary as a sanctuary of God where true worship may be offered. There are stories which imply that from the first the Muslims sometimes performed their acts of worship in the Ka'bah. There was no attempt to change the sacral character of Mecca and its shrine. The later Qur'ānic attacks on idols seem to have been aimed at stopping the cults at other shrines but not at the Ka'bah. So far as the latter was concerned, these attacks only made it necessary to remove certain idols. In all this there was nothing to justify the belief that Muḥammad's religion would seriously reduce the trade of Mecca.

The only way in which the Qur'ān seems to have threatened trade was by its attacks on shrines outside Mecca (to be described presently). One of the shrines attacked was that of aṭ-Ṭā'if, the smaller commercial centre higher up in the mountains, where some of the rich Meccans now had estates. The closing of the shrine there would affect adversely those who were concerned with its trade, and it is therefore significant that a very early letter of which the text has been preserved attributes the beginning of active opposition to Muḥammad to some Meccans with property in aṭ-Ṭā'if.

This reason, however, presumably counted with only some of the Meccans. There is no record of Abū-Jahl having any connexion with aṭ-Ṭā'if. There must, then, have been some more general reason for his hostility. Reflection brings to light two points. Firstly, the influential merchants of Mecca must have seen that the Qur'ān, in criticizing false attitudes to wealth, was attacking their whole way of life. It must have stung them to be called 'niggardly' and to have it asserted that they were not the lords of creation they thought they were. They would also realize that such teaching would gain Muḥammad wide support if he became politically minded. He might even be able to revive the League of the Virtuous against Makhzūm and its associated clans.

In the second place, there was a threat to the political power and influence of the rich merchants in Muḥammad's very claim to receive revelations from God. Deep in the Arab heart was the feeling that the best man to rule a tribe or clan was the man who was outstanding in wisdom, prudence and judgement. If they accepted Muḥammad's claim, would they not also have to admit in the long run that he was the man best fitted to direct all the affairs of Mecca? The threat was not an immediate one, but a future one. It was in ten or twenty years' time that Muḥammad's power might be irresistible. The men of the previous generation, who still dominated Meccan affairs in the years round about 613, were not so bitterly opposed to Muḥammad as his contemporary Abū-Jahl. The latter would be more conscious of the threat to his own power in the future.

Just what part the remnants of pagan religion played in making Abū-Jahl an opponent of Muḥammad it is difficult to say. Superficially one would say that paganism was a very weak motive in his case. The only thing that gives one pause is that the Qur'ān in later Meccan passages vehemently attacks idolatry. If practical belief in the old religion was very slight, why does the Qur'ān spend so much time attacking it? It will be easier to answer this question if we first describe an incident which probably occurred while Muḥammad was in the house of al-Arqam.

THE INCIDENT OF THE 'SATANIC VERSES'

The accounts of this incident vary somewhat in details, so that it will be best to begin with the points that are certain and then go on to those that are dubious rather than select one complete account of the incident and then criticize parts of it.

At some time Muḥammad must have recited as part of the Qur'ān certain verses which apparently permitted intercession to idols. One version of these is :

Did you consider al-Lāt and al-'Uzzā
And al-Manāt, the third, the other ?
Those are the swans exalted ;
Their intercession is expected ;
Their likes are not neglected.[1]

Then, some time later, he received another revelation cancelling the last three verses here and substituting others for them :

Did you consider al-Lāt and al-'Uzzā
And al-Manāt, the third, the other ?
For you males and for Him females ?
That would be unfair sharing.
They are but names you and your fathers named ; God revealed no authority for them ; they[2] follow only opinion and their souls' fancies, though from their Lord there has come to them guidance. (53. 19–23)

Both the first version and the second version were proclaimed publicly, and the explanation given for the change was that

[1] The word translated 'swans exalted' is obscure ; it presumably means that these are a kind of angelic being.
[2] The worshippers of the idols.

Satan had managed to slip in the false verses of the first version without Muḥammad noticing it.

This is a strange and surprising story. The prophet of the most uncompromisingly monotheistic religion seems to be authorizing polytheism. Indeed the story is so strange that it must be true in essentials. It is unthinkable that anyone should have invented such a story and persuaded the vast body of Muslims to accept it. Moreover there is a passage in the Qur'ān which describes something of this kind.

> Before thee God sent no messenger nor prophet but, while he desired, Satan interposed (something) towards his desire; but God abrogates what Satan interposes; then God perfects His verses; God is knowing, wise. (22.51).

This verse has been variously interpreted, but the above translation accords with one of the traditional interpretations. Muḥammad, it is said, had been greatly desiring to find some way of making it easier for the rich merchants to accept Islam, and, when Satan made the interpolation, he failed to notice it for what it was. Whether we accept this story or not—and there may be some truth in it—it seems certain that Muḥammad recited the 'satanic verses' as part of the Qur'ān and later recited another revelation abrogating them.

One of the most interesting aspects of the incident is the lights it throws on Muḥammad's outlook at the time. Even though he sincerely believed that these verses came to him from outside himself, yet he cannot at first have found anything in them that he regarded as contrary to the religion he was preaching. Does this mean that he was a polytheist at this time? There are several reasons for thinking that the answer to this ought to be, No.

To begin with, it is to be noticed that the three goddesses were specially connected with three shrines within a day or two's journey of Mecca. Al-Lāt was the goddess of the neighbouring town of aṭ-Ṭā'if, al-'Uzzā had a shrine between that town and Mecca, and there was a shrine of Manāt between Mecca and Medina. It seems likely, then, that for Muḥammad's hearers the primary effect of the 'satanic verses' would be to legitimize worship at these three shrines. Similarly the primary effect of abrogation would be to stop such worship. In accordance with this the three shrines were destroyed when Islam became dominant in the region.

How did Muḥammad justify this from a monotheistic standpoint? It must be remembered that the outlook of Muḥammad's more enlightened contemporaries has been described as a *vague* monotheism. The word 'goddesses' should not be allowed to suggest deities of the kind met in Greek mythology. Semitic religion does not produce such stories about its divinities. It has a less personal conception of the divine. A deity is a power specially connected with certain places and certain objects. The names in point mean respectively the Goddess, the Almighty and the Disposer (who allots men their several fates). Perhaps the enlightened Arabs of the day regarded these as various manifestations of a single divine power, just as in later times the Muslims spoke of the ninety-nine names of God. The phrase 'daughters of God' would not be incompatible with this, for the Arabs used the ideas of daughterhood, fatherhood and sonship to express abstract relations. In this way Muḥammad and his followers could have regarded the 'satanic verses' as authorizing the worship of the divine at the three shrines indicated, and yet not have felt that they were compromising their monotheism.

There is also a simpler explanation of the Muslims' failure to recognize the contradiction immediately. The Christians and Jews believed in the existence of a secondary and subordinate kind of supernatural being, angels, and the belief in angels, jinn and other supernatural beings was still a living part of the traditional Arab outlook. Muḥammad and his followers may have looked on the 'goddesses' as beings of this kind. Indeed there are passages in the Qur'ān which show that they must have regarded the matter in this light, at least for a time; this was after the attack on their worship had begun.

For a full understanding of the incidents—the publication of the 'satanic verses' and their abrogation—it is necessary to look at them in a wide context. For a time, even if Muḥammad's professed followers were not numerous, there was general approval of his mission. The ordinary people were sympathetic. Only the rich merchants were hesitant. Yet even they were not completely hostile. They saw the danger that through his contact with a supernatural source of wisdom Muḥammad would become the man in Mecca whose views were most authoritative. They also thought that one of the roots of Muḥammad's activity was his dissatisfaction with his own position in Mecca. In particular they saw that he was excluded from the inner circle of rich merchants who monopolized the enterprises in which the big profits were to be made. It therefore occurred to them that they might reduce this dangerous activity of Muḥammad's by admitting him into this inner circle, letting him share in their profits and power, and intermarrying with his family. They were inveterate bargainers, however, and in return for these concessions to Muḥammad they wanted him to compromise in some way with the older cults.

How was it that the intellectual struggle between Muḥammad and the rich merchants of Mecca came to be focused on the question of idols? The history of religious polemics shows that the points on which controversy centres are not always the fundamental ones, but those where the issue is sufficiently clear for both sides to feel that 'here is ground on which it is worth while doing battle'. The rich merchants had first been attacked in the Qur'ān because of their 'pride in wealth' and selfish use of their position of privilege (though their mercantile activities doubtless raised the standard of living in Mecca as a whole). They could not defend their conduct, however, in any way that would clearly justify them in the eyes of the ordinary people. A few of them, however, were threatened with loss of trade at the shrines outside Mecca; and the others probably realized that their chief hope of gaining the support of the ordinary people was to present themselves as defenders of the old religion. This was why they asked Muḥammad to say something good of their goddesses or otherwise to acknowledge some validity in the old rites.

At first Muḥammad was not prepared to make a stand on this issue. Whatever they had asked for, they received, in the 'satanic verses', an acknowledgement of the efficacy of worship at the three shrines. How long it was before the verses were abrogated we cannot tell. The earliest and best sources give no indication of the interval before the abrogation. It may have been weeks or months. It was presumably long enough for Muḥammad to realize that the compromise was not going to work. Perhaps he felt that the priests of the goddesses were going to be regarded as his equals. Perhaps he felt that his new religious movement was going to be indistinguishable from paganism. He therefore accepted and proclaimed the new revelations which came to him. One was the abrogation of the 'satanic verses' and their replacement by others. Another, traditionally the reply he was to give to invitations to compromise, was the following:

O unbelievers,
I worship not what you worship,
You are not worshipping what I worship,
I am not worshipping what you worship,
You are not worshipping what I worship;
To you your religion, to me my religion. (109)

The abrogation of the ' satanic verses ' meant that the cults at the three shrines were no longer recognized in any way. This marked the beginning of vigorous opposition to Muḥammad. It was begun by some Meccans with property at aṭ-Ṭā'if, doubtless incensed by this disregard for the shrine and goddess there and by the consequent loss of trade. Others of the rich merchants joined in. Here was a suitable issue on which to press home the attack on Muḥammad. Perhaps, too, changing circumstances made them feel insecure, and in their insecurity they naturally tended to look to the old religion, for which, while their success was unbroken, they had had little use.

For Muḥammad also this seemed to be a good issue on which to join battle. Perhaps as time went on he learnt something more of the attitude of Jews and Christians to idols, and saw that he would be in line with them in having no truck with idolatry. The passage just quoted emphasized the distinct character of his religion and its difference from paganism. Other passages made use of the phrase ' daughters of God ' in an *argumentum ad hominen*—the Arabs set great store by sons and prided themselves on having them ; was it fair that God should have only daughters ? It was insisted that idols are powerless to benefit or harm a man, and cannot intercede for him on the Last Day ; indeed, on the Last Day the idols would disown their worshippers.

So the struggle went on. In the intellectual sphere the issue between Muḥammad and the rich merchants of Mecca became that of many gods or God (who is one). Islam came to regard ' the giving of partners to God ' as one of the greatest sins. This attitude is crystallized in the first half of the confession of faith which runs : There is no god but God.

The Migration to Abyssinia

The beginning of the migration to Abyssinia is probably

to be dated after the abrogation of the 'satanic verses', perhaps about 615. The main facts are tolerably clear, but the underlying reasons are obscure. The widely accepted form of the story among Muslims is contradicted by many details in the early sources. This is that there were two distinct migrations, since the first party returned on hearing of the 'satanic verses' and Muḥammad's reconciliation with his opponents, but found on their return that the verses were abrogated and the struggle more bitter. The following is an attempt at a critical reconstruction of the events.

The universally admitted facts are that a number of Muslims went to Abyssinia round about the year 615. Of these some came back to Mecca and went to Medina along with Muḥammad in 622, while others remained in Abyssinia until 628. Lists have been preserved of the names of those who went to Abyssinia, of those who returned to Mecca, and of those in the party which returned straight to Medina in 628. There are some discrepancies in the lists, chiefly with regard to minor figures; but there is no doubt about the main participants. The most important questions to be answered are why these Muslims went to Abyssinia, and then why some of them remained there so long. A subordinate question is whether the initiative for this migration was the emigrants' or Muḥammad's.

The difficulties of the situation after the abrogation of the 'satanic verses' must have had something to do with the migration. Once the policy of opposition to Muḥammad had been adopted, the leading merchants and their friends took steps to make life difficult for their younger brothers and cousins and other members of their families and clans who were attracted to Muḥammad's movement. In one way this would be mild as a form of persecution, but in other ways it might be extremely annoying and frustrating. It mostly happened within the family or clan. There was no public judicial or police system in Mecca. Crime was kept in check by the blood-feud. That meant that each clan exacted vengeance or a blood-wit for injuries to its members. Apart from this it was dangerous for a man to lay hands on a member of another clan. Within the clan, however, the power of the leading men was almost unquestioned. If the head of a family decreed that measures were to be taken against a Muslim member of it, they would be taken, and no redress would be possible, since there would be no one to whom appeal could be made.

There is a curious fact which supports the assertion of the sources that it was the difficulty of the situation which made the Muslims go elsewhere. Apart from two exceptions all the early Muslims known to us who remained in Mecca belonged to a group of five clans, headed by Muḥammad's clan of Hāshim. This group seems to be a reconstituted form of the League of the Virtuous. It is thus the focus of the opposition to the leading merchants with their monopolistic practices. Muḥammad had attacked the attitudes of the merchants, and they were now open enemies of his movement; so it was natural for their political opponents to be friendly with Muḥammad. This did not mean that they all became Muslims, but it did mean that this group of clans did not create difficulties for those of their members who followed Muḥammad. This would explain the clan attachment of the Muslims remaining in Mecca. They were those who were not being persecuted in any way by their clans. Of the two belonging to the 'persecuting' clans one was a blind poet, and so in a special position. The other was al-Arqam, who, with a large house of his own, was sufficiently independent not to be troubled by hostile measures.

Thus there are strong grounds for thinking that these Muslims went to Abyssinia to avoid persecution. This can hardly be the whole reason for the migration, however, since it does not account for some of them staying on in Abyssinia after the Muslims had settled in Medina and were no longer troubled by persecutors. Are there any other reasons for the migration?

Perhaps they went to engage in trade. This was the normal occupation of Meccans, and there must have been opportunities in Abyssinia. Those who made a living there until 628 presumably did so by trading. Apart from the migration of the Muslims there were trade relations between Mecca and Abyssinia. So we may be certain that the Muslims traded. But this could not have been the sole reason for leaving Mecca. To run away from their native town in this way at a critical stage in the development of Muḥammad's reform movement, was tantamount to a betrayal of the movement; and the chief among the emigrants were not weak men of this type.

Could it be, then, that Muḥammad had some plan in mind, and sent them to Abyssinia in furtherance of it? Could he have been hoping for military help which would enable him to seize control of Mecca? The Abyssinians would have been glad of an excuse for attempting to regain their lost dominion in Arabia; and their allies, the Byzantines, who had just been seriously defeated by the Persians, would have approved of a diversion on the Persian flank. Or was Muḥammad hoping to make Abyssinia a base for attacking Meccan trade, as he later made Medina? Or was he attempting to develop an alternative trade route from the south to the Byzantine empire, out of reach of Meccan diplomacy, and so to break the monopoly of the Meccan merchants? Whatever may have been in Muḥammad's mind, the Meccans were apparently alarmed, and immediately sent two men to the Negus of Abyssinia and from him, it is said, demanded the repatriation of the emigrants. This was not granted, but the envoys may nevertheless have thwarted Muḥammad's ultimate aims by informing the Nẹgus of his weakness in Mecca.

There remains another important possibility. Was there a sharp division of opinion within the nascent Islamic movement? Of the Muslims who remained in Mecca the most important after Muḥammad was Abū-Bakr; but he came from a very weak clan. Were the Muslims from the influential clans ready to follow him and to support the policies he favoured? There are slight traces of rivalry between his group and that led by 'Uthmān ibn-Maẓ'ūn. The latter belonged to the same generation as Muḥammad and Abū-Bakr. Before Muḥammad began to preach he had lived a disciplined life and avoided wine. At some later time he wanted to introduce into Islam an ascetic note of which Muḥammad disapproved. With his puritan zeal and influential connexions he would find distasteful a policy advocated and supported by uninfluential men like Abū-Bakr. There were others, too, who for various reasons may have been averse to the policies adopted by Muḥammad with Abū-Bakr's support. What these policies were we cannot say. Perhaps the emigrants disliked some attitude adopted by Muḥammad to meet the growing vehemence of the opposition, such as an increased involvement in politics.

If there is some truth in this last suggestion, then it would be in keeping with what we know of Muḥammad's character that he should quickly have become aware of the incipient schism and have taken steps to heal it. This might have been by suggesting the journey to Abyssinia in furtherance of some plan to promote the interests of Islam. Since the ostensible aims were not attained, it is not surprising that we are not told the precise nature of the plan. 'Uthmān ibn-Maẓ'ūn and the others who returned to Mecca before 622 were soon reconciled with Muḥammad and Abū-Bakr, and this shows that the break can never have been complete.

The migration to Abyssinia, then, however certain as a fact, remains obscure in its interpretation. It gives a tantalizing glimpse of conditions in the little band of Muslims after the appearance of vigorous opposition.

The Intellectual Argument

The Qur'ān reflects the war of words and ideas between Muḥammad and his opponents throughout the remainder of his life at Mecca. As well as expounding and defending the new religion, it quotes the arguments used against it. No dating is possible, but the main points made on the two sides are clear.

One of the main criticisms of the message of the Qur'ān was that its teaching about the resurrection of the body was absurd. The Meccans, regarding the body as an essential part of the man, could not conceive how a human body could be restored to life after it had mouldered in the grave. In their eyes this was a crushing retort to Muḥammad's assertions.

> When they are warned they reck not ;
> When they see a sign, they mock,
> And say, This is magic manifest ;
> When we are dust and bones, shall we be raised,
> Or our fathers from of old ? (37. 13–17)

This question was not simply a debating point against Muḥammad, but was in line with their real beliefs.

> They say, There is naught save our present life ; we die and we live ; only Fate destroys us. (45. 23)

The Qur'ān was not concerned with resurrection in any abstract way. For the Qur'ān resurrection was involved in the teaching about the Last Judgement, and that teaching was important as providing a sanction on an individualistic basis for virtues like generosity to which the Qur'ān was recalling men. The pagans of Mecca did not directly attack what the Qur'ān said about generosity. It is easy to be selfish in practice, but not so easy to defend selfishness as an ideal. All the Qur'ānic teaching on this point, however, would be discredited if the resurrection could be disproved ; and the indisputable fact of mouldering bodies seemed to the opponents of Muḥammad a clear disproof of a vital link in the chain of his ethical and eschatological doctrine.

The Qur'ān meets this criticism by calling attention to the ' signs ' of God's power and activity. Some passages show God's existence and power in a general way, but others are explicitly concerned with His power to raise men from the dead. His creation of man through the process of conception and the slow development of the embryo in the womb, and His subsequent provision for sustaining man's life are taken as ' signs ' that He is also able to restore the bodies that have lain in the grave.

> Does man reckon he will be left to himself ?
> Was he not a drop of seed emitted,
> Then became a blood-clot ? He formed, He moulded,
> Made of him mates, male and female.
> Is not That One able to raise the dead ? (75.36–40)

Despite such arguments, however, the opponents remained unconvinced.

On the question of idols and the unity of God the Qur'ān took the initiative in attacking, and the pagans were on the defensive. The chief points in this connexion have already been mentioned. One further point, however, was the appeal by the pagans to the customs of the fathers, and the implied criticism of Muḥammad for deviating from established usage. It was a deep-seated conviction among the Arabs that the right way for men—the way through which they achieved something of value—was adherence to established usage. This conviction was transferred to Islam, where the word for 'heresy' is simply 'innovation'. When Muḥammad's opponents, then, insisted that they had found their fathers practising a certain religion and that it was best for them to follow in their fathers' footsteps, this was an assertion that would meet with a deep response from many Arab hearts.

The answer of the Qur'ān to this implied criticism was in the stories of the prophets of former times. The stories give encouragement to Muḥammad and his followers in their troubles. They must sometimes have felt they were deserting their ancestors, especially when they were asked difficult questions about the present or future state of deceased pagans. The stories of the Old Testament prophets and others helped them to realize that, as themselves followers of a prophet, they had a distinguished spiritual ancestry. They also were members of a community with its roots deep in the past and, like most Arab tribes, able to boast of the excellence of its stock and the great merits of the forerunners.

Besides these arguments about the message of the Qur'ān there were criticisms of Muḥammad's position as 'messenger of God'. The extent of the criticisms shows that from the first Muḥammad must have claimed that the words which came to him were a revelation from God. One of the lines of attack used by the pagans was to admit that Muḥammad's experiences were real and that they had a supernatural cause, but to hold that this cause was not God but jinn, and that Muḥammad was possessed by jinn, or mad. Poets, not to speak of soothsayers and sorcerers, were also inspired by jinn, and so to link Muḥammad with any of these groups had a similar effect to saying he was possessed.

All such assertions about the origin of the revelations had the effect of making men think that the warnings need not be taken seriously. The supernatural beings who produced the revelations might be either malevolent or lacking in knowledge. The people who made these allegations may have believed them, or they may merely have been trying to discredit Muḥammad. In either case a reply had to be made. The passage describing Muḥammad's visions (discussed above) comes as a refutation of the suggestion that the revelations are of demonic origin.

Another line of attack on Muḥammad's prophethood was the allegation that he had had a human assistant. No name is given in the Qur'ān, but later Muslim sources mention several persons whom his opponents named as his assistants. What grounds there were for the charge it is difficult to say. Muḥammad, it has been argued, was completely sincere in holding that the revelations were not the product of his normal consciousness. It remains possible, however, that he had heard some of the stories recounted by the persons mentioned, though not in the same form or with the same point as when they appeared in the Qur'ān. If he had thus heard the stories, there would be some plausibility in the allegation. The opponents were certainly doing all they could to discredit Muḥammad.

Finally there were attacks on Muḥammad's position and his motives. They said he was not a sufficiently important person to be a messenger from God, since he was weak and of no account. Others demanded that his mission should be accompanied by miracles, or suggested that God normally sent angels as messengers. At least onc passage makes it likely that the opponents asserted that Muḥammad was moved by personal ambition. Such an assertion is also implied by the repeated counter-statements that Muḥammad is not a controller, but only a warner whose function is to warn his fellow-countrymen that there is a Judgement followed by eternal reward and punishment, and by the insistence that Muḥammad, like other prophets, seeks reward not from men but only from God. It would be only natural that the rich merchants, with their materialistic outlook, and their knowledge of Muḥammad's difficult circumstances, should imagine that he like themselves was moved by a desire for wealth and power. His whole conduct throughout the Meccan period makes it improbable that political ambition was among his dominant motives, though, when power came to him at Medina, he did not shrink from it, but regarded political leadership as having been thrust upon him by God.

The Boycott of the Clan of Hashim

Round about the year 615 the leadership of the opposition to Muḥammad passed from the older men to one of his own generation, Abū-Jahl of the clan of Makhzūm. The older men would have liked to effect some reconciliation with Muḥammad and to induce him to compromise, but Abū-Jahl was bent on crushing the new religious movement. A passage in the earliest biography seems free from exaggeration :

> It was the wicked Abū-Jahl who used to incite the men of Quraysh against the Muslims. When he heard of the conversion of a man of high birth with powerful friends, he criticized him vigorously and put him to shame. 'You have left your father's religion,' he said, 'although he is a better man than you ; we shall make your prudence appear folly and your judgement unsound, and we shall bring your honour low.' If he was a merchant, he said, 'By God, we shall see that your goods are not sold and that your capital is lost.' If he was an uninfluential person, he beat him and incited people against him.

This illustrates both the vigour of the opposition and its limitations. It has always to be remembered that the system of public security in force in Mecca was the protection by each clan of its members. Most of the clans were sufficiently strong to cause serious inconvenience to anyone who maltreated a clansman or confederate ; and thus there was little scope for physical violence.

Western scholars have argued that the extent of the persecution of the Muslims at Mecca has been exaggerated. This seems to be borne out by a careful study of the earliest sources (such as the passage above). On the other hand there is great bitterness in the Qur'ānic description of the treatment of the Muslims by pagan Meccans. The strength of feeling is perhaps due to the fact that Abū-Jahl and his supporters went as far as they could in the way of persecution and did things that would not have been tolerated by the older Arab tradition.

It was within his own clan that Abū-Jahl was able to do most. A uterine brother of his own and two other young men of like high standing were inclined to adopt Islam, and two of them had been in Abyssinia. After their return Abū-Jahl made life difficult for them, and for a time they were incarcerated by their families and latterly prevented from joining Muḥammad at Medina. A confederate of the clan and his aged parents were regularly exposed to the heat of the midday sun, and the mother is said to have died from this. For such persons little could be done by the other Muslims.

Abū-Jahl and his associates had also many opportunities of exercising economic pressure. In the case of a creditor who had no effective protection from any clan one of them refused to pay a legitimate debt. It must have been difficult for the less influential men to resist pressure of this kind. Abū-Bakr is said to have had 40,000 dirhams when he became a Muslim and only 5,000 when he left Mecca in 622. He is also said to have used his money to buy slaves, but only seven slaves are mentioned and we hear of a slave costing 400 dirhams. So the presumption is that the decline in his fortune was mainly due to various forms of economic pressure by the opponents of the Muslims.

Physical violence, because of the system of security, was limited to persons like slaves or those who could find no clan to protect them. Of the latter one who is often mentioned was a blacksmith and another a trader of Byzantine origin. In normal times these men would have no difficulty in making a living in Mecca ; but it was different when they joined a movement with powerful enemies. It was also possible for a clan to disown formally one of its members. This tended to lower the clan's honour and was not usually done unless there was a strong reason. It seems, however, to have happened in the case of Abū-Bakr, for we hear of him accepting the protection of a nomadic chief who lived near Mecca and also of him undergoing the indignity of being bound to a fellow-clansman. In any case his clan was not powerful.

Muḥammad himself still enjoyed the protection of his clan, though that did not exempt him from minor insults, such as having his neighbours' rubbish and waste dumped at his door. Abū-Jahl is said to have appealed more than once to Muḥammad's uncle Abū-Ṭālib, who was head of the clan, either to stop his nephew proclaiming the new religion or else to withdraw his protection from him.

Abū-Ṭālib stood firm. For one thing it would have been dishonouring to the clan to disown Muḥammad, since there was no likelihood of their persuading him to give up his religion. It would also have further weakened a clan whose strength was declining, for he was one of their promising young men. There was probably also a deeper reason, however. Although Abū-Ṭālib and most members of the clan did not accept Muḥammad's teaching, this had economic implications in which they were interested. It was in line with the policy of the clan and of the whole League of the Virtuous in opposing the attempts of the rich merchants in other clans to establish monopolies. It would therefore be natural for the clan of Hāshim to give Muḥammad a certain measure of general support, though without endorsing his religious assertions. Indeed it was not only the Muslims of the clan who were protected. Abū-Ṭālib also gave protection to his sister's son, whose father belonged to Abū-Jahl's clan of Makhzūm, and who was presumably in danger of being ill-treated by his father's clan.

Abū-Jahl continued to work assiduously against Muḥammad. He failed to isolate Muḥammad from his clan, but he managed to isolate the clan of Hāshim from the other clans in the League of the Virtuous. It was perhaps about 616 that he brought into being a grand alliance of nearly all the clans of Mecca against Hāshim. A document was drawn up and signed, and a boycott of Hāshim instituted. None of the clans taking part was to have any business dealings with Hāshim, and there was to be no intermarriage. The boycott was apparently maintained for over two years.

The situation of Hāshim cannot have been as serious as it sounds. There is no record of any complaint of undue hardship, nor of recriminations against Muḥammad. The last point tends to confirm the view that Muḥammad's religion was not the sole reason for the boycott. Hāshim must have been able to carry on trade in one form or another. Perhaps they sent their own caravans to Syria ; and they would be able to sell to the nomads who came to Mecca. Besides, several members of the boycotting clans were closely related by marriage to Hāshim and presumably did not keep the boycott with absolute strictness.

Thus the boycott must be adjudged a comparative failure. It came to an end, not by Hāshim yielding, but by the break-up of the alliance organized by Abū-Jahl. The lead was taken by members of the clans formerly in league with Hāshim and by a pagan member of the clan of Makhzūm whose mother was another sister of Abū-Ṭālib's. Perhaps with the passage of time these former allies of Hāshim had realized that the boycott was strengthening the wealthy clans which were trying to extend monopolistic controls over Meccan trade and was consequently weakening their own position.

The boycott may not have been a complete failure, however. In the course of it there was one important defection from the clan of Hāshim, Abū-Lahab, and the clan's subsequent acceptance of him as chief may indicate that there was more discontent than is usually allowed.

The various forms of hostility to Islam did not at once stop men from becoming Muslims. One important accession to their ranks was 'Umar ibn-al-Khaṭṭāb, who later became the second caliph. For a time he was an active opponent. When he heard that his sister and her husband had become Muslims he was so incensed that he struck his sister, causing blood to flow. The sight of blood, however, led to a swift revulsion of feeling. In a mood of repentance for the hurt he had done his sister he listened to the Qur'ān being recited and was so moved that he straightway went to Muḥammad and professed faith in Islam. 'Umar was one of the two or three most important men in his clan, which was relatively weak and uninfluential, and after his conversion—which may have taken place before the boycott began—the clan took no further part in active opposition to the Muslims. Those members of the clan who were still in Mecca in 624 sent a contingent to Badr, but it withdrew from the Meccan army before the battle.

'Umar seems to have been the last important convert to Islam during the Meccan period. The successful defiance of the boycott by Hāshim indicated that the two parties had reached a stalemate. Soon after its ending, however, various events occurred which caused Muhammad's position to deteriorate rapidly.

The Betrayal by Abū-Lahab

Within a short time of one another, probably in the year 619, Muḥammad lost by death both his uncle and protector Abū-Ṭālib and his faithful wife and helpmate Khadījah. What the latter meant to Muḥammad in these years of opposition we can only conjecture. When he first came to think that God was calling him to be a prophet, she encouraged him to believe that the call was genuine. In later days, when his resolution wavered, she comforted him, and doubtless gave him the support he needed. Her death would therefore compel him to be more self-reliant, and that may have been necessary for the ultimate success of the religious movement. While Khadījah was alive Muḥammad took no other wife, but he married again shortly after her death. This might indicate the need for spiritual companionship, but it is more likely that Muḥammad's motives were of a political kind. The woman, Sawdah, was herself an early convert, and she had been married to a Muslim who had died. Muḥammad may have regarded it as incumbent on himself, the head of the little group of Muslims, to marry her so that she might not have to marry someone outside the group. As for Muḥammad himself there are signs that deepening religious experiences were taking the place of human companionship.

The repercussions of the death of Abū-Ṭālib were much more serious for Muḥammad. Abū-Ṭālib was succeeded as chief of the clan of Hāshim by his brother Abū-Lahab. The latter had joined the ' grand alliance ' against Hāshim during the boycott, but when he became chief he at first promised to protect Muḥammad as his brother had done. Mere self-respect and the honour of the clan would dictate such a course. Nevertheless he had really joined the camp, or one of the camps, of Muḥammad's opponents. He had managed to marry the sister of Abū-Sufyān of the clan of 'Abd-Shams, a very rich merchant of the same generation as Abū-Jahl, and the latter's chief rival for the position of most influential man in Mecca. Perhaps this marriage was itself the bribe which detached Abū-Lahab from the traditional policy of Hāshim. On the other hand, the marriage may have been earlier, and the ties of affinity may merely have made it easier for Muḥammad's opponents to work upon Abū-Lahab. At a time when Abū-Lahab and Muḥammad were looked upon as the two brightest young men of the clan, two daughters of Muḥammad had been engaged to two sons of Abū-Lahab, but these engagements were now broken off.

Before long Abū-Lahab found an excuse for depriving Muḥammad of the protection of the clan. He is said to have been put up to it by Abū-Jahl and a member of the clan of 'Abd-Shams who was friendly with him. He asked Muḥammad about the present position of his grandfather. Muḥammad gave an evasive answer which seemed satisfactory, but the two instigators made him go back and ask Muḥammad directly whether his grandfather was in hell. Muḥammad had to say that he was. Such remarks about a former chief of the clan were tantamount to an insult to the whole clan, and the present chief could therefore, without any loss of self-respect, refuse to protect him any longer. The refusal may not have been absolute. Perhaps there were conditions for protection, such as the abandonment of preaching, which Muḥammad could not accept. Whatever the details, the result was that Muḥammad lost the protection of his clan and could no longer carry on in Mecca as he had been doing. His bitterness is reflected in a sūrah of the Qur'ān (111) which denounces Abū-Lahab and his wife.

Unable to propagate his religion any longer in Mecca, Muḥammad had to look round for another base. The first place he thought of was aṭ-Ṭā'if. It was the nearest town to Mecca, being about forty miles away to the east. Because it was higher up in the mountains it had a better climate, and many of the richer Meccans had houses and estates in or near it. At one time it had been a commercial rival of Mecca, but now it was under Meccan control.

Muḥammad made the journey to aṭ-Ṭā'if and entered into negotiations with one of the leading men and his brothers. This group belonged to the section of the inhabitants who were cooperating with the Meccans, but Muḥammad may have thought that they were becoming restive under Meccan domination. It seems clear that he was not merely looking for a protector, but was intent on the further propagation of the movement he had inaugurated at Mecca. Whether he had in view the possibility of hostilities with Mecca, such as later developed at Medina, is not certain. It is likely that he suggested some way of removing Meccan control from the trade of aṭ-Ṭā'if. The group he approached, however, did not feel strong enough to throw down the gauntlet to Mecca. On the contrary they were afraid that they might have been compromised by having entered into discussions with Muḥammad, and they not merely rejected the proposition he made, but encouraged the town rabble to fling stones at him.

In great dejection Muḥammad set out to return to Mecca. At one of the points where he stopped for a night, while he was engaged in worship, a company of jinn is said to have come and listened and to have gone off believing. The Qur'ān (72. 1) shows that Muḥammad had some experience of this kind, and we may well believe that at this critical period of his life, when things were becoming more and more difficult for him, he would increasingly 'take refuge with God'. What may have been another experience of this type is referred to briefly in the Qur'ān (17. 1) and was expanded in later Islamic tradition into most elaborate accounts of a miraculous journey first to Jerusalem and then to each of the seven heavens.

Muḥammad was unable to enter Mecca again until he had been guaranteed protection by the leader of some clan other than his own. With this journey to aṭ-Ṭā'if his protection by his own clan must have come to an end. Whether Abū-Lahab set a time-limit, within which he had to leave Mecca, or whether the journey broke some condition about not propagating Islam, must remain uncertain. It was only the third leader, too, whom he approached, who was willing to protect Muḥammad, and doubtless this protection had conditions attached which greatly restricted Muḥammad's activity. He was, however, at least able to return to Mecca eventually.

During this same difficult period after the death of Abū-Ṭālib Muḥammad is said to have tried to gain the support of some of the nomadic tribes while they were in the neighbourhood of Mecca attending one or other of the fairs. Four tribes are named. The pasture grounds of one were comparatively near, and, as later events show, a section of this tribe was attracted to Muḥammad. The others came from a much greater distance and were either wholly or partly Christian. Perhaps Muḥammad hoped that for this reason, or because of some matter of local politics, one of these tribes would accept his message and give him protection. He may even have been thinking about the possibility of unifying the Arabs. Nothing came of all his approaches, however, and he had to continue in patience.

IV

THE EMIGRATION TO MEDINA

The Appeal from the Medinans

The first light began to dawn for Muḥammad in his darkness with an event which happened at the pilgrimage season in the summer of 620. Among the pilgrims with whom Muḥammad came into contact were six men from Medina. They were impressed by his personality and his message, and they thought that he might be able to help them to overcome the difficulties which were then besetting Medina. At the pilgrimage in the summer of 621 five of these six came back bringing seven others. The twelve represented most of the parties or bodies of opinion among the Arabs of Medina, and they are said to have made a promise to Muḥammad to accept him as prophet and obey him and to avoid certain sins. This was known as the First Pledge of al-'Aqabah.

Following upon this Muḥammad sent back to Medina with these men a trusty Muslim, well-versed in the Qur'ān, whose ostensible duty was to instruct the people of Medina in Islam, but who was doubtless also expected to inform Muḥammad about the political situation in Medina. During the winter things went well in Medina for the new movement. There were converts from nearly all the Arab clans, and the converts were of sufficient importance to make it certain that nearly all the clans would publicly support an agreement with Muḥammad. By June 622 it was possible to collect a representative party of seventy-five Muslims from Medina to make the pilgrimage to Mecca. The party, which included two women, met Muḥammad secretly by night and pledged themselves not merely to accept Muḥammad as prophet and avoid sins, but also to fight on behalf of God and His messenger. This was the Second Pledge of al-'Aqabah or the Pledge of War.

Such is the traditional account. Some Western scholars have doubted whether there was more than one pledge, and it may be allowed that all the details of the traditional account are not necessarily sound. Yet there must have been several meetings between Muḥammad and the men of Medina before they agreed on the basis on which he was to go there. It may not have occurred to the Medinans that he would deliberately go out to attack and provoke the Meccans, and they may have been thinking only of defending him when he was attacked; but it is also possible that they foresaw that there would be trouble with the Meccans. In either case they must have promised to protect him; otherwise he would quickly have been killed by his enemies from Mecca. How was it that the men of Medina, in contrast to those of Mecca, so easily accepted Islam and the prophethood of Muḥammad?

The Troubles of Medina

The situation in Medina was absolutely different from that in Mecca. In the immediate neighbourhood of Mecca no agriculture was possible, but only the pasturing of camels, and so the very existence of the town depended on commerce. Medina, on the other hand, about 250 miles to the north, was an oasis of twenty square miles or more, and gained its livelihood chiefly from growing dates and cereals. There was some commerce, for there was a market in the area inhabited by the Jewish clan of Qaynuqāʿ, who were not merely traders but goldsmiths and manufacturers of weapons and armour. There may also have been some caravan trade with Syria but it cannot have been on the same scale or had the same importance as the caravan trade of Mecca.

The inhabitants of Medina were of different origins. When Muḥammad went in 622 there may be said to have been eleven main groups—to be called 'clans' here—as well as a number of smaller ones. Three of the main groups professed the Jewish faith. It is not clear whether they were descended from Jewish refugees or from Arab families which had adopted Judaism. In either case there had been much intermarriage between Jews and Arabs, and in their general manner of life the Jewish clans were hardly distinguishable from the Arabs. At one time the Jews had had political control of Medina, and the remnant of the previous Arab settlers had become dependent on them. Perhaps it was the Jews who developed agriculture at Medina, as they did in other parts of Arabia.

The eight main Arab clans were descended from families which had settled in Medina when it was already dominated by the Jews. In the earlier part of the sixth century they had wrested their independence from the Jews, and they were now much the stronger. The Jewish clans of an-Naḍīr and Qurayẓah, however, still retained some of the best lands on the higher ground in the south of the oasis, and were superior to the small groups of Arabs, belonging chiefly to the clan of Aws-Manāt, who lived either interspersed among the Jewish settlements or close to them. Despite such dependents the Jewish clans only maintained themselves by entering into alliances with Arab clans, and in these alliances the Jews were the inferior partners.

There was no compact town in the oasis, but numerous settlements scattered among the palm-groves and fields. Each clan had a number of little forts or strongholds to which they retired when attacked. It was the general view in Medina that these strongholds could not be taken by storm; so, once one side in a battle had gained their strongholds, the fighting ceased. Probably the leading members of a clan inhabited the strongholds permanently; others may only have gone into them in time of danger.

In the century before Muḥammad's arrival there had been a steady increase of violence and fighting between the clans.

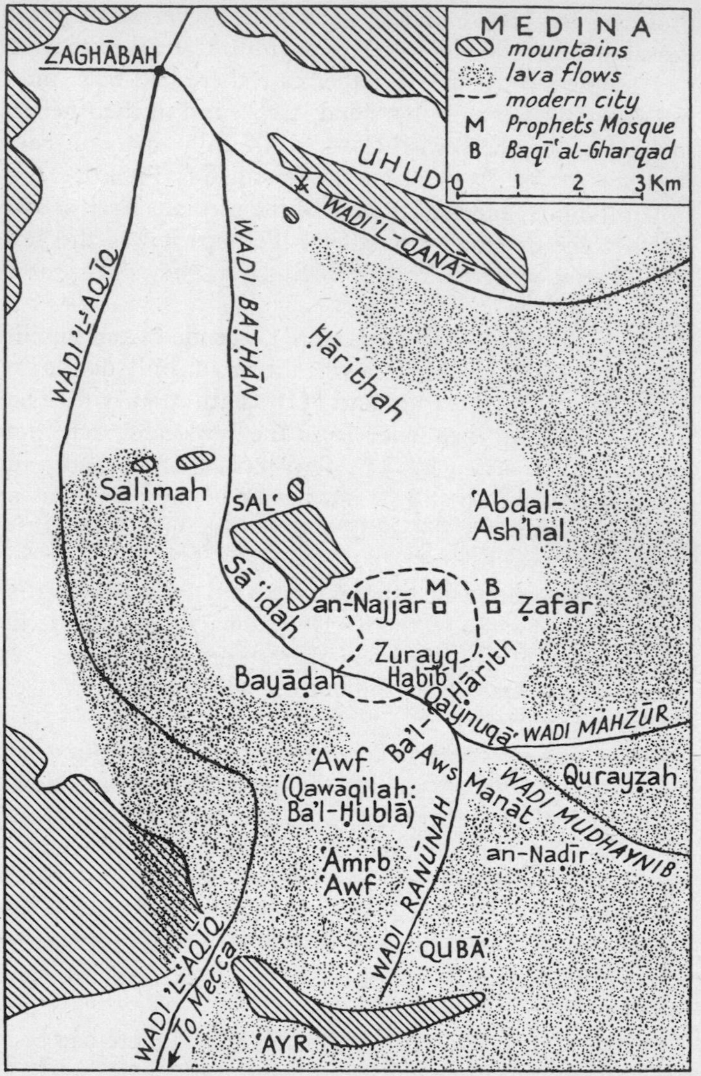

THE OASIS OF MEDINA

Perhaps it was due to the increasing pressure of population on the available resources. This cannot be the whole of the reason, however, for until some years after Muḥammad's death there was still virgin land available for cultivation, though it was doubtless marginal land which gave a poor return. In some of the later fighting the avowed aim of clans was to seize the lands of their weaker neighbours. At first the fighting was between single clans, but as time went on strong leaders were able to induce several clans to ally themselves together under their leadership. Because of this the numbers involved in a fight were constantly becoming larger. Finally the climax came in a battle about 618 at a locality called Bu'āth. Most of the Arab clans of Medina were engaged in this battle, and also, as their allies, the Jewish clans and some nomadic clans from the neighbourhood. There was heavy slaughter. Hostilities came to an end because the two sides were exhausted, but peace was not made. After this Medina lived in a state of tension. There were one or two instances of men being murdered when they went through the territory of a neighbouring clan at night.

The alliances mostly coincided with the division of the Arab clans into two tribes, the Aws and the Khazraj, and these two tribes are usually said to have constituted the Arab population of Medina. There were one or two exceptions, however, in which clans opposed the rest of their tribe. This shows that there was no strong loyalty to the tribe. It is thus not surprising that the tribes are not mentioned in the Constitution of Medina (a document to be discussed later), but only the clans. The new situation created by Muḥammad's presence in Medina made the squabbles between the clans rather petty, so that less is heard of them and more of the tribes. After Muḥammad's death, when horizons had been further widened by the vast conquests, the rivalry of the Aws and the Khazraj ceases to be a political factor of importance, and the two tribes came to be known jointly as the Anṣār. This word means the Helpers, *sc.* of Muḥammad, and was a name of honour conferred on them.

The fundamental trouble underlying the fighting and the tension at Medina was that the nomadic outlook and ethic, to which the men of Medina still adhered, was not suited to the conditions of agricultural life in an oasis. As it became more difficult to gain a livelihood from the soil of Medina for the growing population, quarrels would arise and blood would be shed. To deal with this situation nomadic custom had only the method of the blood-feud. If a man had been injured or killed, his kinsmen exacted the equivalent from the individual responsible or his family or clan—' an eye for an eye, and a tooth for a tooth '. The equivalent might be an actual eye or an actual life, but it was also becoming common, as already mentioned, to accept a hundred camels in place of the life of an adult male. In the wide spaces of the steppe this method was tolerably successful since contacts were few, but in the restricted area of an oasis it was unsatisfactory. Here there were too many disputes, and therefore too many possibilities of disagreement about what constituted a fair equivalent for what. There was one celebrated occasion in the sixth century when a great nomadic chief had been killed ; his brother, the avenger of blood, killed a youth of the slayer's tribe, but would not accept his life as equivalent for more than his brother's shoelatchet. The youth's tribe naturally did not accept this, and there was a fierce war between the two tribes for many years. If this could happen in the desert, it was no wonder that life in Medina was difficult.

In pre-Islamic Arabia there were men of wisdom who were frequently resorted to as arbiters in disputes, if the two parties were not too enraged to accept arbitration. The arbiters had no powers to execute judgement, but they bound the two parties by oath to accept their judgement. This procedure, however, was too slow and clumsy for the numerous disputes in an oasis. What was needed was a single judge with executive powers. Had Muḥammad not come to Medina such an office might have been established, though it would have been difficult to find a man whom all would accept as impartial. One of the leading men of the Khazraj, 'Abd-Allāh ibn-Ubayy, had remained neutral at the battle of Bu'āth, and it was thought that, but for Muḥammad's arrival, he might have become king of Medina; yet it would have been difficult for him to unite all the men of Medina behind him, since he would always be suspected of partiality.

For the men of Medina in this situation much of the attraction of inviting Muḥammad lay in the fact that he would be neutral and would be able to decide their disputes impartially. One of his great-grandmothers had belonged to a Medinan clan, but it was uninfluential and his connexion with it was not regarded as infringing his neutrality. He was careful, too, not to ally himself by marriage with any Medinan clan. It was also helpful in this connexion that the Medinan Arabs, doubtless influenced by Jewish ideas of the coming of the Messiah, were ready to accept Muḥammad as a prophet. Because of his rejection by the Meccans he was also free from the suspicion of being an agent working for the extension of Meccan domination over Medina.

For several reasons, then, Muḥammad was a most acceptable person to the Medinans. They were hopeful that he might deliver them from their troubles, and establish a new era of peace. With such thoughts seventy-five of them promised at al-'Aqabah to defend him as they would their own kin. This opened the way for the Hijrah.

The Hijrah

Even before the final pledge was given to Muhammad by

the Medinans (early in July, 622), one or two of his Meccan followers had moved to Medina. After the pledge, when it was clear that Muḥammad himself was going, small bands of his followers began to leave Mecca quietly and make for Medina. Perhaps the Meccan pagans did not realize what was happening. At least no attempt was made to interfere with the Muslims, and they all reached Medina safely. In the heat of the summer months the journey of some 250 miles probably took about nine days. Eventually about seventy of Muḥammad's followers had reached Medina and been given hospitality by the Muslims there. In Mecca the only Muslims remaining, who were able and willing to make the journey, were Muḥammad, Abū-Bakr, 'Alī, and some of their families.

By thus sending his followers on before him, Muḥammad ensured that there would be no repetition of his failure at aṭ-Ṭā'if. Even if there was some change of mind among the Medinans he would have this body of committed Meccan followers to support him. This arrangement also meant that Muḥammad was in Mecca to the last possible moment to encourage any waverers among the Muslims.

It was about the middle of September before Muḥammad himself was ready to set out. Shortly before he did so the Meccan pagans are said to have become suspicious, and to have plotted to kill Muḥammad himself. Some young men, one from each of the clans, were to thrust their swords into him simultaneously, so that the blood-guilt would be shared by nearly the whole of Mecca, and the avengers of blood would have no option but to accept blood-money. The story goes that this plan was foiled when Muḥammad slipped away by night and left 'Alī sleeping on his bed in his green cloak. The ruse was eventually discovered, but nothing was done to 'Alī, and Muḥammad was already away.

While we may perhaps be a little sceptical about this story, it seems clear that there was a real danger for Muḥammad. This was in the period between his leaving Mecca and his arriving in Medina. So long as he remained in Mecca he was under protection—presumably that of the man who had agreed to protect him on his return from aṭ-Ṭā'if. He would be under the protection of the Medinans as soon as he reached Medina. Between the two towns, however, his blood could be shed with impunity, it would seem. He therefore took great care over the arrangements for his journey. Camels were hired from a nomad from the neighbourhood of Mecca. He and Abū-Bakr left their homes together, but, instead of making for Medina, they hid in a cave not far away, close to which a freedman of Abū-Bakr's was in the habit of pasturing sheep. Here they remained for three days till the hue and cry which the Meccans had raised had died away. Then they set out on two camels, a small party of four men, for they were accompanied by Abū-Bakr's freedman, while the owner of the camels acted as a guide. They went by devious and unfrequented routes and met no enemies. At last on 24th September, 622, they reached the settlement of Qubā' on the edge of the Medinan oasis. The Hijrah had been safely accomplished.

The Arabic word *hijrah* (which still sometimes appears in the Latin form *hegira*) does not mean 'flight' but is best translated 'emigration'. It has the connotation not of geographical transference, but of separation from one's family and clan and attachment to others. The Islamic era, used for dating events by all the older Muslim writers, begins on the first day of the year in which the Hijrah took place, viz. July 16, A.D. 622. The calculation of equivalent Islamic and Christian dates is a complicated matter, however, for the Islamic year contains twelve lunar months or 354 days, so that in each Christian century there are about 103 Islamic years.

Qubā' was not to be Muḥammad's final abode. He spent two or three days there, doubtless forming his own assessment of the political situation. He would at once realize that Qubā' was not the best place for his permanent residence. It lay in the higher ground to the south of the oasis. Nearby were two strong Jewish clans and their Arab associates, who had not joined in the invitation to Muḥammad and the pledge. Proximity to them would be a constant source of weakness.

Muḥammad therefore set out one morning and headed for the lower ground a mile or two to the north. He professed not himself to make the final choice of site for his house, but simply to accept the spot where his camel stopped. It was quite a suitable one, a plot of ground belonging to two orphans within the district of the clan of an-Najjār to which one of Muḥammad's great-grandmothers had belonged. This was a numerous clan, but, for reasons which are not clear to us, it was less important politically than several smaller clans, and had no vigorous leader. In this way Muḥammad obtained relative security for himself, and avoided the appearance of siding with one of the factions in Medina.

Muḥammad obtained lodging in a neighbouring house, paid the orphans for the ground, which was being used for drying dates, and set about having his house built. His followers from both Mecca and Medina helped, and he himself took a hand in the work. While the primary purpose of the structure was presumably to shelter Muḥammad and his family and to facilitate the transaction of administrative business, it had a large courtyard, and this may have been partly intended for the public worship of the Muslims. As time went on this aspect became more important, until, after the death of Muḥammad and his wives, the buildings and courtyard came to be used solely as a mosque. After many transformations this is now the prophet's mosque of Medina. Muḥammad's wives had apartments along the east side of the courtyard. The work of building the house was not completed until August 623.

The First Months in Medina

There are practically no events with a precise date that are recorded for the first six months of Muḥammad's life at Medina. Much must have been happening. The lines must have been laid down on which the new state and the new religion were to develop. It would no doubt be fascinating to have the exact dates of the various passages of the Qur'ān which were revealed during these six months. We have to be satisfied, however, with inferences which may not always be quite correct. The things which were happening were not things which caught the imagination. After the excitement of the subsequent years they remained no more than a hazy recollection. In the absence of notable events, then, we must try to give a general account of the situation in which Muḥammad and the Emigrants from Mecca found themselves during those first months in Medina.

A document has been preserved which is commonly known as the Constitution of Medina. It appears to be authentic, but there is uncertainty about its date. Some scholars place it near the beginning of the Medinan period, which would be its natural place. On the other hand, there are signs that in the document as we have it there are articles from different sources. One group of articles deals with the same topics as another group, and one article is actually repeated. Again, though several Jewish groups are mentioned, there is no explicit reference to the three main Jewish clans, and they do not seem to be included by implication. They could hardly have been omitted altogether. The third of these Jewish clans was liquidated in summer 627. The document would therefore seem to have taken its present form after that date. Many of the articles, however, are presumably older, perhaps belonging to the agreement between Muḥammad and the Medinans made while he was still at Mecca. The document may therefore be accepted as evidence for the political situation in Medina at the beginning of Muḥammad's residence there.

The document commences:

> In the name of God, the Merciful, the Compassionate!
>
> This is a writing of Muḥammad the prophet between the believers and Muslims of Quraysh and Yathrib (sc. Medina) and those who follow them and are attached to them and who crusade along with them. They are a single community distinct from other people.

There follow nine articles mentioning nine clans or groups of people, and stating that each is to be responsible for blood-money incurred by a member of the group and for ransoming a member of the group who is captured. The first group to be mentioned, the Emigrants of Quraysh, are Muḥammad's Meccan followers. The other eight are Arab clans, or groups of clans, three from the tribe of the Aws and five from the Khazraj. Of the remaining articles about twenty deal with various aspects of the relations of the believers to one another and to the unbelievers, while about fifteen treat of the rights and duties of the Jews. A number of Jewish groups are mentioned, mostly not by name but simply as 'the Jews of (that is, attached to) such-and-such an Arab clan'.

This document, the Constitution of Medina, may be taken to show that the people of Medina were now regarded as constituting a political unit of a new type, an *ummah* or 'community'. In some ways it was like a federation of nomadic clans or tribes. It was bound together by their solemn agreement with one another. There are many instances of such federations in pre-Islamic history under men of outstanding personal qualities. In this case, however, it was not Muḥammad's military prestige that drew men to accept him as leader, but his prophethood. The 'community' thus had a religious basis. It must have been almost impossible, however, for the Arabs of Muḥammad's time to think of any political unit except in terms of the one political unit with which they were familiar, the tribe or kinship-group. There are stories in the sources for the life of Muḥammad in which the Byzantine emperor is spoken of as if he was a nomadic shaykh dealing with his fellow-tribesmen who considered themselves as good as he. In its relations to other bodies, whether friends or enemies, the 'community' acted very much like a tribe. Muḥammad, like a nomadic chief, received a share of any booty taken on raids, but only a fifth instead of a quarter. For these and other reasons it is not unfitting to describe the 'community' as a 'super-tribe', as has been done.

Muḥammad was by no means the ruler of this community. The Emigrants were treated as a clan, and he was their chief, but there were eight other clans with their chiefs. If the Constitution is good evidence at this point, he was only marked off from other clan chiefs by two things. Firstly, the people primarily concerned in this agreement which we are calling the Constitution are *believers*, and that implies that they accept Muḥammad as prophet. That should mean accepting as a binding rule whatever comes as revelation, and attributing to Muḥammad a certain prestige as the recipient of revelation and perhaps a wisdom beyond that of ordinary men, at least in religious matters. It does not mean the acceptance of his opinion in matters not covered by revelations.

Secondly, however, the Constitution states that 'wherever there is anything about which you differ, it is to be referred to God and to Muḥammad'. It seems likely that it was contemplated in the original agreement between Muḥammad and the Medinans that he would be able to act as arbiter between rival factions and thus help to maintain peace in the oasis. In a passage of the Qur'ān (10. 48) one of the functions of prophets is thus described :

> Each community has a messenger, and when their messenger comes judgement is given between them with justice, and they are not wronged.

But, if this seemed a good idea to the Medinans so long as Muḥammad was far away in Mecca, some of them may have felt hesitation after he came among them and his prestige and power began to grow. Certainly, there are several exhortations in the Qur'ān to the believers to take their disputes to Muḥammad for settlement ; and from the repetition of the exhortation we may conclude that the practice was not always followed.

In these early months, then, Muḥammad can have been no more than the religious leader of the Medinan community. In strictly political matters he was only the head of the ' clan ' of Emigrants, and probably less powerful than several other clan chiefs. He probably first became a force in the politics of Medina after his military success at Badr in March 624. Even after that there were still one or two men of comparable influence, and Muḥammad's undoubted political ascendancy began with the failure of the siege of Medina in April 627.

Before the Hijrah most of the main Arab clans in Medina had accepted Muḥammad as prophet. Apparently they did so as clans, and therefore all the members of the clan must have become at least nominally Muslims. There were one or two exceptions, however, notably a group of clans usually known collectively as Aws-Manāt. Their homes and plantations were scattered among those of the strong Jewish clans of an-Naḍīr and Qurayẓah, and they probably had close links with these Jews. When the Jews refused to accept Muḥammad as prophet, they would naturally side with them. It was only after some of the leaders had died or been killed that these clans as a whole accepted Islam. They appear to be included in the Constitution in its present form (as al-Aws).

Besides these clans which did not at first enter the community, there was at least one important individual who so disapproved of his clan's policy of accepting Muḥammad and his religion that he abandoned Medina for Mecca. This was a man called Abū-'Āmir ar-Rāhib. The nickname ar-Rāhib, ' the monk ', was given to him because in the years before 622 he had practised some forms of asceticism. He was so incensed against Muḥammad that, along with a band of Medinan followers, he fought against the Muslims at Uḥud in 625. This man's story would have made one expect that he would have eagerly embraced Islam, and his hostility is thus all the more remarkable. Perhaps he saw the political implications of Muḥammad's position from the start and disliked them.

This ' pagan opposition ' of men like Abū-'Āmir, who refused to acknowledge Muḥammad as prophet, is to be distinguished from the ' nominal-Muslim opposition ', consisting of those Medinans who nominally became Muslims but who opposed Muḥammad politically. This is the group usually known as the Hypocrites. Their opposition probably only became active after Muḥammad's victory at Badr in 624. At first the Qur'ān refers to them as ' those in whose hearts is disease '. About the time of Uḥud in 625 the Qur'ān begins to refer to them as the ' Hypocrites ', perhaps because after preparing to fight they withdrew from the battle. From 625 to 627 they were a thorn in Muḥammad's side, but in 627 he was strong enough to force a show-down which revealed their weakness. There is mention of another group of Hypocrites about the year 630, but they are probably not identical with the first, though they may be connected with Abū-'Āmir ar-Rāhib.

The Jews of Medina were also among the opponents of Muḥammad, though the names are given of one or two who became Muslims.

The Jews had been in Medina for a considerable time, and their presence must have helped to spread monotheistic ideas there and to facilitate the acceptance of Muḥammad's prophethood. They consisted of about a score of clans, of which the most important were an-Naḍīr, Qurayẓah and Qaynuqā'. The last, as mentioned above, had no lands, but conducted a market and practised the crafts of the goldsmith and armourer. The other two possessed some of the richest lands in the higher and more southerly part of the Medinan oasis, and there were weak Arab groups with dwellings among them and politically dependent on them. Each Jewish clan was in alliance with one or other of the strong Arab clans, and was probably the weaker partner. Thus the Jews were divided among themselves, and did not form a compact body.

Although the Jews of Medina probably had no extensive knowledge of the Jewish religion and scriptures, they had sufficient to realize that the claims of Muḥammad were incompatible with Judaism. In this they were agreed. As allies of the Arab clans the Jews were in a sense included in the new community at Medina. There may even have been a direct treaty between some of them and Muḥammad. Muḥammad, however, hoped for more than this, and presumably devoted much of his time in the first weeks after the Hijrah to trying to obtain some acknowledgement of his prophethood from the Jews.

From an early stage in his career Muḥammad had been aware that the message revealed to him in the Qur'ān was similar to the teachings of Judaism and Christianity. Perhaps he regarded his claim to be a prophet as implying an essential identity of message with previous prophets. Presumably it was after the emigration to Medina began to be contemplated that he tried to model Islam more on Judaism. Before he left Mecca he is said to have chosen Jerusalem as his *qiblah* or direction to be faced in prayer, in accordance with the Jewish practice. The Fast of 'Āshūrā, the Jewish Day of Atonement, seems to have been observed by the Muslims in Medina; and the special Friday worship of the community as a whole, which became distinctive of Islam, is somehow or other connected with the Jewish preparation for Sabbath worship on the Friday.

This adoption of Jewish practices did not make the Jews any friendlier to Muḥammad. He was anxious for some degree of recognition from them, for he realized that without their support the whole structure of ideas on which his religion was built was in danger of collapse. He seems to have been prepared to allow them to keep their forms of worship and other distinctive religious practices if they would recognize him as a prophet parallel to their own prophets. The Jews, however, became increasingly hostile, and used their knowledge of the Old Testament to criticize Muḥammad's claim that the Qur'ān was the speech of God. In a largely illiterate environment it was easy for them to assert and appear to prove that the Qur'ān was mistaken in various matters mentioned in the Old Testament. And the conclusion of the argument, of course, was that the Qur'ān was not the speech of God and that therefore Muḥammad was not a prophet. In view of the gravity of this matter it must have been one of Muḥammad's chief preoccupations during the early months.

Altogether, then, Muḥammad's position in these months was still precarious. The community was established in Medina, but it was far from being firmly established. It was really only being tried out, and it had yet to approve itself in the eyes of the bulk of the inhabitants of Medina. Life in the oasis was still conducted mainly on the basis of previous customs. Being Muslims only meant for the Medinans the observance of certain cult forms, refraining from fighting with other Muslims, and perhaps some hospitality to the Emigrants. And all that was required of the ordinary Muslim at this time in the way of a religious cult may have been attendance at the midday prayers on Friday. Those who were more enthusiastic for the new religion probably also engaged in worship at least morning and evening, and perhaps also at midday; but there is no good evidence that the five standard prayers of later Islam had been definitely fixed during Muḥammad's life-time. The night-vigils, however, which had been popular with some of the Muslims at Mecca, were stopped by revelation at some date after the Hijrah when the Muslims became more involved in mundane affairs.

The ideas of the Qur'ān were thus by no means the only factor determining the course of life in Medina. Yet they were certainly important in guiding Muḥammad on his dangerous course between rocks and shoals. When action on any matter became necessary, he was often able to devise a course of action which led to a fuller realization of the principles of his religion. One of the most noteworthy features of all this development is the suitability of the religious ideas first proclaimed in Mecca to the different situation in Medina. In the growth of all the great world-religions it is found that ideas specially relevant to the situation in one small region are capable of application much more generally. The adaptation of Meccan Islam to circumstances in Medina is a striking example of this phenomenon. The chief feature in the Meccan situation was the increase of commerce and wealth, and, with that, of individualism. There was nothing on a comparable scale at Medina. The one thing they had in common was that in both towns men from a nomadic background, and still retaining much of the social, moral and intellectual outlook of the desert, were attempting to live a settled life. The Islamic religion had been trying, not very successfully, to deal with this problem in its Meccan form. This gave it a certain relevance to the Medinan form of the problem, and this relevance was greatly increased by placing more emphasis on the function of the prophet or messenger.

The framework of the life of the Muslims at Medina was determined for them by various economic and other material factors. In dealing with the difficulties which arose from time to time, however, Muḥammad was guided by the fairly coherent set of ideas found in the Qur'ān. That these ideas were adequate and appropriate to the various situations was one of the foundations of his success. Another was his own wisdom, tact, patience and other statesmanlike qualities. It is interesting, as one runs through the course of events, to see the importance of these fundamental ideas and how they were progressively adapted to the needs and problems of Medina.

V

THE PROVOCATION OF THE MECCANS

The First Expeditions or Razzias

One or two domestic events are dated in 623. The most important was the consummation of Muḥammad's marriage with 'Ā'ishah, which took place in April, when the bride can only have been about nine. She had been betrothed to him a a year or two earlier at Mecca, but had continued to live in her father's house. Indeed she may have gone on living there for some months after April 623. Eventually she moved to one of the apartments opening off the courtyard of the series of buildings which was both Muḥammad's home and office and also the mosque for the common worship of the Muslims.

The sources do not comment directly on her tender years, though they describe how she went on playing with her toys, and how Muḥammad entered into the spirit of her games. 'What are these,' he would say, and she would answer, 'Solomon's horses.' This relationship between a man of fifty-three and a girl of ten must have been a strange one, more like father and daughter than husband and wife. We must remember, of course, that girls matured much earlier in seventh-century Arabia. There were no children to the union, but 'Ā'ishah seems to have been as happy as a girl could be in a polygamous household. Her marriage was clearly for the political reason of binding together Abū-Bakr and Muḥammad, and just as Abū-Bakr was Muḥammad's chief lieutenant, so she was his chief wife, even though three years earlier after the death of Khadījah he had married Sawdah, a Muslim widow of about thirty, as noted above.

Most of Muḥammad's own marriages, as well as those he arranged for his daughters and his close associates, are found to have political reasons of one kind or another. In the following August (or perhaps not till June 624) his daughter Fāṭimah was married to his cousin 'Alī. This indicated that 'Alī was one of Muḥammad's close associates, and bound him to him. 'Uthmān ibn-'Affān, later the third caliph and one of the leading Muslims, had been married at Mecca to an older daughter of Muḥammad's, Ruqayyah.

Important as these matters were for later history, the chief feature of the year 623 was the adoption of the practice of organizing razzias against Meccan caravans. The first is usually held to have taken place in March. Muḥammad sent out his uncle Ḥamzah (who was only four years older than himself) with a party of thirty men on camels to go towards the Red Sea coast and try to ambush a Meccan caravan returning from Syria. Apart from the fact that the Muslims accomplished nothing it is not clear what happened. It is stated that the caravan was accompanied by 300 men under the leadership of Muḥammad's opponent Abū-Jahl; and the size of this force alone would have justified the Muslims in not carrying out the plan for the ambush. There seems to have been some risk of fighting, however, for a nomad chief, who was allied to both sides, is said to have intervened to keep the peace.

This was the first of a number of 'expeditions' or razzias organized by Muḥammad and the Muslims in the course of 623. In April another leader with a body of sixty men tried to intercept another Meccan caravan. On this occasion one of the Muslims is said to have shot some arrows—the first warlike act on behalf of Islam—but the caravan had a strong guard and discretion was thought to be the better part of valour. Another in May of perhaps only eight men reached the road from Mecca to Syria a day after the caravan had passed. The failure of all these efforts must have been very disheartening for the Emigrants, who alone were involved.

Whether because of the general discouragement and the ensuing tensions, or for some other reason, Muḥammad himself led further expeditions in August and September and again in December. All were directed against Meccan caravans, and all were unsuccessful, at least in their primary aim. The mere demonstration, however, of this readiness to attack Meccan caravans in favourable circumstances must have increased the anxieties of the Meccans and at the same time shown the nomads of the region that Muḥammad meant business. Some small clans or tribes made alliances with Muḥammad in the course of his expeditions, probably pacts of non-aggression. The failures were doubtless largely due to the fact that Muḥammad's opponents in Medina gave the Meccans information about his plans.

An insight into the conditions in which Muḥammad was working is given by an incident which occurred about September. A band of nomads, probably friendly to the Meccans, descended on pasture grounds not far from Medina and drove off a number of the Muslims' camels that were grazing there. As soon as news reached Muḥammad and his followers they set out in pursuit. After about three days, however, it was clear that they would be unable to catch up with the freebooters, at least before they joined up with friends who would protect them, and they therefore returned to Medina.

Simple as these events are in the telling, they involved momentous decisions for the whole future of the Islamic community, and it is worth while trying to understand them. A useful starting-point is to ask how Muḥammad expected the Emigrants to gain their livelihood after they reached Medina. He cannot have expected them to farm lands in the oasis, and he cannot have intended them to be permanently dependent on the hospitality of the keener Medinan Muslims. He cannot have reckoned on the opposition of the Jews and the consequent elimination of those of them who were traders, since up to the Hijrah and for some months afterwards he hoped the Jews would recognize him as a prophet. It seems certain, then, that he expected that the Muslims would make a living either by engaging in trade themselves or by preying on the trade of Mecca. These alternatives are not exclusive, of course. It would probably have been impossible for them to organize caravans to Syria until Meccan trade with Syria had been seriously dislocated, and until the tribes along the route thought the Muslims sufficiently strong to make protection of their goods (for a fee) more profitable than raiding. And there are indications that from the first some of the Muslims did business in the Jewish market at Medina.

When one looks at all the alternatives, however, it seems clear that even before he left Mecca Muḥammad must have looked on raids on Meccan caravans as a possibility, even a probability. In the raids the Muslims were taking the offensive. Muḥammad cannot have failed to realize that, even if the raids were only slightly successful, the Meccans were bound to attempt reprisals. In these little raids, then, he was deliberately challenging and provoking the Meccans. In our peace-conscious age it is difficult to understand how a religious leader could thus engage in offensive war and become almost an aggressor.

The first thing to be said in explanation of Muḥammad's behaviour is that the raid or razzia was a normal feature of Arab desert life. It was a kind of sport rather than war. The Arabs had their wars indeed, but these were much more serious affairs. The razzia was directed against the camels and other animals of an unfriendly tribe, less frequently (and only when things were more serious) against their womenfolk. A body of raiders would try to take by surprise a few camel-herds and their charges, while the rest of the clan or tribe was far away. For the time being the raiders would have overwhelming force, and little resistance would be offered. The raiders had then to try to rejoin the main body of their tribe before a superior force from the tribe attacked could overtake them. The Arabs generally tried to avoid hand-to-hand fighting on approximately equal terms. They seldom deliberately attacked except when they had the advantage of surprise or of overwhelming superiority, however temporary. Thus the loss of life in razzias was usually small. Loss of life, of course, was always a serious matter, since it could lead to a bitter blood-feud, and both sides would try to avoid it when there was no specific hostility between them. When the killing was accidental or incidental, it was becoming customary in the early seventh century for the injured tribe to accept a blood-wit of camels, though the conservatives described this disdainfully as 'accepting milk instead of blood'.

The next point to consider is that Muḥammad and his contemporaries thought of a religious community in a different way from the modern West. For us a religious body is a group of people who come together for common worship, and perhaps for some other limited purposes; but for Muḥammad the religious community was a body of people associated with one another in the whole of their lives, that is, was also a political unit. He had originally thought of a prophet as a man sent to a particular tribe or people, that is, to a political unit. When his own tribe would have none of him, he began to use the word *ummah* or 'community' for that group, out of all to whom the prophet's message was addressed, which accepted it. At Mecca the Islamic community was not unlike a modern Western religious community, but with the Hijrah the conception was further developed. Islam became, at least nominally, the religion of a political community, and the latter ceased to be merely a political community. As the years passed and the Islamic religion permeated into more aspects of the common life, the members of this unique political and religious body had no other way of describing it than to say it was an *ummah*. It was neither a tribe, nor a federation of tribes, nor a kingdom; and these were the only political units with which they were familiar.

The razzias mentioned so far were not undertakings of the whole community but solely or primarily of the Emigrants. The expedition to Badr in March 624 is usually said to have been the first on which the Helpers (or Medinan Muslims—in Arabic *Anṣār*) took part, though some may have taken part, as it were privately, in earlier expeditions; the number of participants given for some of the expeditions led by Muḥammad personally is much greater than the number of Emigrants in Medina. This distinction between the activities of the Emigrants and the Helpers is reflected in a Qur'ānic passage (8. 73–75) which speaks of the former as 'those who believed and emigrated and strove with goods and person in the way of God' and of the latter as 'those who gave shelter and help'.

The Emigrants went on razzias because they thought they had been badly treated by their fellow-Meccans. One verse describes them as 'those who after persecution emigrated, then strove and patiently endured' (16. 111); 'strove' here implies 'went on razzias'. Another passage (22. 40 f.) makes their treatment by the Meccans the justification for their hostile activity: 'permission is given (sc. by God) to those who are fighting because they have been wronged . . . those who were driven from their homes for no reason but that they say "God is our Lord"'. It is conceivable, however, that this verse was an answer to the complaint of some of the more nominal Muslims in Medina that the razzias were endangering the safety of all Medina; the answer would consist in saying that they have been ill-treated because of their belief in God, and that God approves of their striking back.

Thus, whether Muḥammad incited his followers to action and then used their wrongs to justify it, or whether he yielded to pressure from them to allow such action, the normal Arab practice of the razzia was taken over by the Islamic community. In being taken over, however, it was transformed. It became an activity of believers against unbelievers, and therefore took place within a religious context. The Emigrants were described as 'striving with goods and person in the way of God'. They were promoting one of the purposes of the Islamic community in trying to establish a region in which God was truly worshipped. As this character of their activity became clear to the Emigrants, there was no reason why they should not call on the Helpers to share in it. If it was God's work, all Muslims should share in it. Besides, the Meccans seem to have been reinforcing the guards on their caravans, and more participants were necessary if the razzias were to be successful. A verse (5. 39) which was probably intended to encourage the Helpers to join in the razzias runs: 'O believers, fear God . . . and strive in His way.' Thus it was because of the religious character of the Muslim expeditions that the Medinans were invited to share in them.

This transformation of the nomadic razzia has wider implications than are apparent from the English translations used. The word translated 'strive' is *jāhada*, and the corresponding verbal noun is *jihād* or 'striving' which came in the course of time to have the technical meaning of 'holy war'. The change from the razzia to the *jihād* may seem to be no more than a change of name, the giving of an aura of religion to what was essentially the same activity. Yet this is not so. There was a change in the activity which came to be of the utmost importance as time went on. A razzia was the action of a tribe against another tribe. Even if two tribes were very friendly, their friendship might cool, and in a few years a razzia might be possible. *Jihād*, however, was the action of a religious community against non-members of the community, and the community was expanding. If members of the pagan tribes raided by the Muslims professed Islam, they at once became exempt from further Muslim raids. Consequently, as the Islamic community grew, the raiding propensities of the Muslims had to be directed ever further outwards. It was this 'religious' character of the *jihād* which channelled the energies of the Arabs in such a way that in less than a century they had created an empire which stretched from the Atlantic and the Pyrenees in the West to the Oxus and the Punjab in the East. It seems certain that without the conception of the *jihād* that expansion would not have happened.

The First Bloodshed

The serious implications of engaging in razzias against the pagan Meccans became obvious when Meccan blood was shed on a razzia in January 624. The story of this razzia leads to a number of interesting points.

A little band of from eight to twelve Emigrants was sent out under the leadership of 'Abd-Allāh ibn-Jaḥsh. They were told to proceed eastwards for two days, and then to open a sealed letter which had been given to 'Abd-Allāh. By this method no disaffected person in Medina was able to learn the ultimate destination and inform the enemy. When 'Abd-Allāh opened the letter, he found instructions to proceed to a place called Nakhlah far to the south on the road between Mecca and aṭ-Ṭā'if and there to ambush a Meccan caravan returning from the Yemen. He was also to tell the other members of the party of the destination and to give them an opportunity of withdrawing. As the operation would be a highly dangerous one, it was desirable that all who took part should do so willingly. No one retired at this point, but two members of the party disappeared. When they returned to Medina several days *after* the successful raiders, they had a good story about how their camel had strayed and they had become cut off from the main body. It may well be true that this is the story they told, but it does not follow that the story was true or that it was believed.

'Abd-Allāh and the rest of the party reached Nakhlah, found the caravan, and joined up with it. There was no difficulty about this, for they pretended to be pilgrims to Mecca and they were still in one of the sacred months when all bloodshed was forbidden. In this way they were able to accompany the caravan until they found an opportunity for attack. Perhaps they intended from the first to break the taboo of the sacred month. Perhaps they had hoped to avoid violating the month, but came to realize that before the end of the sacred month the caravan would have reached the sacred territory of Mecca, which was equally taboo. Whatever the exact situation, the Muslims made a surprise attack on the guards of the caravan during the sacred month. Since nothing of this kind had been expected on the southern route from Mecca, there were only four guards. One was killed, two were taken prisoner, and the fourth escaped. The latter presumably took the news to Mecca as quickly as possible, but the Muslims had no difficulty in reaching Medina safely with the caravan and their two prisoners.

There must have been jubilation in Medina, especially among the Emigrants ; but there were also misgivings. The latter seem to have been more widespread than Muḥammad expected. He is said to have kept the booty undistributed, and not to have accepted the fifth of it that was offered to him, until the matter was cleared up. (It is doubtful, however, whether the practice of giving Muḥammad a fifth of any booty captured in a Muslim raid had yet been established.)

The misgivings were ostensibly because of the violation of the sacred month. Some thought that there was a contradiction between Muḥammad's call to worship God and his profaning of the sacred month. Some perhaps thought that this profanation would bring the wrath of the divinities upon them in some form or another. Others, even if they spoke about the divinities, may have been more concerned about the danger of the wrath of the Meccans. Apart from the normal demand for vengeance for the life taken and apart from annoyance at the loss of the caravan, the Meccans must have been infuriated that this should have been done under their very noses, as it were. Those Medinans who were not too friendly to Muḥammad must have been perturbed at the serious turn things were taking. The Meccans had been thoroughly provoked, and were certain to retaliate.

Muḥammad's hesitation in the face of Medinan misgivings came to an end when he received a revelation (2. 214) to the effect that, while fighting in the sacred month was serious (with the connotation of sinful), keeping people from the way of God, and disbelief in Him, and the expulsion and persecution of His people are more serious than killing. There is no mention of the material and mundane dangers from the Meccans. It is interesting, too, that the sacredness of the month is not denied. All that is asserted is that violation of the month is less heinous than certain forms of opposition to the Islamic religion. It may be that Muḥammad himself did not believe there was any real sacredness in the month, since its sacredness was linked up with the old religion, but had to reckon with a continuing belief in it, especially among his Medinan followers. On the other hand, he had from an early time regarded God as Lord of the Ka'bah (Q. 106. 3), and later considered that the sacredness of Meccan territory derived from Him (2. 119; 3. 91), and also the sacredness of certain months (9. 36). With regard to the months two attitudes were possible for a Muslim in accordance with the principles of his religion. One—that adopted in the verse just mentioned (9. 36)—was to hold that it was God who made the months sacred and that therefore unbelievers could not expect to receive any benefit from their sacredness. The other was to hold that the sacredness of the months was pagan, and that therefore the Muslim need not observe it. One would imagine Muḥammad to have taken the second position as long as he was trying to make his religion more Jewish. Just while he was wondering what to do about this expedition, however, he was finally turning away from the Jews and making his religion more Arabian; and he may therefore have been moving from the second position to the first.

Such was the expedition to Nakhlah and its consequences. There is much about it that is obscure. The version given of some of the details is only one of several, and motives have usually to be inferred from external facts. Yet it is clear that Muḥammad had here, more or less deliberately, thrown down the gauntlet to the Meccans. They were the strongest and wealthiest people in this region of Arabia, perhaps in the whole of it. Trivial as this incident was, it gave a blow to their prestige which they could not afford. From this moment they must have been planning how to 'teach a lesson' to this upstart in Medina.

The Break with the Jews

The story is told how one day while Muḥammad was leading the public prayer of the Muslims he received a revelation commanding him to face Mecca instead of Jerusalem. He and the Muslims with him had begun the prayers facing Jerusalem, but when this revelation came they all turned round and faced Mecca instead. This happened at a place of prayer in the district of the clan of Salimah, and the site was afterwards known as the Mosque of the Two Qiblahs. It is significant that the change should have first been made here, for before the Hijrah it was a member of the clan of Salimah who had wanted to face Mecca instead of Jerusalem. The date given is 11 February 624.

In reality the change may not have happened so quickly and smoothly as this story suggests. The verses about the change in the Qur'ān (2. 136–147) give the impression of having been revealed at different times. It has therefore been suggested that there may have been an interval between dropping the Jerusalem *qiblah* and adopting the Meccan. Even if this is not so, Muḥammad must have hesitated before making the change. Apart from the purely religious or intellectual question, the change probably involved relying on a different grouping of clans from the one on which he had hitherto relied.

The sources say nothing explicitly about this, but, if one looks closely at the persons who did most to help Muḥammad during March and April 624, one gets the impression that political changes were also taking place. In particular, the break with the Jews, symbolized by the change of *qiblah*, involved an estrangement from 'Abd-Allāh ibn-Ubayy, who was friendly with some of the Jews and probably hoped for their support in realizing his ambition of becoming prince of Medina. It may be at this point that the Hypocrites (to use the later name) became definite opponents of Muḥammad's policies. Muḥammad's provocation of the Meccans doubtless contributed to their dislike of him. At the same time, one of the most important men in Medina, Sa'd ibn-Mu'ādh, threw in his lot actively with Muḥammad and the policies which were now becoming apparent. He was the chief of the clan of 'Abd-al-Ash'hal, and, though his clan had been at war with Salimah, had a close friendship with an important section of Salimah. Sa'd's support for Muḥammad included bringing more than two hundred of the Helpers on the expedition which led to the battle of Badr and taking a part in the subsequent action against the Jewish clan of Qaynuqā‘. From this time until his death he is reckoned as the foremost of the Helpers or Medinan Muslims. It would therefore seem that the widespread disapproval of the affair at Nakhlah, the break with the Jews, the turning away from ‘Abd-Allāh ibn-Ubayy and the turning towards Sa‘d ibn-Mu‘ādh are linked with one another. The change of *qiblah* could thus be interpreted as a gesture to some of the anti-Jewish clans of Medina, to win their support and to show that Muḥammad was committing himself to them.

The break with the Jews had many aspects. There were other changes in outward forms. Hitherto the Muslims, or at least the Helpers, had apparently observed the Jewish fast of the Day of Atonement, and Muḥammad had commanded all Muslims to do this in 623 (probably July). In February or March 624, however, the fast of the month of Ramaḍān was made obligatory instead of that of the Day of Atonement. Ramaḍān began on 26 February in 624, and some sources speak of the Muslims trying to fast while on the expedition to Badr in early March. It seems more likely, however, that it was not instituted until after Badr, and was then intended to be a celebration of the victory, as the Jewish fast was of the deliverance of the Israelites from Pharaoh and his host at the Red Sea.

The most important aspect of the break with the Jews was the intellectual. The Jews were attacking the whole set of ideas on which Muḥammad's position was based. They declared that some of the things in the Qur'ān contradicted the ancient scriptures in their hands, and must therefore be false; in that case they could not be a revelation and Muḥammad could not be a prophet. This was very serious. If many of the Muslims thought that what the Jews were saying was true, the whole structure of the community so carefully built by Muḥammad would crumble away. Especially with the increasing disapproval of his policies from a political standpoint, he needed the support of men who whole-heartedly believed in the religious aspect of his mission. The Jews were doing what they could to deprive him of such support, and as the possessors of the scriptures they were able to act effectively.

At the centre of Muḥammad's attempt to 'contain' the attacks of the Jews was the conception of the religion of Abraham. The Qur'ān had all along insisted that its message was identical with that of previous prophets, and notably with the messages of Moses and Jesus, the founders of Judaism and Christianity respectively. This idea could not be excised from Islam. It had been an important part of the claim presented to the pagan Meccans, and was asserted or implied in a great many passages. Yet it was difficult not to admit that the Jews were correct in pointing to the differences. The only alternative to the inference that the Qur'ān was false was to show that the differences were due to deviations on the part of the Jews. It need not be supposed that Muḥammad thought this out logically. However the ideas first occurred to him, after they had occurred he saw their appropriateness to the situation.

The religion proclaimed by Abraham, it was asserted, was the true religion of God in its purity and simplicity. It was identical with the religion preached by all the prophets, including Muḥammad. If the Jews and Christians had something different, then the differences were due to them. Some of the special rules imposed on the Jews might indeed have been commanded by God, but these were intended only for the Jews and were by way of being a punishment on them. Some of what the Jews alleged to be the revealed scriptures were not that, but additions they themselves had made—

presumably a reference to the Jewish oral law. The Qur'ān also accuses the Jews and Christians of 'altering' the scriptures and of 'concealing' them. In the Qur'ān the former charge may mean no more than that the Jews and Christians gave false interpretations of some passages, but in later Islam it has been taken to mean that the Bible as a whole or large parts of it are corrupt and therefore unworthy of trust. The second charge means that the Jews kept silent about certain verses in which the Muslims considered that Muḥammad was foretold.

This new way of looking at things could be supported by various facts which the Jews could not deny. They could not deny the Muslim assertion that Abraham was not a Jew, for they had to admit that he lived before the Jewish religion was revealed, whether that is made to begin with Jacob or, as the Muslims normally did, with Moses. And when the Muslims argued that there was nothing surprising in the Jewish rejection of Muḥammad, since they had rejected many of the prophets sent to them and mentioned in their own scriptures, the Jews could not deny that there was some truth in this latter matter.

The Qur'ān also went on to criticize Jewish exaggerations of their claim to be the chosen people. There was an old Arab custom that in certain cases a man might be challenged to take an oath calling down some dire calamity or even eternal perdition upon himself if some assertion he had made was false. The Jews were challenged to swear in this way that they were the friends of God and that they alone would be in Paradise. The challenge presumably did not worry the Jews, but by not responding to it they would weaken their position in the eyes of the Arabs. Another telling argument of the Qur'ān against the exclusive claims of the Jews was that the Christians made similar claims, and that both could not be true.

The identification of the Islamic religion with the religion of Abraham made it easy to incorporate various Arab ceremonies. The Ka'bah was said to have been founded by Abraham, and some use was made of the view, derived from the Old Testament, that the Arabs were descended from Ishmael.

This religion of Abraham was at first called the *ḥanīfīyah* or *ḥanīf* religion. The word *ḥanīf* has been much discussed by Western scholars. It appears to have been used previously by Jews and Christians for 'pagan', and also to have been applied to followers of the Hellenized (and philosophical) form of the old Syro–Arabian religion. In pre-Islamic Arabia, though there were men who were attracted by monotheism and who are called *ḥanifs* by later Muslim writers, they do not seem to have applied the word to themselves. In the Qur'ān it is given a new turn and means a monotheist who is neither a Jew nor a Christian. The Christians continued to use it for 'pagan', and to taunt the Muslims with it. This may have been why it passed out of favour with the Muslims. For a time they were content to say they followed 'the religion of Abraham, the *ḥanīf*'. Eventually, however, they came to prefer the form 'the religion of Abraham, the *ḥanīf*, the *muslim*'. *Muslim* is a participle meaning 'surrendered' (*sc.* to God). It was appropriate to apply it to Abraham, who along with his son whom God had told him to sacrifice 'surrendered himself (to God)' (Q. 37. 103). *Islām* is the corresponding verbal noun with the meaning 'surrender (to God)', and is a good name for a religion. Though it is convenient to speak of Muḥammad's religion from the first as Islam, this name may not in fact have been given to it until late in the Medinan period.

The conception of Islam as a restoration of the pure religion of Abraham offends modern Western standards of historical objectivity. Yet from a sociological standpoint it must be admitted that it was effective in its original environment. It enabled Muḥammad to maintain with only a slight modification the set of ideas on which his religion was based, and to parry the hostile criticisms of the Jews. It was the adaptation of a set of ideas to a new situation in which the practical attitudes and activity based on the ideas were no longer appropriate. With the Jews behaving as they were, Muḥammad could no longer support his claim to prophethood by the testimony of the Bible, as he had done at Mecca. He had to revise his attitude to the Jews. But the conception of the religion of Abraham was no after-thought—a justification for a course of action already decided on. The position rather was that Muḥammad was being forced by circumstances to take up new attitudes to the Jews, to the pro-Jewish Medinans (like 'Abd-Allāh ibn-Ubayy) and to the anti-Jewish Medinans (like Sa'd ibn-Mu'ādh). He had also to do nothing to disturb the faith of his loyal followers, as he would have done had he abandoned a large part of his former revelations. In this situation there could be no practical decision until there was an idea on which to base it. The decision to give up trying to conciliate the Jews and their friends and the decision to accept the conception of his religion as the religion of Abraham (with the related complex of ideas) were two aspects of one decision.

The modern Westerner ought also to be ready to admit that the conception of the religion of Abraham is not entirely without foundation. Islam may not tally with what objectively we consider the religion of Abraham to have been. But Islam belongs in a sense to the Judaeo-Christian tradition, and that tradition may be described as the tradition which begins with Abraham. Islam is thus a form of the religion of Abraham—a form, too, well suited to the outlook of men whose way of life was closer to Abraham than that of the bulk of Jews and Christians.

THE BATTLE OF BADR (15th March 624)

While Muḥammad was dealing with the various matters which have just been mentioned, he received information about a large Meccan caravan which was setting out from Gaza to return to Mecca. Perhaps several smaller caravans, after narrowly escaping from the Muslims on the way north, had joined together for greater safety. It would presumably be easier to give adequate protection to a large caravan than to several smaller ones. It is reported that the merchandise in this caravan of 1,000 camels was worth 50,000 dīnārs, and that nearly everyone in Mecca had a share in it. About seventy men accompanied it, and it was commanded by Abū-Sufyān ibn-Ḥarb, one of the most astute men in Mecca.

In view of the importance of the caravan Muḥammad raised the largest possible force to intercept it. In this he now had the active support of Sa'd ibn-Mu'ādh. This enabled him to collect over 300 men—according to one list, 238 Helpers and 86 Emigrants. This was by far the largest force he had so far commanded, and was probably the first on which the Helpers were officially present. If the figure of 150 to 200 participants given for some of the earlier expeditions led by Muḥammad is correct, there must have been some Helpers present; but they were doubtless some of the poorer Medinans who were attracted by the prospect of plunder. It is said that Muḥammad's agreement with the Medinans only bound them to defend him within the territory of Medina. If that was so, then the earlier razzias or expeditions were enterprises of the Emigrants alone, in which the Medinan clans were not concerned as clans, even if a few individuals joined them. The presence of Sa'd ibn-Mu'ādh and over 200 Helpers at Badr, however, following on the events of the last two months, indicates a change of policy on the part of the Helpers. Some at least are now prepared to give active support to Muḥammad's policy of provoking the Meccans.

Meanwhile, perhaps through Muḥammad's enemies in Medina, word reached Mecca of the grave danger in which the caravan would be placed. The Meccans, led by Abū-Jahl, set about raising a large force. The chief of a neighbouring tribe, of which a section had a blood-feud with the Meccans, gave his word that they would not attack Mecca, even if it was stripped of defenders. Eventually about 950 men set out. Abū-Jahl probably hoped to overawe Muḥammad and his followers, to scare away any potential recruits, and to stop them attacking Meccan caravans in the future.

The various parties converged on a place called Badr, where there were some wells. It was the point on the coast road from Syria to Mecca that was most easily reached from Medina. Muḥammad had set out about five days before the battle, and Abū-Jahl about nine. Muḥammad's main objective was the caravan. Abū-Sufyān, however, was aware of his intentions, and by forced marches and devious routes managed to elude the Muslims. It looked as if the great expedition was going to be a failure. For the Muslims merely to return home, however, would have looked like a sign of cowardice in the face of the superior Meccan force. They therefore remained in the neighbourhood, and camped at the wells of Badr on the evening of 14th March.

Meanwhile Abū-Jahl got word that the caravan had escaped. Some of the Meccans are now said to have wanted to go home. The only remaining cause of war between them and Muḥammad, they said, was the blood of the man killed at Nakhlah; and one of the Meccan leaders offered to pay blood-money himself to keep peace. Abū-Jahl, however, skilfully shamed him into withdrawing his offer. He was more fully aware than others of the danger Meccan trade was in from Muḥammad, and must have hoped to do something to stop it or at least to reduce it. He may also have been moved by personal considerations ; the right to command in battle apparently belonged to Abū-Sufyān, so that it was only in his absence with the caravan that Abū-Jahl could command a force like this, and he wanted to make the most of his opportunity. The rest of the Meccans, with some knowledge of this personal motive and of the rivalry between Abū-Jahl and Abū-Sufyān, were not wholeheartedly in favour of continuing in the field. Two clans completely withdrew, but the remainder were persuaded not to hurry home. On the evening of 14th March their camp was not very far from that of the Muslims.

Neither party was probably keen to fight. It was more in keeping with Arab custom to try to impress the other side without actually having to fight them. The bulk of the Muslims presumably thought they had come to plunder a caravan whose guards were greatly inferior to themselves. Most of the Meccans doubtless thought they were so strong that the Muslims would keep at a safe distance. Even Abū-Jahl may have thought this, though he may also have hoped there might be an encounter. It is difficult to know what was in Muḥammad's mind. If it was his policy to provoke the Meccans, and if he thought the Muslims were more than a match for the pagans, then he may have tried to create a situation in which the Muslims could not honourably avoid a battle.

This was in fact what happened. Both sides unexpectedly found themselves so close to the enemy that they could not retire without disgrace. A reconnoitring party of Muslims is said to have captured a water-carrier of the Meccans. When questioned, the man told the truth about Abū-Jahl's force, but the numbers were so large that the Muslims thought he was lying and punished him. Muḥammad himself then appeared and cross-questioned the man and realized that he was speaking the truth. Perhaps Muḥammad already had some information about the Meccans. Certainly, whether in this way or some other, Muḥammad had definite news of the Meccans before they had much news of him, and this gave him the tactical initiative.

When he heard that Abū-Jahl was not far away, Muḥammad gave orders to block up the wells, all except the one nearest Mecca, round which he stationed his men. The enemy, presumably now in need of water, was thus forced to fight, and to fight on ground of Muḥammad's choosing. On the morning of the 15th they advanced towards the wells. They seem to have known that Muḥammad was in the neighbourhood, but at the same time to have been astounded to find him so placed that they could not obtain water without fighting. Even if they were not in need of water, they could not now retire without dishonour.

The battle appears to have opened with a number of single combats between champions, as was the normal custom of the Arabs. In these the Muslims had the advantage, and many leading Meccans were killed, including Abū-Jahl. There was also arrow-shooting on both sides, which was responsible for some deaths. Finally there was a general mêlée which turned into the flight of the Meccans. Apart from this it is difficult to say much about the course of the battle, though the anecdotes are plentiful. There was no dubiety about the result, however. Muḥammad's little force of 300 had utterly routed a much larger force of Meccans and killed many of their leaders. The list of Meccan dead varies from forty-five to seventy, and there was a similar number of prisoners (lists are extant with sixty-eight and sixty-nine names respectively). In achieving this victory the Muslims lost only fourteen men, six Emigrants and eight Helpers. Muḥammad himself did not take part in the fighting but, with Abū-Bakr at his side, directed it from a hut or shelter nearby; he spent much of the time in prayer, and is also said to have had a religious experience.

The Muslims had a large amount of booty. To prevent the quest for loot interfering with the pursuit of the enemy, Muḥammad announced that the booty, apart from the spoils of those killed and the ransoms for those taken prisoner, would be divided equally among those who took part in the battle. The ransoms must have amounted to a considerable sum, for many of the prisoners came from wealthy families. Those who were not sufficiently influential or wealthy to be ransomed, Muḥammad usually set free without any ransom. Generosity in any form was always admired by the Arabs, but Muḥammad may also have been beginning to realize that one day it would be important for him to win the Meccans to his side. For some weeks after the battle many Meccans visited Medina to arrange for ransoms.

Life was not entirely idyllic, however. One or two of the prisoners were treated with harshness and ferocity—an indication of the roughness of the age. The common attitude was that a man might do what he liked with his prisoner, but that it was normally better to consider what was profitable or advantageous for himself and his clan. At Badr at least one pagan, who was being led off by a Muslim captor, was set on and killed by a group of Emigrants who particularly hated him. The captor, of course, lost the ransom. Such excesses Muḥammad put a stop to. Yet even he had two prisoners executed. One had written verses about him, and the other had said that his own stories about things Persian were as good as the tales of the Qur'ān. Throughout his career Muḥammad was specially sensitive to intellectual or literary attacks of this kind. They were for him an unforgivable sin. Matters like the treatment of prisoners are important in that they show us grim features of the environment in which Islam was born.

Lack of unity among the Meccans contributed to their defeat. Of the 950 who set out from Mecca perhaps only 600 or 700 were left, and not all of these were convinced of the wisdom of Abū-Jahl's policy. At the same time they were over-confident, since, partly because of their wealth, their dominant position in western Arabia was now unquestioned. They had not been involved in any serious warfare, however, since about 590, and a more luxurious life may have made them softer. Yet when the records of the Meccan Emigrants and the Medinan Helpers in the battle are scrutinized, there does not appear to be any marked difference between them in fighting quality; and so one must be hesitant in ascribing softness to the Meccan pagans. What is probably true, however, is that many of the pagans were men past their prime, whereas the Emigrants were mostly younger men at the height of their physical power. All the Muslims, too, would tend to fight more bravely because of their belief in a future life, while Muḥammad's confidence, grounded in his steadfast belief in God, would inspire confidence in his followers.

The Significance of Badr

The defeat at Badr was a serious disaster for the Meccans. Of the fifteen or twenty most influential and experienced men in Mecca a dozen had been killed. Abū-Sufyān was safe, and indeed controlled Meccan policy for the next three years; and there were other younger men coming forward. Yet the loss of so much ability and experience was a catastrophe.

The loss of prestige was even more serious, though its effects did not appear immediately. Comparatively small forces had been involved in the battle, and Medina clearly had neither the strength nor the necessary skills to take the place of Mecca as commercial capital of western Arabia. Yet the prestige of Mecca had been shaken. Old enemies like the tribe of Hawāzin, doubtless began to wonder how long it would be before they could have another trial of strength with the Meccans. Meanwhile the issue between Muḥammad and the Meccans was the more urgent. Abū-Jahl had clearly been right in his view of the seriousness of Muḥammad's challenge to Mecca's position. After Badr they could no longer neglect that challenge. They could only restore their prestige if they met the challenge and crushed Muḥammad. To this all their efforts must now be bent. Muḥammad could therefore expect a vigorous riposte from the Meccans, and would have to make it his primary task in the ensuing months so to organize matters in Medina that he would be able to parry that riposte. Would he be able in a short space of time to increase the number of his active supporters and decrease the number of opponents ?

It would be a mistake, however, to think of Badr simply as a political event. For Muḥammad and his followers it had a deep religious meaning. There had been those weary years of hardship and opposition at Mecca. Then there had been the long months at Medina when nothing seemed to be going right. Now came this astounding success. It was a vindication of the faith that had sustained them through disappointment. It was God's vindication of their faith in Him, His supernatural action on their behalf. The Qur'ān develops this religious interpretation of the event in various passages, e.g. ' You did not kill them, but God killed them ; you did not shoot (and strike) when you shot, but God shot, to let the believers experience good from Himself ' (8. 17).

So the victory at Badr came to be regarded as the great deliverance God had effected for the Muslims, comparable to the deliverance he had effected for the Israelites at the Red Sea. The destruction of Pharaoh and his hosts and the escape of the Israelites was the *furqān* or ' salvation ' given to the prophet Moses (the Arabic word is an adaptation of the Syriac *pūrqāna*). Similarly the disaster to the Meccans was the Calamity foretold for them in the Qur'ān, and the victory granted to Muḥammad was his *furqān*, and a ' sign ' confirming his prophethood. In the light of this interpretation the mood of the convinced Muslims was one of great elation. Muḥammad and the more thoughtful were aware of the great danger ahead, and put all their energies into preparations to meet it. Yet even they seem to have been carried away somewhat by the general elation.

VI

THE FAILURE OF THE MECCAN RIPOSTE

Consolidation at Medina; the expulsion of Qaynuqā'

Of the tasks confronting Muḥammad after Badr one of the most important was the consolidation of his position in Medina, and the removal of some of the sources of weakness. The victory of Badr itself, following upon the decision of Sa'd ibn-Mu'ādh to give him active support, had greatly strengthened him. In the sources there are many little straws to show which way the wind was blowing. Larger numbers of Helpers were now ready to take part in Muḥammad's expeditions. The prospect of booty attracted to Medina poor nomads from the neighbouring region. Some of the leading men of Medina also began to think again. One, a rival of Sa'd's, who may before Badr have thought it to his advantage not to espouse a losing cause, and who therefore stayed away, now came and apologized to Muḥammad, saying that he thought it was only a raid for booty and that had he known there was to be fighting he would certainly have been present. Muḥammad handled the truants very gently and did all he could to reduce the opposition to himself.

Yet he was also capable of sternness. In the flush of victory two Medinans, a man and a woman, who had written poems against him, were killed by persons related to them. The woman belonged to one of the few clans which had not accepted Islam, and the man's clan was probably not wholly Muslim. The tenor of the verses of both was that it was dishonourable for the people of Medina to allow an outsider to control their affairs, a man who confused right and wrong (perhaps an allusion to the violation of the sacred months), and who aimed at being a king. Muḥammad probably did not know about the plans beforehand, but he did not express any disapproval afterwards, and none of the next of kin of the two persons dared to exact vengeance for their death. On the contrary a number of waverers became Muslims, and it was probably as a result of these events that all the Arab clans of Medina officially accepted Islam.

Another political assassination may be mentioned here, though it did not take place till some five months later in early September 624. The victim was Ka'b ibn-al-Ashraf, the son of a nomadic Arab father and a Jewish mother, but usually reckoned as belonging to his mother's clan of an-Naḍīr. His offence was that after Badr he was so disgusted with Muḥammad's success that he went to Mecca and composed anti-Muslim verses which had a wide circulation. Muḥammad, always sensitive to attacks of this kind, instigated one of the Muslim poets, Ḥassān ibn-Thābit, to satirize Ka'b's Meccan hosts. This was felt so keenly by these hosts that Ka'b was obliged to return to Medina, but he did not cease to make propaganda against the Muslims. (All this illustrates the power of the poets of that age.)

Muḥammad seems to have let it be known that he would gladly be rid of Ka'b. Five Muslims, at least one of whom was a foster-brother of Ka'b, hatched a plot and obtained from Muḥammad permission to say what they liked about himself. The milk-brother by his relationship and by his complaints about the hardships suffered under Muḥammad, such as lack of food, gained Ka'b's confidence. He agreed to give them a loan and to accept arms as a pledge. To receive the arms he left his house in the middle of the night. At a quiet spot the five set upon him, and not without some difficulty killed him. All five were members of clans in alliance with an-Naḍīr, and therefore the question of a blood-feud could not arise.

In the gentler or (should we say ?) less virile age in which we live men look askance at such conduct, particularly in a religious leader. But in Muḥammad's age and country it was quite normal. Men had no claims upon you on the basis of common humanity. Members of your tribe and of allied tribes, and those protected by your tribe, had very definite claims ; but outside this circle no one had any claim at all. That is to say, in the case of a stranger or enemy there was no reason why you should not kill him if you felt inclined. The only consideration that might hold you back was the ability of his kinsmen to exact vengeance, or respect for your own word in the case where you had been induced to accept him as a guest before you realized who he was. A man like Ka'b ibn-al-Ashraf was a clear enemy of the Islamic community, and so there was no obligation to consider him in any way. Since those who assassinated him were from a clan in alliance with his and on which his own clan was dependent there was no likelihood of a blood-feud developing. So far were the Muslims who killed him from having any qualms about it that one of them, describing the return from the deed wrote that they returned ' five honourable men, steady and true, and God was the sixth with us '. Because this was a normal way of acting one could carry out such a deed believing that one was serving God and meeting with His approval.

The other side of this picture is that Muḥammad himself had to be constantly on his guard against possible assassins. The story is told of one such, a poor Meccan, who was persuaded by the chief of his clan to make an attempt on Muḥammad's life while ostensibly arranging for his son's ransom. He sharpened his sword and poisoned it. When he reached Medina, he was admitted to Muḥammad's presence, though some of the Muslims were suspicious at the sight of his sword. Muḥammad, however, showed no fear and asked him to step forward and say why he had come. He maintained it was only to arrange the ransom, but Muḥammad told him of his arrangement with his clan-chief that he would kill Muḥammad and was able to give so much detail that the man was convinced of Muḥammad's supernatural knowledge, acknowledged his prophethood and became a Muslim.

Of all the events of the year 624 after Badr the expulsion of the clan of Qaynuqā' in April (or perhaps a month or two later) did most to consolidate Muḥammad's power. The ostensible reason for this was a petty quarrel between some Jews of Qaynuqā' and some Muslims who were doing business in the market there. While an Arab woman was sitting at a goldsmith's, a Jew contrived to fasten her skirt with a thorn in such a way that when she stood up a large part of her person was exposed. The bystanders laughed, and a Muslim who was present, regarding the trick as an insult, killed the perpetrator and was himself killed. The Jews then retired to their strongholds, and shortly afterwards Muḥammad and a large party of Muslims came and besieged the Jews.

Little credence need be given to the story of the trick, for it also appears in legends of pre-Islamic Arabia; but there may well have been some quarrel between Muslims and Jews. The deeper reasons for Muḥammad's action, however, are obvious. The Jews were not prepared to become full members of the Islamic community, and therefore he had broken with them. They still had agreements of some sort with him, but he would be on the look-out to take advantage of any failure to fulfil the letter of the agreements. This is presumably what happened here. He was aware, too, of the close relations between the Jews and some of those who were opposing his new policy of active hostility towards Mecca. He may also have been moved (though probably only very slightly) by a conflict of interests between Qaynuqā' with their market and the Emigrants. Certainly it is probable that after this most of the internal trade of Medina was in the hands of the Emigrants.

The siege lasted for fifteen days, and then the Jews surrendered. It was arranged that they were to leave Medina, taking their wives and children, but leaving behind their arms and probably their goldsmith's tools. Three days were granted to them to collect money owing to them. Then they moved off, first to the not very distant Jewish colony of Wādi-l-Qurā, and then after a month to Syria.

They had been allies of 'Abd-Allāh ibn-Ubayy and other Medinan Arabs. The others, however, were now active Muslims, and denounced their alliance. Only 'Abd-Allāh ibn-Ubayy tried to stop the expulsion. He had an interview with Muḥammad, but, as he tried to force his way into Muḥammad's presence, the man on guard pushed him so violently against the wall that his face bled, and he was apparently not in a position to exact vengeance or compensation. He urged upon Muḥammad the important contribution Qaynuqā' could make to his forces in the event of further fighting with the Meccans—they were said to have 700 fighting men, of whom about half were armoured. But Muḥammad insisted that they must leave, though he was prepared to be lenient about the other conditions. This failure of their Medinan allies to support them, and the indication of the comparative weakness of 'Abd-Allāh ibn-Ubayy, doubtless convinced the Jews that it was best to yield on the terms offered. The whole affair shows how much the political climate in Medina had changed since the beginning of 624.

Another form of consolidation that was in evidence in the year following Badr was the binding together of the leaders of the Emigrants by marriage relationships. The marriage of Muḥammad's cousin 'Alī with his daughter Fāṭimah may not have taken place until June 624. The first child of this marriage, Muḥammad's grandson al-Ḥasan, was born early in March 625. In September 624 Muḥammad married another of his daughters, Umm-Kulthūm, to 'Uthmān who later became third caliph. 'Uthmān had previously been married to Umm-Kulthūm's sister Ruqayyah, but Ruqayyah had died about the time of Badr. This marriage was thus the renewal of a previous tie. Finally about the end of January 625 Muḥammad himself married Ḥafṣah, the daughter of 'Umar, who became second caliph. This both forged a link with one of his most important lieutenants, and also provided for Ḥafṣah, whose previous husband had been one of the handful of Muslims killed at Badr. These marriages, like all the marriages Muḥammad contracted himself or arranged for his followers, had thus a definite political purpose, whatever else may have been involved.

The Expeditions of 624 after Badr; Meccan Preparations

Consolidation of his position in Medina, however, was only one of Muḥammad's tasks. Another and even more urgent one was to get ready for the Meccan riposte that was now inevitable. The prosperity of Mecca depended on its prestige. To maintain their far-spread commercial operations the Meccans must make it clear to all their neighbours that this was only a temporary lapse, that they were still stronger than Medina and that they were capable of removing this threat to their trade. From the Meccans Muḥammad could expect nothing but an intensification of the struggle. He had therefore to make the most of the time available to him. It is against this background that his expeditions during the rest of 624 are to be understood.

At Mecca the news of Badr was received at first with incredulity and then, as the magnitude of the disaster was realized, with a dismay that inhibited effective action. Abū-Sufyān took control of affairs. He forbade mourning for the dead, professedly to prevent the Muslims from gloating over their plight and to avoid dissipating the energies required for revenge, but perhaps really to avert a complete collapse of morale. He publicly announced that he himself had vowed to have nothing to do with oil or women till he had carried out a raid against Muḥammad. He also got all those with shares in the caravan he had brought back safely to agree to devote the profits to war preparations.

After a time the pent-up feelings swept away the prohibition of mourning. Perhaps it had served its turn. Ka'b ibn-al-Ashraf, the Medinan Jew, in his poems encouraged the expression of grief in order subsequently to stir up the desire for revenge. The leaders began to plan how they might restore their position. Meanwhile there were prisoners to be ransomed.

Some ten weeks after Badr, about the end of May, Abū-Sufyān, in fulfilment of his vow, led a party of 200 men to raid Medina. His primary aims were doubtless to restore confidence among the Meccans and to show the world that the day of Mecca was not yet over. He may also have hoped to learn something about the political situation in Medina. With this small force—less numerous than the Muslims at Badr—he cannot have intended to inflict any serious damage on Muḥammad. It is unlikely that he expected a large number of Medinans to join him. His control of news leaving Mecca must have been very good, for he apparently reached the outskirts of Medina without Muḥammad's knowledge. A former friend, the chief of the Jewish clan of an-Naḍīr, gave him a meal and some information about the local situation, but nothing more ; and he decided to retreat immediately. To fulfil his oath two houses were burnt and some fields laid waste.

This was a typical razzia, characterized by surprise and speed, but achieving little. As soon as he heard of Abū-Sufyān's presence in the neighbourhood, Muḥammad collected at least 200 men and set out in pursuit. He was not quick enough, however, and was unable to catch up with the Meccans. Yet the latter were hard-pressed, and abandoned some excess provisions, consisting mainly of barley-meal. This was picked up by the Muslims who because of it called the expedition 'the barley-meal raid'.

Later in this same year—in July, in September and at the end of October—Muḥammad personally led three expeditions. The number of participants is reported to have ranged from 200 to 450. The latter figure shows an increase of over a hundred on the force Muḥammad had at Badr. It is to be explained partly by the greater readiness of the men of Medina to take part in the Muslim raids and partly by the beginning of an influx of nomads into Medina. The latter point is worth noting. It is impossible to give exact statistics; but from this time there are found in Muḥammad's entourage men from some of the poorer and weaker tribes of the region to the west and south-west of Medina—the tribes in whose territories the Muslims had shown themselves during 623. Some of these men looked after camels for Muḥammad. One at least was thought sufficiently capable to be left in charge of Medina on certain occasions when Muḥammad was absent on an expedition. Such people were closely attached to Muḥammad himself, and would always support him against any combination of Medinan clans. Some were officially given the status of 'Emigrants'; others may rather have been regarded as persons protected by the 'clan' of Emigrants.

Unlike the expeditions of 623 these three expeditions in 624 were directed against tribes to the east and south-east of Medina. In the first and third the tribe of Sulaym is mentioned. Now this tribe had close contacts with the Meccans because these were interested in the mines which were found in its territory. The second expedition was against tribes a little to the north of Sulaym, either identical with or closely related to some tribes which two years later sent a strong force to help the Meccans. The inference is that all three expeditions had the aim of deterring these nomadic tribes from supporting the Meccans. They were given ocular proof that, if they took active measures against Muḥammad, he was in a position to avenge any injuries he suffered.

Meanwhile the Meccans were bending all their energies to retrieving what they had lost. No caravans were sent to Syria during the summer by the coast road which passed between Medina and the sea. After the blow to Meccan prestige many of the tribes along the route, especially those near Medina, would be more favourable to Muḥammad than to the Meccans. To ensure the safety of a caravan it would require to be accompanied by a very large force ; and even that would not rule out the possibility of a battle with the Muslims, since the larger the force the more difficult to keep its movements concealed. At this juncture, therefore, Abū-Sufyān judged it wiser not to dissipate his strength on a caravan, but to concentrate on preparing a military expedition against Medina.

A group of Meccans, however, rivals of Abu-Sufyan, decided to risk sending a caravan by a route well to the east of Medina. They found a reliable guide, and despatched a caravan worth 100,000 (silver) dirhams. Unfortunately Muḥammad got word of the caravan, and against it sent his adopted son, Zayd ibn-Ḥārithah, with a hundred men. They were successful in capturing the whole caravan. The men in charge of it, knowing what had happened at Badr, were doubtless terrified at the prospect of fighting against Muslims and made good their escape. This was in November 624.

The Battle of Uḥud (23rd March 625)

About 11th March 625 the main army set out from Mecca. Some of the allied detachments may have joined them as they progressed. By the time they reached Medina they had a force of 3,000 well-equipped men; 700 had coats of mail. There was a camel for each man for the journey, and 200 horses to form a cavalry force in the battle. No major tribe had been induced to join the Meccans. The allies who sent detachments were minor tribes which, even if nominally independent, were in fact largely dependent on Mecca. Abū-Sufyān had the chief command of the expedition. Not merely had his drive been behind the preparations for it, but it was the privilege of his clan to provide the commander-in-chief in war. The general direction of the campaign, however, he shared with others, notably Ṣafwān ibn-Umayyah (of the clan of Jumaḥ) who had been coming to the fore as the chief rival of Abū-Sufyān and was the chief person behind the ill-fated caravan of November 624.

The army advanced by easy stages and reached the oasis of Medina on Thursday 21st March. The best road for an army was through a wādi to the west of the oasis, from which there was convenient access to the oasis by its north-west corner. This was the route followed by the Meccans. No attempt was made by the Medinans to attack them as they marched, and they entered the northern part of the oasis without opposition. For their camp they chose a site here, a little to the south of the hill of Uḥud. In this neighbourhood there were fields of corn, now in the ear, and they deliberately pastured their animals in them in order to provoke the Medinans to come out to fight.

On Thursday evening a scout brought Muḥammad exact information about the strength of the Meccans, and some of the Helpers kept guard at his door all night. Early on Friday the Muslims held a council of war. Muḥammad, 'Abd-Allāh ibn-Ubayy and some of the senior men were for remaining in the centre where the strongholds and other buildings were close to one another; in this way the enemy would be forced to undertake a combination of siege and house-to-house fighting. Younger men, however, together with one or two men of weight, argued that to allow the Meccan army to lay waste the fields (as it was doing) would make them seem cowards and ruin their reputations in the eyes of the nomadic tribes, and that therefore it was better to go out. Muḥammad was eventually won over to the latter view and the decision taken to go out. Some of the hotheads cooled down and said they were willing to accept Muḥammad's original plan, but he, very properly, stuck to the new decision with the remark that once a prophet has put on armour he must not take it off until God has decided between him and his enemy.

Later in the day the Medinan forces set out in the direction of the enemy camp. Muḥammad is said to have rejected the help of a Jewish contingent, allies of 'Abd-Allāh ibn-Ubayy, because they were not believers. Some distance short of the enemy they halted for the night. Very early next morning, using their superior knowledge of the terrain, they made their way unobserved to a position on the lower slopes of the hill of Uḥud. The enemy camp was thus between them and the main settlements of the oasis. To protect the left flank Muḥammad stationed a party of fifty archers on a mound or spur a little to the east.

Shortly before the battle began 'Abd-Allāh ibn-Ubayy and his followers left the field. It is probable, as the reports suggest, that this had something to do with the decision not to remain in the strongholds as he had advocated. In this case, however, it is strange that he went out even part of the way. Whatever the precise thought in his mind, it must have been based on a selfish calculation of some sort. A passage of the Qur'ān almost certainly refers to this (3. 160–62):

> Your misfortune on the day the two hosts met was by God's permission, so that He might distinguish the believers from the

> Hypocrites. It was said to them, ' Come, fight for God, or defend yourselves '. They said, ' If we knew fighting (*sc.* with a hope of success, or, would actually take place), we would follow you '. Nearer to unbelief were they then than to belief. They spoke with their mouths what was not in their hearts, but God knows what they conceal. Those who had remained behind said to their brothers, ' Had they listened to us, they would not have been killed '.

This passage is important because it probably marks the introduction of a new way of referring to those opponents of Muḥammad's who had up till now been ' those in whose hearts is disease '. They are now ' hypocrites ' or ' those who play the hypocrite '. The change of name also means increasing bitterness between the two parties, especially since 'Abd-Allāh ibn-Ubayy made no secret of his joy at Muḥammad's discomfiture. Even with this defection Muḥammad had a larger army than at Badr, reported to be about 700 men. The Meccans were vastly more numerous, but the quality of many of their troops may not have been good.

Muḥammad had chosen his ground skilfully. He had in a sense left the main part of the oasis exposed to the enemy; but he probably calculated that the numerous little forts or strongholds scattered over the oasis were capable of resisting any Meccan assaults and that the Meccans were not likely to waste time on them. The Meccans would therefore require to attack his own force. To do so they would have to go forward across a wādi and then move towards the hill. The hill slopes would prevent them attacking him with their cavalry, and would also keep them from making much use of their numerical superiority.

The battle may have opened with an attempt by the cavalry to rush Muḥammad's position, but, if so, they were driven back by the Muslim archers. Then the Meccan standard-bearer moved forward, perhaps with a view to single combat, but soon a general mêlée developed round the standard. The clan which had the privilege of bearing the standard fought with great gallantry against heavy odds. Nine clansmen were killed defending the standard—a large number for a small clan. The standard did not fall into Muslim hands, however, but the Meccan infantry gave way before the Muslim onslaught, perhaps even fled. Just how far the Muslims advanced is not certain. Some reports state that they entered the Meccan camp, but others assert that they gained no booty (though the two points need not be contradictory).

As victory was almost within their grasp, there was a sudden reversal of fortune. The cavalry on the Meccan right under Khālid ibn-al-Walīd, observing some disorder in the Muslim advance and a movement of the archers away from their station to join the advance, quickly overran the few remaining archers and attacked the Muslim flank and rear. A scene of great confusion followed, especially as the cry went up that Muḥammad had been killed. Muslims wounded other Muslims—in at least one case mortally. Muḥammad was not in fact killed, but for some time there was a fierce hand-to-hand struggle round him. He received two or three wounds on the face and leg, and himself inflicted a spear wound on one of the Meccans, from which the man subsequently died. Eventually Muḥammad and the group round him reached the slopes of the hill. Here the Muslims rallied and were given some sort of order. A section, however, had become separated from the main body and had made for a stronghold nearer the centre of the oasis ; of these many, perhaps most, were killed.

The position on the hill—with the Muslims perhaps a little higher up than before the battle—still had the advantages for defence which Muḥammad saw when he first chose it. In particular it was beyond the reach of the Meccans' chief offensive arm, their cavalry. The attacks on the hill soon ceased, therefore, though the Meccans remained on the field for some time longer. At last, with a final taunt to the Muslims, Abū-Sufyān ordered withdrawal. Though the battered Muslim force was now licking its wounds on the hill of Uḥud, Abū-Sufyān did not attempt to attack any part of the oasis or even to march through it, but headed for Mecca by the route by which he had come.

In trying to make an assessment of the battle of Uḥud the first question to ask is the purely military one : who won the battle ? who had the advantage in it ? Some Western scholars, not without justification from the early Muslim accounts, have thought that it was a very serious defeat for the Muslims and a great victory for the Meccans. From the military standpoint this view is mistaken. The strategic aim of the Meccans was nothing less than the destruction of the Muslim community as such, or—what amounts to the same thing—the removal of Muḥammad from his position of influence in Medina. This aim they completely failed to achieve. They had indeed killed about seventy-five Muslims for the loss of twenty-seven of their own men, and thus more or less avenged the blood shed at Badr (though according to some versions there would still be an excess of Meccan dead). But they had boasted that they would make the Muslims pay several times over for Badr, and now they had at most taken a life for a life. They had had the better of the fighting as measured by casualties, but they had failed to do what they intended to do. They had recently thought that they had all western Arabia under their control, and now they had shown themselves unable to do little more than hold their own against Muḥammad. What humiliation for the proud merchant princes of Mecca ! It was an intimation that the end of their commercial empire was at hand.

The failure of the Meccans is underlined by their failure to press home the advantage they gained in the closing stages of the battle. Abū-Sufyān was certainly aware of the strategic necessity of destroying Muḥammad's power, and apparently knew before he left the battlefield that the claim of a Meccan to have killed Muḥammad was false. Why then did he withdraw ? Why did he take no further action ? The answer is that there was little he could do. He could not repeat the attack on Muḥammad's position, for he had a number of wounded and most of his horses had received arrow-wounds. Besides, set battles were not in the Arab tradition of fighting. It would also be unwise to move further south into the oasis. He knew that 'Abd-Allāh ibn-Ubayy and an important part of the Medinan forces had not been engaged, and might attack him if he appeared to move against them. There were also other Medinans who had not joined in the march to Uḥud, but who had no doubt been making preparations to defend their strongholds. He may also have been hoping to win over 'Abd-Allāh ibn-Ubayy by diplomacy, having heard something of his coolness towards Muḥammad. The decisive fact, however, was probably that his infantry had been roughly handled by the Muslims in the first part of the battle, and shown to be greatly inferior. Their morale must now have been very low. With the cavalry out of action the wisest course was clearly to return home.

For Muḥammad, on the other hand, the purely military result of the battle was not wholly unsatisfactory. The Muslims had shown themselves almost equal to the Meccans. Their infantry was more than a match for their opponents. The Muslim casualties were mostly due to the enemy cavalry, and the Muslims were still too poor to have a cavalry squadron of their own. Despite this weakness, however, Muḥammad had managed to hold his own against the Meccans, and that was all he needed to do at the moment. For the future much would depend on how many men he could attract to his community and whether he could maintain its fighting qualities. About seventy of the Muslim casualties were Helpers, and that might increase the opposition to him in Medina. The casualty list would also reduce Muslim prestige somewhat in the eyes of the nomads.

On the whole, however, these debit items were of a secondary nature. The main thing was that Muḥammad's position in Medina was still intact. The battle was essentially a draw. The Muslims lost considerably more men, but apart from that the draw was distinctly in their favour. The practical conclusion to be drawn was that the two sides would require to meet at least once again to settle the issue. In the meantime the task of both was to increase their strength as far as possible. This was not only a military matter, however. Muhammad was able to attract military support because his was a religious movement and because he was being carried forward in the stream of emergent social forces. The Meccans, on the other hand, were attempting to retain a position of privilege that was no longer appropriate in the new circumstances. How was each side going to fare in the months ahead ?

Yet if the battle of Uḥud was not a military defeat for Muḥammad, it might almost be called a spiritual defeat. This was because Muḥammad and the Muslims had regarded the victory of Badr as a special mark of God's favour to them—a confirmation that the work of spreading Islam in which they were engaged was indeed work to which God was calling them. In their elation after Badr they seem to have drawn exaggerated inferences from this premise. They can hardly be blamed for this. It is a tendency to be seen in religious men in all ages. Addressing the God-fearing man the Psalmist said :

> There shall no evil befall thee,
> neither shall any plague come nigh thy dwelling.
> For (God) shall give his angels charge over thee,
> to keep thee in all thy ways. (90. 10 f.)

The Muslims seem to have concluded that in future they would always be victorious. There was a verse of the Qur'ān (8. 66) which seemed to justify confidence not merely in their military superiority, but even in their invincibility.

> O prophet, urge the believers to fight : 'if among you are twenty steadfast men, they will vanquish two hundred ; if among you a hundred, they will vanquish a thousand . . .'

Perhaps when Muḥammad thought it best not to go out to fight, he realized that this was somewhat exaggerated or else thought that many of the Muslims were not 'steadfast'.

Because of this intellectual context in which it took place the battle had a devastating effect on most of the Muslims. If Badr was a sign of God's favour, were their casualties at Uḥud a sign of his disfavour ? Or was he completely neutral with regard to them ? The average Muslim must have been seriously troubled by such thoughts. He would be aware of the large number of Muslim dead, but not of the place of the battle in the whole strategy of Muḥammad's struggle with the Meccans. The Qur'ān gives some indications of how the problem was dealt with.

The chief point was to explain how God, without abandoning the Muslims, could allow such misfortunes to befall them. It was not possible to say that they were the result of superior numbers or of the greater offensive power of their cavalry. The Muslims had been encouraged to think that God would give them victory over vastly superior forces. It is noteworthy, however, that in the Qur'ān as we now have it the verse quoted above about one Muslim being more than a match for ten adversaries is followed by another (8. 67) which states that God has reduced His demands on the Muslims, knowing their weakness; and now only expects one Muslim to be a match for two adversaries ! Even with this modification, however, there was still a problem. It was solved by placing the blame on the Muslims themselves.

> God was indeed faithful in his promise to you, letting you kill them ; but you slacked off, and were at variance, and disobeyed, after He showed you your desire ; some of you wanted this world, some the next ; then He distracted you from them (and let you fare badly) to test you ; but He has pardoned you, for He is gracious to the believers ; you were making for the hill, turning aside for none, while the Messenger was calling you from behind, so He recompensed you sorrow upon sorrow, that you might regret neither what missed you nor what befell you . . . (3. 145–47)

In other words, the misfortunes of the Muslims at Uḥud were permitted by God, partly as a punishment for disobedience and partly as a test of their steadfastness. At the same time the Muslims were shown (ib. 172 f.) that the comparative good fortune of the Meccans did not mean that God was showing favour to them ; their success would not be for their ultimate good, but would lead to further disobedience against God, which would ultimately bring punishment upon them.

Such were the problems, military and religious, that the battle of Uḥud created for Muḥammad. The difficulties were not insuperable, but sufficient to call out the best in Muḥammad and the Muslims. The experience of adversity at this stage in the development of Islam made the Muslims more capable of seizing the opportunities which later came to them.

The Aftermath of Uḥud

Muḥammad and the Muslims buried the dead on the battlefield, and returned to their homes late in the evening of 23rd March. Overnight Muḥammad had time to reflect on the position and realized, if he had not done so already, that he had suffered no irretrievable disaster, and that much depended on his actions in the immediate future. On the following morning, therefore, he summoned those who had been with him at Uḥud to set out in pursuit of the retreating Meccans. It was the normal and expected thing for an Arab to do when he had been the victim of a raid. Muḥammad had presumably no intention of attacking the Meccans, any more than they can have thought seriously of attacking him. It was an act of defiance and a demonstration of strength.

The Meccans spent Saturday night at a place called Ḥamrā'-al-Asad only a few miles from Medina, but they had left it before the Muslims arrived at it on the Sunday. They remained in the vicinity, however, for they had to avoid giving any grounds for the impression that they were fleeing from Muḥammad. To make his demonstration the more impressive and to ensure that the Meccans did not try to return to the attack Muḥammad kept his men hard at work all day collecting wood, and then at night lit many fires to suggest that his force was much larger than it really was. The ruse seems to have worked. A friendly nomad also helped to lower the morale of the Meccans by exaggerating the number of Muslims. Abū-Sufyān, of course, was trying to spread disquieting rumours among the Muslims. But Muḥammad did not flinch, and no attempt was made to bring him to battle. After a day or two the Meccans set off home.

Long before they reached Mecca Abū-Sufyān and the other leaders must have realized that their position was critical. They had made a great effort and had not succeeded. Unless they could do much better they were faced with disaster. For the expedition of Uḥud they had collected all the available men from Mecca itself and also some detachments from surrounding friendly tribes. The only way to raise a more powerful army was to attract the active support of some of the great nomadic tribes to the east and north-east. With great energy the Meccans set about doing this, using all the means at their disposal—propaganda about Muḥammad's weakness, memories of the prestige of Mecca, promises of booty and even straight bribes.

Muḥammad had a good information service, and during the next two years he was at pains to forestall any hostile moves. As soon as he heard of a concentration of tribesmen threatening Medina, he sent out an expedition to break it up. Such was the expedition to Qaṭan in June 625. The nomads dispersed at the approach of the Muslims, but the latter captured a little booty. Perhaps it was as a result of seeing the Muslims in action that nine men of one of the tribes here professed Islam and went to live at Medina. Even if the men did this because of some personal rivalry within the tribe, it is a good example of how Muḥammad's strength was growing. Later in June (according to the most likely date) Muḥammad was informed of the gathering together of a large force by a nomadic chief Sufyān al-Liḥyānī, and to this information he responded by either ordering or conniving at the assassination of Sufyān by one of the Muslims.

The attempted concentrations of nomads which Muḥammad thus prevented are an indication that the Meccans were having some success in rousing the tribes against Muḥammad. Two disasters which befell parties of Muslims shortly afterwards are pointers in the same direction.

The first was that at the well of Ma'ūnah, also in June 625. Involved in this was the tribe of 'Āmir, within which two men, uncle and nephew, were rivals for the chiefship. For the moment the uncle was the stronger and was able to carry a large part of the tribe with him, but the nephew also had a following. The uncle was inclined to become a Muslim, doubtless hoping with Muḥammad's backing to consolidate his position in the tribe. To achieve this end it was necessary that a sufficient number of tribesmen should become Muslims along with him. He therefore asked Muḥammad to send some young men to instruct his tribe, and formally undertook to protect them. Such protection had to be confirmed by the tribe as a whole, but the uncle, despite the opposition of his nephew, persuaded the tribe to honour his undertaking.

Foiled at this point the nephew then went to some clans of another tribe (Sulaym) which happened to be near, gave them information of the approach of the Muslim party, and urged or induced them to attack it. This they did and killed all the Muslims except two, a nomad from near Medina, who may have been related to some of the attackers, and a Medinan who was left for dead on the field but eventually arrived home. The nomad who escaped happened to meet two men of the tribe of 'Āmir on his way back with the news, and killed them in revenge for his comrades. Unknown to him, however, these men belonged to a section of the tribe which was in alliance with Muḥammad. So Muḥammad was in the curious position that, after losing nearly forty men, he had to pay blood-wit for two, instead of receiving any; and the sources even say that he had to pay it to the very man, the nephew, who was really responsible for the Muslim deaths. The solution of this paradox seems to be that, though the nephew was morally responsible, the blood had actually been shed by another tribe.

If we neglect the puzzles in this story (which have not been fully expounded here), certain general points stand out. Muḥammad was now trying to gain a foothold in a part of Arabia where his prestige and influence did not yet count for much, that is to say, where men were not afraid of his power to retaliate. His relative weakness here was doubtless due in part to Meccan propaganda and to the connexion between the Meccans and the tribe of Sulaym. It was important for Muḥammad, however, to have as many allies as possible, and he was prepared to take the risks involved in meddling in the internal politics of the tribes. He must have known about the rivalry of the uncle and nephew, for Abū-Bakr, his chief lieutenant, was an expert in genealogy, and that would include knowledge of the political relations of the different sections of a tribe. The sending of young men to the tribe of 'Āmir was therefore the taking of a calculated risk. The result was unfortunate for those concerned, but the tribe of 'Āmir as a whole never became hostile to Muḥammad.

A week or two later in July 625 the Muslims suffered another similar loss. The victims were seven men whom Muḥammad had sent to be instructors to a tribe which said it wanted to accept Islam. This was merely a pretext, however. At a spot on the road to central Arabia the guides from the would-be Muslim tribe abandoned the seven. They had in fact been bribed to act in this way by the tribe of Sufyān al-Liḥyānī, who had just been assassinated by a Muslim. This tribe now fell upon the Muslim party, killed four who resisted and, after making fair promises, took the other three prisoners and led them in bonds to Mecca. On the way one of the three gained his freedom and died sword in hand. The remaining two were sold in Mecca to relatives of men killed at Badr, who did not consider that their blood had yet been avenged. After the sacred month was over the two prisoners were taken outside the sacred area, summoned to recant from Islam, and, when they refused, put to death not altogether painlessly. The wider implications of this event are similar to those of the disaster at the well of Ma'ūnah. Muḥammad was urgently trying to extend his power even in districts where risk was involved.

The Second Expulsion of Jews

The news of the loss of two small parties of Muslims must

have thrown a gloom over Medina. The losses were perhaps not considerable in themselves. The list of those killed at the well of Ma'ūnah has less than twenty names, all Emigrants or Helpers, and this suggests that, even if there were more killed, they were allied nomads. Even so, however, the losses would be felt keenly among people for whom every individual counted as an individual. Though there may have been during the period positive achievements of which we have no record, they cannot have been sufficiently spectacular to outweigh the losses. Muḥammad, with his grasp of strategic realities, may not have been unduly perturbed; but the ordinary Muslim, still recovering from the spiritual shock of Uḥud, may have felt that the situation was deteriorating. Muḥammad's opponents in Medina may have thought they would soon be rid of him.

This is the background against which we have to try to understand Muḥammad's treatment of the Jewish clan of an-Naḍīr. One day in August 625 Muḥammad went to their settlement to demand a contribution to the blood-money which he had to pay to the tribe of 'Āmir for the two victims of the man who escaped from the well of Ma'ūnah. There may have been complications. As an-Naḍīr were in alliance with 'Āmir, Muḥammad may have thought they ought to do more than the other inhabitants of Medina, and they may have thought they ought to do less. Whatever the precise point, they professed themselves ready to give a satisfactory answer, but bade Muḥammad make himself comfortable while they prepared a meal. He and his companions seated themselves with their backs to the wall of one of the houses.

Presently Muḥammad slipped quietly away and did not return, and his companions also eventually left. When they found him at his house, he explained that he had had a warning from God that an-Naḍīr were planning a treacherous attack on him—they could easily have dropped a heavy stone on him from the flat roof and killed him as he sat by the house. He therefore at once despatched an ultimatum to an-Naḍīr; they were to leave Medina within ten days on pain of death, though they would still be regarded as owners of their palm-trees and receive part of the produce.

Such an ultimatum seems out of proportion to the offence, or rather to the apparently flimsy grounds for supposing that treachery was meditated. Yet perhaps the grounds were not so flimsy as they appear to the modern Westerner. Both parties knew how some Muslims had treated Ka'b ibn-al-Ashraf; and, in accordance with the ideas of the Arabia of that day, Muḥammad was bound to expect that, if he gave his opponents an opportunity, they would kill him. An-Naḍīr's postponement of a reply created such an opportunity, and was therefore tantamount to a hostile act.

The Jews were at first inclined to submit to the demand, especially when they saw that it was brought to them by one of the leading men of the Arab clan on which they were primarily dependent for support. The foremost man of an-Naḍīr, however, by name Ḥuyayy, was less inclined to submit than some of the other leaders. While Ḥuyayy hesitated, 'Abd-Allāh ibn-Ubayy sent messages to him promising support and speaking of the readiness of some of the allied nomads to attack Muḥammad. The Jews therefore refused to comply with Muḥammad's demand, and he set about besieging them.

The siege lasted about fifteen days. An-Naḍīr lost heart when the Muslims began to destroy their palms. 'Abd-Allāh ibn-Ubayy was doing nothing to help them and they realized that, even if they were able to keep their foothold in Medina, their livelihood would be gone. They told Muḥammad they were ready to fulfil his original demand, but he now imposed less favourable terms. They were to leave their weapons and to have nothing from the palms. To this perforce they agreed, and with a train of 600 camels departed proudly for Khaybar, some seventy miles to the north, where they had estates. The swords, cuirasses and helmets all went to Muḥammad to be used, when needed, for arming the poorer Muslims. By agreement with the Helpers the houses and palm-gardens were allotted to the Emigrants (and two poor Helpers); this meant that they were now able to support themselves and were no longer dependent on the hospitality of the Helpers.

For this expulsion of a Jewish clan there were a number of possible motives, and it is now impossible to say which was dominant in Muḥammad's mind. Perhaps the ostensible reason—the attempt to kill him—was uppermost. In view of the recent disaster many Medinans would be incensed against the Jews because of their connexion with the tribe of 'Āmir. It seems likely, however, that Muḥammad may have been largely moved by the need to cheer up the Muslims after their misfortunes and to strengthen his own position in Medina; and all that he certainly succeeded in doing.

Reforms of Marriage and Inheritance

The loss of life among the Muslims at the battle of Uḥud created certain social problems, especially that of making some provision for the women who had been widowed and the girls who had been orphaned. The basis of the modern Islamic system of polygamy is a verse of the Qur'ān (4. 3) which was revealed not long after Uḥud.

> If you are afraid that you will treat the orphans unjustly, then marry what women seem good to you, twos and threes and fours; if you are afraid you will not deal equitably, then one; or what your right hands possess (*sc.* slave concubines); then you are more likely not to be unfair.

The curious thing about this verse is that it is not saying to men who had had six or ten wives 'You shall not have more than four'. On the contrary it seems to be encouraging men who had had only one (or perhaps two) to marry up to four. How is this to be explained?

There is an immense mass of detail in the sources, but it is fragmentary and not always easy to interpret. The following is in the nature of a provisional account. It has to begin with conditions in Arabia before Muḥammad, and this is precisely where the difficulties are greatest.

There is a considerable amount of evidence to show that, at least in much of Arabia, the social system was on a matrilineal basis. Men and women are reckoned as belonging to their mother's clan. There are tribes whose common ancestor is a woman. At Medina such features are more frequent than at Mecca, where the social system seems in the main to be on a patrilineal basis. It is conceivable, then, that what we have in pre-Islamic Arabia is the mingling of two systems which had previously been in force in two separate groups of people. A more likely hypothesis, however, is that we have a largely homogeneous society which is in transition from a matrilineal system to a patrilineal one. This would fit in with the view expressed above that individualism was growing in Mecca and other parts of Arabia. Individualism means, among other things, that a man appropriates to his personal use what had hitherto been communal property, though perhaps administered by him on behalf of the group. It would be natural for him at the same time to become specially interested in *his own* children and to want to hand on his newfound personal wealth to them.

A matrilineal group consists of a woman and her descendants, male and female. On the basis of such groups social structures of varying kinds are possible. We do not know exactly what happened in Arabia, but it was probably something like this. When the first woman died, her position as head of the household would be taken by her eldest daughter, and she would perhaps be followed by her next eldest sister. Property would belong to the group communally, and would be administered by the chief woman's brother (on the mother's side) or by her eldest son. This means that a man hands on the administration of property not to his own son, but to his sister's son.

Marriage for a woman did not mean leaving the family home. The husband must come to ' visit ' her for longer or shorter periods. One thinks of two desert tribes camping close to one another for a short while, then becoming separated by vast distances. In a number of cases a woman seems to have had two husbands concurrently, one from her own clan and one from some other tribe or clan. One report says that in pre-Islamic times there were some women who had one husband at a time, some who had up to ten, and some who had sexual relations with any man who came to them. This may well be true, but we do not know the exact position in the social structure of the women in question—especially of the last group who are really prostitutes. Perhaps the Muslim author of the report exaggerated the looseness of the marital customs of the days before Islam. What is clear, however, is that in such a system it was not important for most purposes to know who a child's father was ; it was sufficient to know his mother. The child belonged to his mother's family and lived in her family house (or tent). The father would have no house of his own, but, when not visiting his wife, would live in the house of his sister or maternal aunt.

It is against this background that the marriage reforms of the Qur'ān are to be seen. Perhaps the most important is the apparently simple prescription that, when a woman is divorced, she is to have a ' waiting period ' of three months before she remarries. Divorce was and is common in Arabia. The point of this provision is to ensure that there is no doubt about a child's paternity. It implies, of course, that a woman has only one husband at a time. The Qur'ān advocates this but does not insist on it universally, realizing that it was not immediately practicable. The whole structure of a society cannot be changed in a year or two. By desiderating the strict determination of physical paternity, however, the Qur'ān was taking the essential step in transforming a matrilineal society into a patrilineal one.

The exhortation to the Muslims to marry two, three or four wives must be taken to imply that these women had no other husbands at the same time. We do not know in whose house the married couple lived. In some cases it seems likely that the woman continued to live with her own family, and that a man 'visited' his various wives in turn. On the other hand, Muḥammad himself gave an example of a different arrangement, according to which the wives went to live in the husband's house. Muḥammad had a separate room or small suite built for each of his wives round the courtyard of his house. The Emigrants may already have been accustomed to arrangements of this type. Gradually other Muslims would adopt it, until it became in time the normal practice.

The mention of orphans in the Qur'ānic verse quoted suggests that the crux of the problem after Uḥud was not the widows but the unmarried girls who now became wards of uncles, cousins and other relatives. It would be easy for a selfish and unsympathetic guardian to keep his wards unmarried so that he could have unrestricted control of their property. He would allow them to contract the looser kinds of union, but nothing else. This would be all the more irksome in matrilineal Medina if, as seems likely, guardianship now went in the male line. Such is the situation the Qur'ān was trying to meet by encouraging a man to have several wives. It probably did not mean the guardian to marry his ward himself (unless the two were outside the forbidden degrees). The idea would rather be that, if all Muslims had several wives, it would be possible for girls to be properly married as soon as they were old enough.

The net effect of these reforms is to give the family a more individualistic basis and to discourage older customs in which the group counted for more than the individual. Similarly the Qur'ānic rules about the inheritance try to ensure a fair division of property in a society which is moving from a communal basis to an individualistic one. The perennial temptation in such a period of transition is for the strong man who administers property on behalf of his group to treat this property as if it was his own private possession. The Qur'ān gives precise but rather complicated rules about inheritance. Of several rules dealing with the matter one (4. 12) runs as follows:

> In respect of your children God enjoins : the male is to have the equivalent of the portion of two females ; if (the children) are females (only), more than two, they receive (between them) two-thirds of what (the deceased) left ; if only one, she has a half. His parents receive each a sixth of what he left, if he has children ; but if he has no children, and his parents are his heirs, his mother receives a third. If he has brothers, his mother receives a sixth—(all this) after the payment of any bequest he has made and any debt.

What is of interest here is not the details—though it is important to note that women are capable of owning property in exactly the same way as men—but the way in which the Qur'ān fixes a precise share for all persons closely related to the deceased, and thus tries to stop the influential and unscrupulous individual from taking advantage of his weaker kinsmen.

Muḥammad himself demonstrated this new conception of the family. He already had three wives, and in the early part of 626 he married another two. One, Zaynab bint-Khuzaymah, belonged to the tribe of 'Āmir with which he had been trying to foster closer relations. She was also the widow of an Emigrant killed at Badr, whose clan was closely linked with Muḥammad's own. She was only about thirty, but she died a few months after the marriage. The other was Umm-Salamah, the widow of Abū-Salamah, who died from wounds received at Uḥud. Both she and her former husband, though Muslims of long standing, belonged to the clan of Makhzūm, the clan of Abū-Jahl, and one of the chief centres of opposition to Muḥammad at Mecca. This marriage was at the very least a way of providing for an important Emigrant widow, but it may also have been designed to help Muḥammad to reconcile the Meccans.

The most controversial of all Muḥammad's marriages—to anticipate a little—took place about a year later, towards the end of March 627. This was his marriage with another Zaynab, Zaynab bint-Jaḥsh. It was criticized by his contemporaries, and has been the object of virulent attacks by European scholars. Let us try to get this story into perspective.

Zaynab was Muḥammad's cousin, being the daughter of one of his father's sisters. At the time of the Hijrah she was probably a widow, and emigrated to Medina, presumably along with her brothers who were also Muslims. There she was forced by Muḥammad, against her will, to marry his adopted son, Zayd ibn-Ḥārithah. In the course of the year 626 Muḥammad called at Zayd's house to talk to him. Zayd was out, but he saw Zaynab scantily clad, and is supposed to have been smitten by love for her. He went away saying to himself, 'Praise be to God, praise to the Manager of Hearts!' Zaynab told Zayd about Muḥammad's visit, his refusal to enter and his cryptic utterance. At once Zayd went to Muḥammad and offered to divorce Zaynab, but Muḥammad told him to keep her. After this, however, life with Zaynab became unbearable for Zayd, and he divorced her. When her ' waiting period ' was complete, a marriage with Muḥammad was arranged. This was justified by a verse of the Qur'ān (33. 37), which runs as follows :

> You were saying to the man favoured by God and yourself (*sc.* Zayd), ' Keep your wife and fear God '. You were hiding in your heart what God was bringing to light, and fearing the people, though God is rather to be feared. When Zayd divorced her, We gave her to you in marriage, so that for the believers there may be no guilt in (marrying) the wives of their adoptive sons when they divorce them.

About the main outline of the story there can be no dispute, but several details are doubtful, and different views may be taken of the significance of the whole. Like all the marriages Muḥammad contracted himself or arranged for others this had political implications. On her mother's side Zaynab was closely related to Muḥammad, and he probably felt some responsibility for her. Her father's family were, or had been, under the protection of Abū-Sufyān's father, and, at a time when Abū-Sufyān was directing the Meccan campaign against Muḥammad, this aspect of the match cannot have escaped the latter's notice. About the same time two of her sisters were married to two of the leading Emigrants. Indeed her marriage to Zayd showed that she was regarded as a person of importance, since Zayd held a high place in Muḥammad's esteem and, but for his premature death, might have succeeded him.

Unfortunately we do not know why Zaynab was unwilling to marry Zayd in the first place. She can hardly have thought he was not good enough. Yet she was an ambitious woman and may already have been hoping to marry Muḥammad. Another possibility, however, is that she may have been wanting to marry someone of whom Muḥammad disapproved for political reasons. Be that as it may, Zaynab was almost certainly working for marriage with Muḥammad before the end of 626.

The story of Muḥammad's meeting with Zaynab in Zayd's absence and being swept off his feet by her physical attractiveness must be taken with a grain of salt. It does not occur in the earliest source. Moreover, Zaynab was thirty-five or thirty-eight at the time of the marriage, and for an Arab woman of those days that was ' getting on '. All Muḥammad's other wives except Khadījah were younger when he married them, and most of them very much younger. Zaynab may have made the most of such beauty as she still had, but, even if there is a basis of fact underlying the story, one must suspect that it has been touched up in the course of transmission. Later Muslims liked to maintain that there was ' no monkery in Islam ', and their asceticism usually did not include celibacy. It would be in keeping with this to magnify the extent and romantic character of Muḥammad's relation with the fair sex. It is even boasted that his virility was such that he could satisfy all his wives in a single night. The theme of love at first sight seems to belong to this imaginative elaboration of Muḥammad's life-story. It is most unlikely that at the age of fifty-six such a man as he should have been carried away by a passion for a woman of thirty-five or more.

In any case this was not the point that his contemporaries criticized. There is no evidence that the Muslims thought this allegedly sensual and voluptuous behaviour inappropriate for a prophet. Frequent divorce, too, was quite normal. What was criticized in this marriage was its incestuous character. It was incest for a man to marry a woman who had once been married to his son, and an adoptive son was counted as a real son. It was this that roused many of the people of Medina against Muḥammad.

We cannot be sure of all that is involved. The Qur'ānic verse quoted implies that there was something objectionable about treating adoptive sons as real sons, and that it was desirable that there should be a complete break with the past in this respect. In this connexion it must be remembered that 'adoptive son' is used to translate an Arabic term which does not signify any legal process of adoption such as we have nowadays but designates a relation which happened automatically. The Arabic word properly means 'some one who is known as the son of a man who is not physically his father'. Zayd seems to have become Muḥammad's adopted son because he had been a slave of Khadījah's, became her son when he was set free and Muḥammad's when he married her. The relationship was therefore probably closely linked with the matrilineal kinship system and the loose marital relations which accompanied it. Another verse revealed in connexion with this affair says that men are to be ascribed to their real fathers. This would thus be in line with the principle of making clear who a man's father was which lay behind the prescription of the waiting period.

More than this can hardly be said. This item of social reform was desirable, but was it urgent? Or was the marriage with Zaynab urgent for some political reason of which we are not aware? We cannot tell. But both politics and social reform were involved, and at most only a minor role can have been left for romantic love.

Before leaving these family matters we have about the same period a reminder of how unfortunate Muḥammad was in his immediate family. In October 625 he lost by death at the age of six his oldest grandson 'Abd-Allāh, the son of his daughter Ruqayyah (already dead) and the later caliph 'Uthmān. By way of compensation another grandson, al-Ḥusayn, the son of Fāṭimah and 'Alī, was born in January 626.

The Expeditions of 626

After the expulsion of the clan of an-Naḍīr in August 625 there were no expeditions from Medina until April 626. There is some mention of famine about this time, and this may be the reason. Or Muḥammad may simply have been busy trying to build up his strength. Certainly in April 626 he was able to raise a force of 1,500 men and 10 horses to go to Badr—by far the largest number of men he had so far collected.

The story (which may or may not be true) is that before Abū-Sufyān left the field of Uḥud he shouted to the Muslims, 'We would like to meet you at Badr next year!' and 'Umar replied in Muḥammad's name, 'We will be there!' To keep this rendezvous both parties moved towards Badr about a year after the battle of Uḥud. Each tried to scare away the other by exaggerated reports of its strength. Eventually the Muslims spent the eight days of the market and fair at Badr, and did not come into contact with the 2,000 men and 50 horses which Abū-Sufyān had brought out to meet them. Presumably both sides wanted to avoid fighting and merely to make a demonstration of strength. The Muslims seem to have had the better of their opponents in this matter, and the tribes of the coastal region were suitably impressed. Perhaps the Muslims were also able to do some of the trading that was usually in the hands of the Meccans.

In the months that followed Muḥammad, fully aware that the Meccans were straining every nerve to bring about his destruction, must have been constantly on the alert to thwart their intrigues at an early stage. People who would obviously be ready to listen sympathetically to the Meccans were the Jewish clan of an-Naḍīr, now exiled to Khaybar; and it is not surprising to learn that in May 626 their chief was assassinated by a small party of Muslims—a warning that those who plotted against Muḥammad did so at their peril. In the following month information was received that some tribes to the east of Medina were massing with apparently hostile intentions, and Muḥammad with a force of 400 (or 800) men spent some days in their region. They took to the higher ground where it would have been imprudent for the Muslims to follow them, and there was no effective contact ; but once again there was a warning of the danger of taking arms against Muḥammad.

The most interesting expedition of the summer was that to Dūmat-al-Jandal (the oasis now known as el-Jauf), which occupied twenty-five days in August and September. This expedition is important and remarkable in several ways. It was the largest expedition Muḥammad had led so far apart from his second visit to Badr a few months earlier, for he took a thousand men with him. It was also the longest he had undertaken, for Dūmat-al-Jandal was nearly 400 miles to the north. These two facts in themselves make the expedition unique. When one also remembers that this was the route along which Arab armies set out less than a decade later to conquer an empire, it is difficult to avoid the conclusion that there is a connexion between this expedition and the later conquests. Unfortunately the sources are tantalizingly scanty in regard to this and the other expeditions northwards during Muḥammad's lifetime, and our account of the connexion has to be in part conjectural.

It is possibly true that, as is reported, Muḥammad had heard of a hostile concentration at Dūmat-al-Jandal ; but it is unlikely that men from this distant oasis were thinking of marching against Medina. What is probable is that they were somehow able to affect the trade or communications of Medina, and that Muḥammad decided to show his strength before they became involved in activities against him. His rapid march of some 750 miles with this large force must have impressed all the nomads along the route. While his primary aim, then, may have been to deter the northern tribes from joining the Meccan grand alliance against him, what he learnt on the journey about conditions in the north may have shown him the possibility of expansion in this direction. Booty was taken on the expedition, and booty was an inducement to the poorer nomads to throw in their lot with Muḥammad.

There was also a large question of strategy involved. Muḥammad may not have been consciously aware of it before this expedition, but he must have been beginning to think about it soon afterwards. In December 627, for example, the tribe of Muzaynah (to the north-west of Medina) became Muslims, and several other tribes of the lower lands near the Red Sea coast followed them in the course of the next summer. The problem raised by these adhesions to the Islamic community, and even by merely political alliances with it, was how to stop the tribes in the community raiding one another. The razzia was an established feature of nomadic life. It was an outlet for the energies of the men. It may also have performed an economic function. Membership of the Islamic community, or alliance with it, stopped a tribe from raiding the other members or allies. Where was it to find an outlet for its raiding propensities? The size of the expeditions sent northwards by Muḥammad suggests that long before his death he had seen that, if the Islamic community was to avoid internal dissension, it must adopt a policy of expansion beyond Arabia northwards. This expedition to Dūmat-al-Jandal is the first pointer towards things to come.

About December 627 Muḥammad set out on his last expedition before the Meccan grand alliance descended upon him. It was against a small tribe whose grounds were near the Red Sea coast to the north-west of Mecca. That Muḥammad should be able to go into this area where Mecca had hitherto been supreme is a mark of his growing power.

The reason for the expedition was that the chief of the tribe was arming the men for an attack on Medina, doubtless in concert with the Meccans. Muḥammad attacked the small group unexpectedly with overwhelming force. After only a brief resistance all were taken prisoner, and the Muslims were able to return home with a considerable amount of booty. The wives and children of the tribe became slaves of the Muslims. Juwayriyah, the daughter of the chief, fell to the lot of a man who did not want to keep her but rather to have the money for her ransom. In the course of negotiations Muḥammad offered to marry her and she agreed. This was apparently part of an agreement between him and the tribe, as a result of which all the women and children were eventually restored. It is sometimes stated that at first Juwayriyah was merely a concubine, and only later, on profession of Islam, became a wife.

Before the Muslims set out again for home an incident occurred which brought to light the inner tensions still present in Medina. It began quite simply. 'Umar's groom, a man from a poor nomadic tribe, was watering his horse, when another nomad, an ally of some of the Helpers, who may have been fetching water for them, thrust him aside. The two were soon fighting. One called on the Emigrants for help and the other on the Helpers. A number of men were involved in the quarrel and blood began to flow before the fight was stopped. To make matters worse 'Abd-Allāh ibn-Ubayy the Hypocrite, who was taking part in the expedition, used the occasion to make provocative remarks. This man, he would say, who ostensibly came to keep the peace, was only involving them in brawls ; the people of Medina had given their property to these strangers, and now the strangers were going to lord it over them in their own town. He even muttered something about the stronger driving out the weaker when they returned to Medina.

When Muḥammad was informed he took it calmly. To cool heated tempers he ordered them to set off immediately on their return, and kept them on the move for nearly twenty-four hours. He rejected the offer of ʻAbd-Allāh, the son of ʻAbd-Allāh ibn-Ubayy and a keen Muslim, to kill his father. By the time they reached Medina this particular incident had been almost forgotten. But another incident gave ʻAbd-Allāh ibn-Ubayy another opportunity of attacking Muḥammad.

It was Muḥammad's custom to take one or more of his wives with him on his expeditions. On this occasion ʻĀ'ishah was in the party. At the last halt before they arrived back in Medina she had withdrawn out of sight for a little. A necklace dropped in the sand, however, had kept her longer than she had intended, and when she returned to the camp all had departed. She travelled in a closed litter, and she was so light that the men who lifted it on to the back of a camel had not noticed that she was not in it. According to her own story she had then lain down to wait till someone came back for her. She was roused, however, by a handsome young Muslim of her acquaintance who had fallen behind the main body. He discreetly placed her on his camel and led her back to Medina.

In Arabia, as in other places, it was generally assumed that there was bound to be sexual intimacy if a man and a woman were left alone together. Tongues began to wag. ʻAbd-Allāh ibn-Ubayy did what he could to magnify the scandal. In this he had some strange helpers, both men and women who were certainly not Hypocrites, but who apparently had some personal grudge against ʻĀ'ishah or her family. The scandal kept growing for weeks till matters came to a head. It might have caused a serious rift in the Islamic community, especially if Muḥammad had felt he could no longer retain Abū-Bakr (ʻĀ'ishah's father) as his chief lieutenant.

Eventually the question of fact was decided by Muḥammad in favour of 'Ā'ishah. There was no solid evidence against her, and sufficient time had probably elapsed for it to be known that she was not pregnant. It remained to deal with those who had slandered her in what came to be known as 'the affair of the lie'. The lesser scandal-mongers are said to have been flogged. With 'Abd-Allāh ibn-Ubayy Muḥammad had a 'show-down'. He summoned a meeting of the leading men among the Helpers, and asked for permission to take punitive measures against one of them who was attacking his family. This shows that he was not yet by any means the autocratic ruler of Medina, but would have become liable to reprisals by the *lex talionis* had he used violence towards a man without the consent of his clan or tribe. Muḥammad's request was followed by an angry scene. The two groups of clans among the Helpers vied with one another in their professions of loyalty to Muḥammad and suggestions that the other side had been lacking in loyalty, and nearly came to blows. Perhaps Muḥammad deliberately provoked this state of affairs to make them forget their common grievance against the Emigrants. At last things calmed down.

This meeting made it clear that the majority of the Helpers were now behind Muḥammad and that 'Abd-Allāh ibn-Ubayy had little following. He was probably not punished in any way (though some authorities say he was flogged). He seems to have realized that his influence was now too slight for him to achieve anything, and to have taken no further active steps against Muḥammad. He was too old to become an enthusiastic Muslim, and he may sometimes have grumbled. In 628 he took part in the expedition to al-Ḥudaybiyah, and when the Meccans wanted to give him the special privilege of making the pilgrimage, while they denied it to all the other Muslims, he refused and thus proclaimed his solidarity with the Muslims. On his death early in 631 Muḥammad himself performed the funeral rites.

The 'affair of the lie' (together with the failure of the siege a month later) may be said to mark the end of the opposition to Muḥammad by 'Abd-Allāh and his party of Hypocrites. The weakness of his position was that it had no intellectual basis. As a Jewish leader is said to have put it, he did not know what he wanted; he was whole-heartedly committed neither to Islam nor to Judaism nor to the old religion of the Arabs. What moved him was chiefly personal ambition, and he lacked both the statesmanship to see the vaster issues involved and the vision to propound a way of dealing with them that would attract men. He must have seen the need for peace in Medina, but his attempts to meet it were along conservative lines and already discredited. In opposing Muḥammad he had failed to move with the times. Among the Hypocrites, as one source remarks, there was only one young man; and this is significant.

The Siege of Medina

The siege of Medina, known to Muslims as the expedition of the Khandaq or Trench, began on 31st March 627 and lasted about a fortnight. It was the supreme effort of the pagan Meccans to break Muḥammad's power. For it they had gathered a vast confederacy, including some nomadic tribes in no way dependent on them. The Jewish clan of an-Naḍīr, now in exile in Khaybar and eager to regain their lands at Medina, vigorously supported the Meccans in the building up of the confederacy; they even promised half the date harvest of Khaybar to nomadic tribes if they would join in the attack.

In the army collected by the Meccans there are said to have been about 10,000 men, formed into three separate corps. The numbers given for the various contingents, however, do not add up to more than about 7,500. The Meccans themselves had about 300 horses and the nomadic tribes a similar number. As the Muslims had still practically no cavalry—they are said to have had ten horses on their visit to Badr in 626—this was a formidable array against them. The Meccans approached Medina by the same route they had taken two years earlier, but sited part of their camp on the lower slopes of Uḥud to prevent the Muslims taking up the advantageous position there which they had occupied at the battle.

Muḥammad and the Muslims cannot have contemplated this situation without grave anxiety even if they also had good grounds for hope. Their exertions of the last two years had not prevented the formation of the confederacy, but they had prevented a number of tribes from joining it. At the same time they had increased their own strength. Individuals and small groups had come from various quarters to throw in their lot with the Muslims. Some of these were now resident in Medina. The older inhabitants of Medina, the Helpers, were nearly all whole-heartedly in support of Muḥammad's policy. Only some of the Hypocrites were critical of Muḥammad's methods and sceptical of a successful result. A number of them, as the Qur'ān shows, would gladly have kept out of the fighting and might even have gone over to the enemy had there been an opportunity. The Jewish tribe of Qurayẓah—the principal Jewish group left in Medina—seems to have tried to remain neutral. In all Muḥammad could count on about 3,000 men.

With the enemy at least twice as numerous as his own men and vastly superior in cavalry Muḥammad could not afford to meet them in the open. He therefore adopted a form of defence hitherto unknown in Arabia. Wherever Medina lay open to cavalry attack he dug a trench, the Khandaq. Since the oasis was surrounded by lava flows to the east, south and west, it was only on the north that the trench was required, and towards the north of the oasis there was a fair-sized hill, mount Sal', which he incorporated in his front. On it also he established his headquarters, doubtless at some spot with a view of the whole front. Had the enemy crossed the trench mount Sal' would presumably have given the defenders some of the advantages they had at Uḥud.

The idea of the trench may have come from Persia, and the Persian convert Salmān is credited with an important share in the detailed planning. The work was set afoot as soon as it was known that the Meccans had started out—it would have been difficult to arouse enthusiasm for it earlier—and most of the Muslims worked hard at it for six days until it was completed. (It was perhaps subsequently extended southwards along the western edge of the oasis.) The Meccans were wholly unprepared to deal with this obstacle. Sieges were unknown in Arabian warfare. All they could do was to hurl bodies of horsemen at the trench in the hopes of forcing a passage. But the Medinans were in position behind it, and the trench generally gave them a slight advantage over the cavalry.

On one occasion a small party of horsemen managed to cross, but they were too few to accomplish anything of importance, and in the end they retired with a loss of two. Apart from this the Meccans failed to cross the trench at all. They made several assaults by night, but the trench was guarded constantly. One might have expected the Meccans to deploy their infantry over the whole length of the trench and to attempt to break down the defence in this way; but the infantry seem to have been unwilling to engage the Muslims at close quarters, for they probably regarded them as superior in hand-to-hand fighting. Under these circumstances the one hope of the Meccans would have been to make several attacks at once. They seem to have hoped to persuade the Jewish clan of Qurayẓah to attack the Muslims from the south, but nothing came of the negotiations.

About a fortnight was spent in this way. The Muslims proved sufficiently numerous and sufficiently well organized to contain all assaults from the north. The enemy morale sank, the leaders despaired of success, and the great confederacy split up into its several contingents and retired. Exceptionally cold weather and a storm of wind hastened the departure. By about the middle of April the threat to Medina had been removed. The supreme effort of the Meccans had ended in fiasco. Though this was a military operation of the first importance, the casualties are reported to have been only six Medinans and three Meccans.

On the military side the reason for the Meccan failure was the superior strategy of Muḥammad, and probably also his superior information service and secret agents. His use of the device of the trench was particularly well suited to the circumstances. Meccan hopes of victory rested mainly on the superiority of their cavalry, for previous battles had shown that the Muslims were likely to overcome their opponents in an infantry mêlée unless heavily outnumbered. The trench effectively countered the menace from the cavalry and forced the Meccans to fight in conditions where they derived little advantage from their 600 horses.

The Meccans suffered from a further disadvantage. In the campaign of Uḥud they had arrived at Medina about ten days earlier before the grain was harvested. The fields had provided fodder for the Meccan horses, while the sight of their devastation had provoked the Medinans to leave the safety of their strongholds and march out against the enemy. In this year the grain had been harvested a month before the Meccans arrived—probably earlier than usual because of Muḥammad's foresight—and they had great difficulty in obtaining fodder for their horses. As there was no provocation of the owners of fields, the Helpers were content to remain behind the trench. The point seems to indicate slackness or lack of foresight on the part of the Meccan leaders.

The Muslims had a valuable asset in their comparative unity and better discipline, which contrasted with the lack of cohesion in the confederacy and the lack of mutual confidence between the various groups. Of this disunity Muḥammad's diplomacy took full advantage. The main body of nomads in the confederacy had only been persuaded to come by a bribe, and Muḥammad made tentative offers to them of a higher or further bribe to them if they would withdraw. This offer is said to have been of a third of the date-harvest of Medina, but at first they demanded a half, and only after some time agreed to accept a third. Meanwhile some of the leading Helpers protested that Medina had never sunk to such a depth of ignominy, and insisted that the negotiations should be broken off. This Muḥammad did. Whatever the exact details may have been, the nomads had compromised themselves by discussing such matters with him. The whole was a battle of wits in which the Muslims had the best of it; without cost to themselves they weakened the enemy and increased the dissension.

Somewhat similar were the intrigues in which the Jewish clan of Qurayẓah was involved and which had a tragic outcome for it. They seem to have had a treaty with Muḥammad but it is not clear whether they were expected, if Medina was attacked, to give him active support or merely to remain neutral. They are said to have supplied some instruments for the digging of the trench. Later a Jew from Khaybar persuaded them that Muḥammad was sure to be overwhelmed and they changed their attitude. As they would be exposed to Muslim retaliation should the confederacy retire without destroying Muḥammad, they demanded hostages from both the Meccans and their chief nomadic allies. Negotiations over this were protracted. A secret agent of Muḥammad's, acting in accordance with hints from him, so increased the suspicion with which the different parties viewed one another that the negotiations came to nothing and the threatened 'second front' was never opened. The importance of this diplomatic success can hardly be overestimated, for an attack from the south on the Muslim rear by Qurayẓah might have put an end to Muḥammad's career.

The break-up of the confederate army marked the utter failure of the Meccans to deal with Muḥammad. The outlook for them now was dismal. They had exerted their utmost strength to dislodge him from Medina, but he remained there, more influential than ever as a result of the fiasco of the confederacy. Their trade with Syria was gone, and much of their prestige lost. Even if Muḥammad did not attack them, they had no hope of retaining their wealth and position; but he might well use armed force against them, and try to annihilate them as they had tried to annihilate him. It would be strange if some of the Meccans—a practical people—had not begun to wonder whether it might not be best to accept Muhammad and his religion.

The Execution of the Jews of Qurayẓah

As soon as it was clear that the Meccan confederacy had finally departed, Muḥammad issued a fresh summons to the Muslims just as they were beginning to relax. They were to meet him before evening in front of the strongholds of the Jewish clan of Qurayẓah. The Muslims responded to the summons and a siege was instituted which lasted twenty-five days. The reason, of course, was that, while the outward acts of the clan had been correct, they had been intriguing with Muḥammad's enemies and at one point had been on the verge of attacking Muḥammad in his rear. They had thus been guilty of treasonable activities against the Medinan community. Muḥammad, realizing that after the failure of the Meccans his position was very much stronger, was not prepared to tolerate such conduct, and determined to remove this source of weakness from Medina and to teach a lesson to enemies and potential enemies.

The clan of Qurayẓah did not fight back with much vigour. There seem to have been intrigues and divided counsels. Eventually they sent to Muḥammad and asked to be allowed to surrender on the same terms as the clan of an-Naḍīr. They were told that they must surrender unconditionally. They then asked to be allowed to consult with a Muslim friend called Abū-Lubābah, and he went to them. When they asked if he would advise them to surrender, he is reported to have said ' Yes ', but to have put his hand to his neck to signify that they would be killed. Something must be omitted from our sources, however, for we are told that almost immediately on his return Abū-Lubābah realized that he had gravely betrayed the Muslim cause. Probably he had not repudiated his clan's former alliance with Qurayẓah, but had somehow used his influence in their favour.

Despite this alleged hint of their fate from Abū-Lubābah Qurayẓah surrendered unconditionally. Some of the Arab tribe of the Aws are said to have appealed to Muḥammad to forgive Qurayẓah for the sake of the Aws just as he had forgiven Qaynuqā' for the sake of 'Abd-Allāh ibn-Ubayy and the Khazraj. Indeed there seems to have been a strong desire in various sections of the Aws to honour their old alliance with Qurayẓah. Muḥammad met this feeling by suggesting that the fate of the Jews should be decided by one of their Medinan Muslim allies. In this way Muḥammad avoided any likelihood of a blood-feud. The Jews agreed with the suggestion, and Muḥammad appointed as judge Sa'd ibn-Mu'ādh, the leading man among the Aws and indeed among the Helpers generally. He had been gravely wounded during the siege of Medina, and died shortly afterwards. When he was brought to where Muḥammad was, all the Aws and the others present swore to abide by his decision. He decreed that all the men of Qurayẓah should be put to death, and the women and children sold as slaves. This sentence was duly carried out, apparently on the following day.

Some European writers have criticized this sentence for what they call its savage and inhuman character. It has to be remembered, however, that in the Arabia of that day when tribes were at war with one another or simply had no agreement, they had no obligations towards one another, not even of what we would call common decency. The enemy and the complete stranger had no rights whatsoever. When men refrained from killing and being cruel, it was not from any sense of duty towards a fellow-man but out of fear of possible retaliation by the next-of-kin. What surprised Muḥammad's contemporaries at the execution of all the males of Qurayẓah was that he was not afraid of the consequences of his act. The behaviour of the clan during the siege of Medina was regarded as having cancelled their agreement with Muḥammad.

In the case of the Muslims involved in the execution what was uppermost in their minds was whether allegiance to the Islamic community was to be set above and before all other alliances and attachments. The old Arab tradition was that you supported your ally whatever his conduct towards other people might be, provided only that he remained faithful to you. Those of the Aws who wanted leniency for Qurayẓah seem to have regarded them as having been unfaithful only to Muḥammad and not to the Aws. This attitude implies that these men regarded themselves as being primarily members of the Aws (or of some clan of it) and not of the Islamic community. There is no need to suppose that Muḥammad brought pressure to bear on Sa'd ibn-Mu'ādh to punish

Qurayẓah as he did. A far-sighted man like Sa'd must have realized that to allow tribal or clan allegiance to come before Islamic allegiance would lead to a renewal of the fratricidal strife from which they hoped the coming of Muḥammad had delivered Medina. As he was being led into Muḥammad's presence to pronounce his sentence, Sa'd is said to have made a remark to the effect that, with death not far from him, he must consider above all doing his duty to God and the Islamic community, even at the expense of former alliances.

That this was the question at issue and that it was a serious one is shown by some of the details of what happened immediately afterwards. Two of the leaders of the other Arab tribe, the Khazraj, called Muḥammad's attention to dissensions among the Aws over the execution. This served to put the Aws on their mettle, and Sa'd ibn-Mu'ādh, assured Muḥammad that all the devout believers among the Aws concurred in it. Thereupon two of the condemned were given to each of the six clans involved, and these were executed, thereby implicating all the clans in the shedding of the blood of Qurayẓah. The majority of the executions (said to have numbered 600) were probably carried out by Emigrants, though some of the Khazraj who had no alliance with Qurayẓah may have helped. The palms of the clan were divided among the Muslims who had participated in the military operations. This evidence for the persisting vigour of clan attachments and the old ideas connected with them shows that in appointing Sa'd as judge or arbiter over Qurayẓah Muḥammad was not trying to conceal a dictatorial power which at this period he had not in fact acquired, but was dealing with a difficult situation in the only tactful way open to him.

After the elimination of Qurayẓah no important clan of Jews was left in Medina, though there were probably several small groups. One Jewish merchant is named who purchased some of the women and children of Qurayẓah! The remaining Jews were doubtless very circumspect now, and avoided not only hostile activity but also compromising relationships, though at the time of the expedition against Khaybar their sympathies seem naturally to have been with their fellow-Jews.

The continuing presence of at least a few Jews in Medina is an argument against the view sometimes put forward by European scholars that in the second year after the Hijrah Muḥammad adopted a policy of clearing all Jews out of Medina just because they were Jews, and that he carried out this policy with ever-increasing severity. It was not Muḥammad's way to have policies of this kind. He had a balanced view of the fundamentals of the contemporary situation and of his long-term aims, and in the light of this he moulded his day-to-day plans in accordance with the changing factors in current events. The occasions of his attacks on the first two Jewish clans were no more than occasions; but there were also deep underlying reasons. The Jews in general by their verbal criticisms of the Qur'ānic revelation were trying to undermine the foundation of the whole Islamic community; and they were also giving political support to Muḥammad's enemies and to opponents such as the Hypocrites. In so far as the Jews abandoned these forms of hostile activity Muḥammad allowed them to live in Medina unmolested.

VII

THE WINNING OF THE MECCANS

NEW HORIZONS

The great interest of the period from the end of the siege of Medina and execution of Qurayẓah to the conclusion of the treaty of al-Ḥudaybiyah in March 628 is that in it new trends become manifest in Muḥammad's policy. To speak of a reorientation would be to exaggerate, or rather to confess that one had failed to understand his policy so far. Hitherto he had had to concentrate on the struggle with Mecca, and it would be natural to suppose that he had had no thought beyond the defeat of the Meccans and the capture of their city. Soon after the siege, however, it is clear that Muḥammad's aims are much vaster and more statesmanlike; and when one scrutinizes the earlier years slight indications may be found that these wider aims were present all along, or at least since the victory at Badr had shown that great changes were possible.

In trying to discern the underlying aims of Muḥammad's overt actions we necessarily use an analytic and discursive mode of thought. Muḥammad himself, however, thought intuitively and not analytically. He was aware of all the factors we laboriously enumerate, but, without isolating these in his thinking, he was able to decide on a course of action that was an adequate response to them. Even where he was most fully aware of political implications, the religious aspect of events was dominant for him; and he would almost certainly have described his supreme aim at this period as the summoning of all Arabs to Islam. The implied corollary, namely, the political unity of all the Arabs, cannot have escaped Muḥammad, but it remained in the background.

To speak at this stage of *all* the Arabs may seem to be going too far ahead, since Islam had touched only a few tribes in the neighbourhood of Medina and Mecca. But Muḥammad had sufficient width of vision to look beyond immediate concerns, and it would be natural for him to take as his potential unit the Arabian peninsula, or rather the totality of tribal groups with some claim to the name of Arab. Later Muslim tradition actually claims that by 628 he was summoning the rulers of the surrounding empires to Islam, but this is not credible.

One thing, however, that certainly happened was that some of the nomadic tribes within easy range of Medina began to decide that it would be wiser to throw in their lot with Muḥammad. Among these was the tribe of Ashja' (or a section of it). They had sent a contingent of 400 men to join the Meccan army which besieged Medina ; but even at this time one of their leaders had become a Muslim, though the fact was not generally known, and was acting as a secret agent for Muḥammad. After the failure of the Meccan expedition they sent a deputation to Muḥammad, asking for peace in some form. They gave as reasons that they lived closer to Muḥammad than their allies, and were fewer in number ; they were also in distress because of the war. Muḥammad accepted them as allies or confederates. If a document which has been preserved is correctly attributed to this occasion, then he did not insist on them becoming Muslims or paying the legal alms (*zakāt*) which he latterly demanded from those who sought his alliance. Other tribes in a similar position are known to have sought Muḥammad's alliance about this time, but there is no certainty about the exact dates.

Of the events in the period under review one group belong to what may be called the aftermath of the Meccan failure. Such was the raid by an angry chief on Muḥammad's private herd of camels. This man, called 'Uyaynah, had perhaps had some dealings with Muḥammad before he was induced by a bribe to join the Meccan confederacy. It was to him that Muḥammad offered a third of the date-harvest of Medina, and when in the end he got no dates and had to retire without even any booty, he was extremely annoyed. To give vent to his sense of unfair treatment he sent forty horsemen to the pasture-grounds near Medina and made off with about twenty camels. Eight Muslims at once pursued on horseback, recovered half the camels and killed four of the raiders for the loss of one of their own number. Muḥammad, however, seems to have been afraid of a large-scale attack. He collected 500 (or 700) men before following the eight horsemen, and left a deputy to guard Medina with 300 men under arms. It is doubtful whether there was indeed a threat of this kind, but Muḥammad's action is an indication of the anxiety still felt in Medina. Later in the year (about November) Zayd ibn-Ḥārithah with a small party had a mishap at the hands of a section of 'Uyaynah's tribe, but subsequently (about January 628) avenged it.

There were numerous expeditions during the period, and some were directed, in part at least, against tribes which had helped the Meccans. It also appears, however, from remarks in the sources that rain was scanty this year and fodder scarce. Some tribes to the east of Medina had left their usual pasture-grounds owing to lack of rain and had come nearer to the oasis. It may therefore be that the Muslim raids were not so much a requital for what had gone before as a warning not to encroach on the lands of Medina. It was always of the highest importance, however, among the Arabs to show that one was capable of avenging injuries to oneself, one's tribe and one's allies or protégés. This motive of requital would be dominant in the expedition of July 627, led by Muhammad himself, against the tribe of Sufyān al-

Liḥyānī which two years before had treacherously attacked a small party of Muslims.

The Jewish participants in the Meccan confederacy continued their intrigues, offering bribes to Arab tribes in return for military help. Against one tribe which was inclined to accept the offer the Muslims sent an expedition (about December 627) and captured 500 camels and 2,000 sheep—a warning that it was dangerous to fraternize with the enemies of Islam. The Jews themselves were given a similar warning by the assassination of another of their leaders at Khaybar about February 628.

A second group of events during the same period points to the development of closer relationships with the tribes along the road to Syria. At least after the expedition to Dumat-al-Jandal in August and September of 626 Muḥammad knew something of the strategic importance of expansion in this direction. With the immediate threat to Medina from the Meccans removed he devotes considerable attention to this road to the north.

A series of incidents involves a man called Diḥyah ibn-Khalīfah and the tribe of Judham. Diḥyah is reported to have been sent as an envoy to Caesar, that is, presumably to the nearest Byzantine governor at Bostra. This was probably in 627, but we do not know what the message was. We may conjecture that he was giving the Byzantine governor his version of the failure of the Meccans, to prevent them getting help from him. On his way back Diḥyah was robbed of the Byzantine presents for Muḥammad which he was carrying by some members of the tribe of Judhām. He reported the theft to Muḥammad who sent out Zayd ibn-Ḥārithah to punish the offenders. Meantime other members of Judhām were persuading the tribe to accept Islam. Complaints were made to Muḥammad that Zayd's punitive measures were illegal and 'Alī had to be sent to straighten out matters. The details are obscure, but it is clear that at least a section of Judhām entered into alliance with Muḥammad about this time.

Following upon this (about November 627) Zayd set out on a trading journey to Syria—the first mention of a trading journey from Medina by a Muslim. That he was wounded and robbed in the course of it by some nomads does not lessen the significance of the event. A month later 'Abd-ar-Raḥmān ibn-'Awf, who had the reputation of being the shrewdest merchant and financier among the Muslims, led an expedition of 700 men to Dūmat-al-Jandal. Presumably some trade was done. Later, perhaps after Muḥammad's death, the same man appears as the organizer of a caravan of 500 camels. In 627 the prince of Dūmat-al-Jandal made a treaty of alliance with Muḥammad and gave his daughter in marriage to 'Abd-ar-Raḥmān, though he probably remained a Christian.

All this interest in the route to the north cannot be a matter of chance. It is unlikely that Muḥammad was chiefly interested in the northern tribes because they were interested in Islam. They may indeed have shown more interest in Muḥammad's religion than the pagans farther south, because they were to some extent Christian and were possibly discouraged by the Persian occupation of Syria (which lasted from about 614 to 629). His interest in this northward route would be partly due to the importance of Syrian trade in the Meccan economy. By his raids on Meccan caravans he had blocked the path to the north for the Meccans, and alliances with the northern tribes would serve to tighten the blockade if Muḥammad so desired. The expeditions of Zayd and 'Abd-ar-Raḥmān ibn-'Awf were probably designed to bring part of the Syrian trade to Medina. This trade was perhaps more important in the life of the oasis than our sources indicate. As the population grew through the attraction of

Islam and the Islamic community, imports of food would presumably be necessary. The other reason for interest in the northern route was the one that was mentioned above, namely, the necessity of directing outwards the predatory impulses of the Arabs. As time went on this must have come to weigh more and more with Muḥammad, as is shown by the fact that his interest in the route continued after the conquest of Mecca.

A third group of events concerns more directly Muḥammad's relations to Mecca. In contrast to all the activity to the north and east of Medina, he made no attempt to attack Mecca itself. During an expedition in July 627 he seems to have made a feint against Mecca ; but it cannot have caused more than a temporary flurry. More serious was an attack two months later on a Meccan caravan. It was conducted by Zayd ibn-Ḥārithah with 170 men. The caravan was returning to Mecca from Syria by a roundabout route and carried, among other things, silver belonging to Ṣafwān ibn-Umayyah (of whom more will be heard presently). Everything was captured and some prisoners made. The lenient treatment of one of these, however, may be the expression of a new policy of leniency directed to winning over the Meccans. This man, Abū-l-'Āṣ ibn-ar-Rabī', was the husband of Muḥammad's daughter Zaynab. He sought and publicly received her formal protection (*jiwār*), although this was perhaps contrary to the constitution. Muḥammad denied prior knowledge of Zaynab's declaration but asserted he was ready to uphold it, and Abū-l-'Āṣ received back his property that was among the booty.

These events of 627, considered along with what subsequently happened, show that Muḥammad was not preparing for a direct assault on Mecca. His policy was to weaken Mecca by preventing the movement of caravans to and from Syria, while at the same time increasing the number of tribes in alliance with himself and consolidating the strength of this group. The submission (already mentioned) of Ashja', one of the weaker tribes joining in the siege, indicates that the Meccans and their confederates were not able to provide for their allies as Muḥammad was. The *pax Islamica*, as administered by the iron hand of Muḥammad, would bring prosperity for the Arabs, but only if the means of subsistence were correspondingly increased. But the number of camels and sheep the desert could support could not be greatly increased. Consequently the Islamic state was under the necessity of constantly expanding its sphere of influence. From now on Muḥammad seems to be more concerned with the positive building up of strength and prosperity than with the negative aim of defeating the Meccans. Soon it becomes apparent that the Meccans have an important role to play in the positive side of his policy.

The Expedition and Treaty of al-Ḥudaybiyah

This phase of the relations between Muḥammad and the Meccans was brought to a close, which was indeed a consummation, by Muḥammad's expedition to al-Ḥudaybiyah. The outline of the story is as follows. As the result of a dream Muḥammad decided to go to Mecca to make the *'umrah* or lesser pilgrimage (as distinct from the *ḥajj* or greater pilgrimage). He called on the Muslims (and perhaps others) to join him and to bring animals for sacrifice. Eventually he set out on 13th March 628 with from 1,400 to 1,600 men, among whom were nomads of Khuzā'ah. Other tribes which might have been expected to take part made excuses for abstaining. When the Meccans heard of this approaching force, they assumed that Muḥammad's intentions were hostile, and sent out 200 cavalry to bar the way. By taking an unusual route across difficult hilly country Muḥammad circumvented the Meccan cavalry and reached al-Ḥudaybiyah on the edge of the sacred territory of Mecca. At this point his camel refused to go farther, and he decided it was time to halt.

The Meccans threatened to fight if Muḥammad tried to perform the pilgrimage. Messengers came and went between them and him, and eventually a treaty was agreed on. This year the Muslims were to retire, but in the following year the Meccans were to evacuate their city for three days to enable the Muslims to carry out the various rites of the lesser pilgrimage. At a moment when it looked as if the negotiations would break down, the Muslims made a pledge to Muḥammad known as the Pledge of Good Pleasure or the Pledge under the Tree. On the conclusion of the treaty Muḥammad killed his sacrificial animal and had his hair shaved, and the Muslims, apparently after some hesitation, followed his example. Then they set off home.

It is worth while reflecting for a little on some of the details in order to understand what lies behind them. Since a verse of the Qur'ān (48. 27) speaks of God 'giving His messenger a true and right vision', it may be accepted as a fact that the idea of making a pilgrimage first came to Muḥammad in a dream. He regarded this as a promise from God that he would in fact be able to perform the rites, and when he was prevented he was naturally puzzled. But if the idea came in this way, there were practical political reasons for its commending itself to him. He can hardly have hoped to conquer Mecca, for he must have known that the morale of the Meccans was still good, and his force was too small to overcome them in battle. His primary intention was no doubt simply what he said, to perform the pilgrimage; but this had certain political implications, and it was probably in these that he was chiefly interested. The performance of the pilgrimage would be a demonstration that Islam was not a foreign religion but essentially an Arabian one, and in particular that it had its centre and focus in Mecca. A demonstration of such a kind at such a time would impress upon the Meccans that Islam was not a threat to Mecca's religious importance. It would also suggest that Muḥammad was prepared to be friendly—on his own terms, of course.

Unfortunately Muḥammad's proposed action, if carried out, would make it appear that the Meccans were too weak to stop him. This happened in one of the sacred months in which there was supposed to be no bloodshed, but Muḥammad had not shown himself specially observant of sacred times, and was clearly relying, not solely on the sanctity of the season, but partly on the number of his followers. In the light of the failure of the great confederacy at Medina, the unimpeded progress of Muḥammad through Mecca would look bad. It was therefore understandable that the Meccans should decide to oppose. The compromise eventually agreed on saved their face and their prestige, while Muḥammad obtained all he really wanted.

The first provision was that the two parties were to abandon hostilities against one another for ten years. This expressed Muḥammad's peaceful intentions towards the Meccans and gave them a respite from the desperate struggle against his growing power. The provision about the postponement for a year of the performance of the pilgrimage saved the face of the Meccans. At the same time by obtaining permission to perform the rites in the following year Muḥammad achieved his aim of demonstrating his intentions and attitudes ; indeed he had very largely achieved it by the very concluding of a treaty.

A further provision was that Muḥammad was to send back any Meccan who came to him without the consent of his protector or guardian ; presumably clients and minors are chiefly intended. Any Muslim, however, going to Mecca was not to be sent back to Muḥammad. This provision was a concession to the feelings of the Meccans which cost the Muslims little. The son of one of the Meccan negotiators is said to have come to Muḥammad while the negotiations were still going on, and to have been told that he must remain in Mecca. But Muḥammad made the two other negotiators present guarantee his safety in view of the now strained relations between the boy and his father. The fact that this provision was not reciprocal is perhaps mainly an expression of Muḥammad's belief in the superior attractiveness of Islam.

There was yet another provision, namely, that tribes and individuals were to be free to enter into alliance with Muḥammad or the Meccans as they desired. This appears to be harmless, but the appearance is deceptive. Muḥammad set considerable store on it, for on his way to Mecca he is said to have told one of his messengers that he was ready to make peace with the Meccans if they would allow him a free hand with the nomadic tribes. Ostensibly the two sides are being treated equally, and in a sense the provision is a recognition by the Meccans of Muḥammad's equality with themselves. At the practical level, however, the provision is a concession by the Meccans, permitting tribes to abandon their alliance for that of Muḥammad; and the tribe of Khuzā'ah speedily made the exchange.

This is all part of Muḥammad's programme of consolidating his strength and building a complex of tribes in alliance with himself. He is not primarily concerned to weaken the Meccans. By agreeing to a pact of non-aggression for ten years, he had by implication given up the blockade of their trade. Mecca could presumably now resume her caravans to Syria, though her monopoly of this trade had gone. But if Muḥammad had flung this weapon away, he had otherwise increased his military potential, and, if need be, could meet the Meccans at some future date with good hopes of success.

Meantime he was reducing his pressure on Mecca and showing himself disposed to be friendly and ready to respect Meccan feelings.

These facts point to the conclusion that Muḥammad was no longer vigorously prosecuting the struggle with the Meccans, but was angling for their conversion to Islam. Doubtless he had also further aims behind this. Perhaps he was disgusted at the recent refusal of many nomads to join in his pilgrimage and felt that his own fellow-townsmen, if he could win them over, would be a more reliable basis for the new body politic he was establishing. Perhaps he was rather thinking that in the new Islamic state their administrative and organizing ability would be in demand. Certainly from this time on, whatever may have been the case previously, he was aiming at gaining the Meccans for Islam and the Islamic state.

The treaty of al-Ḥudaybiyah was thus favourable to Muḥammad's long-term strategy, but for the moment it left him to deal with the disappointment of his followers at the apparent failure of the expedition. In this crisis smouldering embers of dissatisfaction within Muḥammad himself were fanned into flame, and he acted vigorously. He had been specially incensed when some of the allied nomads refused to join him. They had seen no prospect of booty, and had suspected that the Muslims might not even return safely. Besides making Muḥammad's demonstration less impressive, their action had shown slight interest in Islam as a religion and little loyalty to Muḥammad.

In such a mood Muḥammad took advantage of a critical situation to strengthen his own position in the Islamic community. When the negotiations with the Meccans proved difficult, Muḥammad sent 'Uthmān (later the third caliph) to be his representative in discussing matters with them. 'Uthmān belonged to the same clan as Abū-Sufyān and so had powerful protection in Mecca; there was no sanctity in those days about the persons of envoys. When 'Uthmān was long in returning and a rumour got about that he had been killed, Muḥammad called the Muslims to himself under a tree and made them pledge themselves to him. There are different accounts of the nature of the pledge, but it is most likely that it was a pledge to do whatever Muḥammad had in mind. It was called the Pledge of Good Pleasure because, as the Qur'ān puts it (48. 18), 'God was well-pleased with the believers when they made the pledge to thee under the tree'

A pledge to accept Muḥammad's decision in all things, or at least on this occasion not to make for safety without his permission, was what the situation demanded. The ordinary member of the expedition would be most aware of his present danger and of the impossibility of making the pilgrimage. He would be unable to appreciate the extent of Muḥammad's diplomatic success. It says much for Muḥammad's ability to handle men that in these circumstances he was able to get his followers to agree to postpone their pilgrimage for a year. His control of the Muslims made a great impression on some of the Meccan negotiators, especially since resistance to the decision was by no means absent among the rank and file. Even 'Umar protested; and for a time after the signing of the treaty most of the Muslims were unwilling to sacrifice the animals and shave their hair—a reaction based no doubt partly on religious scruples but partly also on resentment at the terms of the treaty.

As he rode home to Medina at the end of March, Muḥammad must have been well satisfied with the expedition. In making a treaty with the Meccans as an equal he had received public recognition of the position that was clearly his after the failure of the siege of Medina. More important, by ending the state of war with Mecca, he had gained a larger measure of freedom for the work of extending the influence of the religious and political organization he had formed. He had also advanced towards a more autocratic control of the affairs of this organization. From now on in suitable cases he would insist on acceptance of Islam and readiness to obey the Messenger of God as conditions of alliance with himself.

On the other hand, in stopping the blockade Muḥammad had made a great military and economic concession, and what he had gained in return was chiefly among the *imponderabilia*. The treaty was only satisfactory for the Muslims in so far as one believed in Islam and its attractive power. Had Muḥammad not been able to maintain and strengthen his hold on the Muslims by the sway of the religious ideas of Islam over their imaginations, and had he not been able to attract fresh converts to Islam, the treaty would not have worked in his favour. Material reasons certainly played a large part in the conversion of many Arabs to Islam. But other factors of supreme importance were Muḥammad's belief in the message of the Qur'ān, his belief in the future of Islam as a religious and political system, and his unflinching devotion to the task to which, as he believed, God had called him. These attitudes underlay the policy Muḥammad followed at al-Ḥudaybiyah.

This expedition and treaty mark a new initiative on the part of Muḥammad. His had been the activity after the Hijrah which provoked the Meccans. Their riposte had failed. The obvious way for Muḥammad to follow up his advantage would have been to set about destroying the influence of Mecca. Instead of that he tried something new.

The Conquest of Khaybar (May–June 628)

Perhaps it was on the way back from the pilgrimage *manqué* that the idea occurred to Muḥammad of attacking the rich Jewish oasis of Khaybar. The Muslims were disappointed at the apparent fruitlessness of their expedition to al-Ḥudaybiyah, and it was only natural for an Arab like Muḥammad to feel that virtue should not be allowed to go unrewarded. So when he set out for Khaybar some six weeks after his return from Mecca, he allowed only those who had made the Pledge under the Tree to accompany him.

Even if this was one of the points in Muḥammad's mind, however, there were also weighty military reasons for the expedition. The Jews of Khaybar, especially the leaders of the clan of an-Naḍīr exiled from Medina, were still incensed at Muḥammad. They made lavish, though no doubt judicious, use of their wealth to induce the neighbouring Arabs to take up arms against the Muslims. This was a straightforward reason for attacking Khaybar.

The people of Khaybar had some word of Muḥammad's preparations, but his march was executed swiftly and secretly, and they were taken by surprise with inadequate dispositions to resist a siege. Khaybar comprised about five groups of strongholds or small castles, many built on the tops of hills and considered impregnable. The Muslims attacked them piecemeal. There was much shooting with arrows from a distance and apparently some single combats. When the besieged made a sally, the Muslims fought back vigorously, and on at least one occasion followed them inside the gates. Several of the Muslim successes, however, were due to help they received from Jews who wanted in this way to ensure the safety of themselves and their families. When the first two groups of strongholds had fallen, there was little further resistance, and terms of surrender were speedily arranged for the remainder.

In the agreement between the people of Khaybar and Muḥammad a new principle was introduced, which became one of the foundations of the later Islamic empire. This was that the Jews should continue to cultivate the land, but should hand over half the produce to the Muslim owners. These were the 1,600 participants in the expedition or those to whom they had sold their shares. The lands were not assigned to individuals nor (as happened later) to the community as a whole. They were divided into eighteen lots, and each lot assigned to one or more clans. The individual presumably received a numerical share of the dates or other produce of the lot assigned to the group to which he belonged. Muḥammad, as on all expeditions, received a fifth of what had been captured. Here it was a particular district of Khaybar. From the dates it produced he assigned so many loads annually to each of his wives, to Emigrants of the clan of Hāshim and to other persons for whom he was specially responsible. The assessment and collection of the half of the produce was the work of an overseer, doubtless appointed by Muḥammad.

This settlement meant the end of the political influence of the Jews of Khaybar. They were now politically and economically subservient to Medina. Even if they had wanted to carry on their intrigues, they had not the wealth to back them up. They were also lacking in leadership. Several of their chief men were killed in the siege; and two others were executed after the surrender because, contrary to the agreement, they had concealed the family treasure. Three minor Jewish colonies in the region also submitted to Muḥammad on similar terms.

Various factors contributed to this Muslim success. The Jews were over-confident in the strength of their positions in Khaybar, and failed to lay in supplies of water sufficient for even a short siege. Man for man the Muslims were the better fighters, but this did not count for much in a siege except in so far as the besieged were forced to leave their strongholds through lack of water or other supplies. The Muslims seem to have been short of food for a time until they captured one of the strongholds with ample provisions. The lack of fundamental unity among the Jews was a weakness which meant that it was easy for Muḥammad to find Jews who were ready to help him. The Arab allies of the Jews, too, being attached to them chiefly by bribes, were easily detached, partly by fear of Muslim reprisals and partly by Muḥammad's diplomatic skill.

The fall of Khaybar and surrender of the other Jewish colonies marked the end of the Jewish question during Muḥammad's lifetime, for the expulsion of the Jews from the Ḥijāz by the caliph 'Umar belongs to later history. The Jews had opposed Muḥammad to the utmost of their ability, and they had been utterly crushed. Many still remained in their former homes in Medina and elsewhere, but they had lost much of their wealth and had become politically quiescent.

It is interesting to speculate what might have happened had the Jews come to terms with Muḥammad instead of opposing him. At certain periods they could have secured very favourable terms from him, including religious autonomy. On that basis they might have become partners in the Arab empire and Islam a sect of Jewry. How different the face of the world would be now had that happened! In the early months at Medina the seeds were sown of a great tragedy; a great opportunity was lost.

Why was it that things came about in this way? Was there some inevitability about this dénouement of the meeting between nascent Islam and the Jews? There is no easy answer to such questions. Indeed they can only be answered in the framework of a total philosophy. All that the historian can do is to point to some of the factors underlying the events, and to estimate their relative importance.

The essential cause of the quarrel between Muḥammad and the Jews was in the realm of ideas, though there were also material factors present on both sides. Muḥammad must have been aware of the wealth of the Jews and of the advantages that possession of it would give to him. It would be unrealistic to claim that he was not moved at all by the prospect of financial betterment. This prospect may even have had much to do with the timing of his attacks on the Jews. On the Jewish side there was the hope of recovering political supremacy in Medina, perhaps in conjunction with 'Abd-Allāh ibn-Ubayy—a hope that was being rapidly extinguished by Muḥammad's successes. Those who hold that man is moved solely by material factors will find in the points mentioned a sufficient explanation for the clash between the Muslims and the Jews. Such a view, however, is quite foreign to the position from which I am writing this book. Though I have held that material factors created the situation in which Islam was born, I have also maintained that the social malaise they produce does not become a social movement until it has ideas to focus it. Even so, there may seem to be a contradiction between the emphasis on the contribution of material factors to the origin of Islam and the insistence that the differences between Muḥammad and the Jews were not due to material factors but to ideas. Let us look at this question more closely.

The view on which this book is based is that a novel situation (created by material factors) requires novel ideas. The extent of novelty required in the ideas perhaps varies roughly in accordance with the extent of novelty in the situation. Sometimes, as when a new religion is founded, what is central in men's lives is affected, and then the novelty in the ideas is considerable. When ideas, such as those of a new religion, prove appropriate not just to one situation, but to a whole series of situations over generations, then they become woven into the texture of the social life and the culture of those who entertain them. When this has happened, ideas that have proved satisfactory over a long period and have become part of the texture of a people's life, cannot easily be changed. That was the case with the Jews. They believed that they were God's chosen people through whom alone He revealed Himself to men. It was difficult for them to see why they should change this idea because of an uneducated upstart (as they considered him) like Muḥammad.

For Muḥammad the idea that he was a prophet receiving messages from God and with a commission from Him, was the basis of the whole political and religious movement he was leading. Remove this idea and the movement, though it was twenty years old, would collapse. The ideas of Islam were still partly fluid, however, and Muḥammad was able to deal with situation created by the Jews' rejection of him by introducing the idea of the religion of Abraham, corrupted by the Jews and restored in its purity by the Muslims.

The intellectual or ideational conflict between Muḥammad and the Jews became as bitter as it did because it threatened the core of the religious ideas of each. If prophets could arise among Gentiles, the Jews were not God's chosen people, and that was tantamount to having no religion left. If Muḥammad was not God's prophet and messenger, then in his own eyes he could only be a self-deceived impostor. This was at the root of the quarrel.

Even this, however, is not the whole of the matter. In the relations of individuals and groups, especially in the field of religion, there is often a period when the character of their relationship is indeterminate. Then, either suddenly or gradually, they come to a point at which for one at least the relationship has become determinate. They have decided that they and the others are friends or enemies, belong together or do not belong together. From that point things go either all right or all wrong. The Jews possibly reached this point of no return about the time of the Hijrah, though

Muḥammad did not reach his till about a year and a half after that. Once they had decided to reject Muḥammad, the Jews had to justify this decision at least to themselves, and perhaps this was why they indulged, quite unnecessarily, in mocking criticism of Muḥammad. And when, after unavailing efforts to make them change their minds, Muḥammad broke with the Jews, the whole sorry train of events was set in motion.

Increasing Strength

The period between the fall of Khaybar in May 628 and the submission of Mecca in January 630 was one in which Muḥammad was trying in every possible way to increase his strength and organize his growing state smoothly and efficiently. This had indeed been his chief aim ever since the failure of the siege of Medina, but after his treaty with the Meccans he was able to pursue it more vigorously and in fresh directions.

The usual Muslim historical tradition is that immediately after the treaty Muḥammad sent out six messengers (who are named) to the rulers of surrounding countries, summoning them to accept Islam. Modern critical methods, however, show that this tradition is unreliable, and is probably due to the desire of later Muslims to show that Muḥammad thought of his religion as a universal one (and perhaps also to justify the wars against Persia and Byzantium as wars that were fought only after these empires had been summoned to Islam). The kernel of fact behind this story seems to be that Muḥammad did in fact send envoys to the rulers mentioned. They did not all go on the same day, however. Some certainly went several months before the treaty with the Meccans, and others probably several months later. We do not know what messages they conveyed, but it is probable that Muḥammad gave his version of what had been happening in Arabia, tried to forestall Meccan appeals for help, and sought some kind of political agreement. For such agreements Muḥammad would now feel himself sufficiently strong and important.

The message to the Negus of Abyssinia dealt with arrangements for Muḥammad's marriage to Umm-Ḥabībah and probably also for the return to Arabia of Muḥammad's cousin Ja'far and the other Muslims still in Abyssinia. These were the remnants of the party which had emigrated from Mecca about 615. From their residence in Abyssinia of more than a dozen years one argues that they must have found life there congenial, and that therefore Muḥammad must have held out some inducements to them to return. They arrived about the time of the successful conclusion of the operations against Khaybar, and received shares of the spoil.

Umm-Ḥabībah, who came with the party to Medina, was the widow of a Muslim who had become a Christian, the brother of Zaynab bint-Jaḥsh. Umm-Ḥabībah, herself a Muslim, was the daughter of Abū-Sufyān, and Muḥammad's marriage to her, which took place soon after her return, must have been aimed at facilitating a reconciliation with her father.

The envoy to the ruler of Egypt returned (sometime between January 627 and April 629) with a present for Muḥammad of two slave-girls, one of whom, Māriyah, he kept as a concubine for himself; as she remained a Christian, she did not become a full wife. After Khaybar Muḥammad also took as concubine Ṣafīyah, the daughter of one of the chiefs of the Jewish clan of an-Naḍīr; on accepting Islam she seems to have become a full wife. Here again Muḥammad may have thought that this would help to pacify the Jews. On all sides Muḥammad was attempting to reconcile men to accepting him as head of state.

Of the numerous expeditions in the period between Khaybar and the conquest of Mecca some were directed against tribes that were ceasing to oppose Muḥammad but were not yet completely quiescent. These included some sections of the group of tribes known as Ghaṭafān and the tribe of Sulaym. In some cases a member of the tribe who had become a Muslim led a party of Muslims against the pagan members of the tribe ; and it seems very likely there that an old quarrel was being prosecuted in the name of Islam. A second series of expeditions was against the tribal group of Hawāzin. They may not have been important in themselves, but they are significant as an indication of the geographical expansion of Muḥammad's power and as a premonition of the resistance from Hawāzin which culminated at the battle of Ḥunayn.

Once again the most interesting expeditions are three along the road to Syria in July, September and October 629, but once again the information is infuriatingly slight. On the first expedition a small Muslim party of fifteen was wiped out, only the leader escaping. The second, to Mu'tah, was a much larger affair, and for a time Muḥammad may have been thinking of leading it himself. He eventually put it under the command of his adopted son Zayd ibn-Ḥārithah, and gave him 3,000 men. What exactly happened must remain mysterious, for the few items of information preserved by the Muslim historians have become somewhat garbled in the attempt to vilify Khālid ibn-al-Walīd. What seems certain is that there was an encounter of some kind with an enemy force, that Zayd and his two immediate subordinates were killed but very few other Muslims, and that the army returned safely to Mecca under the command of Khālid ibn-al-Walīd.

The most mysterious fact is that in an encounter between 3,000 men on one side and perhaps 10,000 on the other (one report gives the figure of 100,000), the casualty list should contain the general and two staff officers of one side, but only about a dozen of the men. Was it a sudden raid or skirmish? We do not know. A smaller expedition the following month may have been intended to wipe out any disgrace or dishonour incurred by the Muslims. Together the three expeditions indicate that Muḥammad was continuing to show an interest in the route to the north.

With his power over a wide area as secure as power could be in Arabian conditions, Muḥammad was in a position to march on Mecca as soon as he found an occasion for interference.

Mecca in Decline

For many years there had been two rival groups among the leading merchants of Mecca. One, which we may call the Makhzūm group was led by Abū-Jahl until his death at Badr in 624. The other was led by Abū-Sufyān. From the debacle of Badr to the abortive expedition of the grand confederacy Meccan policy was dominated by Abū-Sufyān. This was partly due to the loss of so many leading men at Badr, for the new generation in the Makhzūm group had not found its feet. There are indeed hints of opposition to Abū-Sufyān at least on points of detail, but the urgency of the situation in which Mecca found itself made a large measure of unity inevitable. After the failure of his grand alliance in 627 Abū-Sufyān was somewhat discredited in the eyes of many Meccans, even of some of his own clan. He was probably also despondent in himself, for he must have realized that the ruin of Mecca was imminent. He seems to have sunk back exhausted by his efforts, and allowed younger men to take the reins.

By the time of Muḥammad's expedition to al-Ḥudaybiyah in March 628 power seems to have been chiefly in the hands of a group of three men, Ṣafwān ibn-Umayyah, Suhayl ibn-'Amr and 'Ikrimah, the son of Abū-Jahl. All belonged to the Makhzūm group, but they did not see eye to eye. Ṣafwān had been most prominent as a rival to Abū-Sufyān in the years since Badr, but 'Ikrimah strongly opposed his views on some points. Suhayl perhaps held the balance between the other two, and he was entrusted with the final negotiations for the treaty with Muḥammad.

After the first breath of relief at the signing of the treaty Mecca must have become a city of despair. The older men and those with vested interests would want to carry on, but the younger men must have seen that there was no future for them in Mecca. The son of Suhayl ibn-'Amr is said to have made his way to the Muslim camp to profess Islam at the very time when his father was arranging the treaty ; and (as mentioned above) he was handed back to his father in accordance with the terms of the treaty. This was the first of a stream of converts to Islam. For those who were full citizens there was nothing to prevent them throwing in their lot with Muḥammad if they so desired.

A series of events which must have begun soon after the signing of the treaty illustrates the strange way in which Arab custom worked. A man called Abū-Baṣīr was under the protection of a Meccan clan. He had been incarcerated by the clan for his Muslim sympathies, but managed to escape and make his way to Muḥammad. On his heels, however, came an envoy of the clan with a letter demanding his extradition. Muḥammad acknowledged the justice of the demand, and, when Abū-Baṣīr protested, said that God would make a way out of his difficulties and would not allow him to be seduced from his religion.

The envoy, his freedman and the prisoner had not gone many miles on their way back to Mecca before Abū-Baṣīr seized an opportunity. When they halted for lunch he won the confidence of the others by sharing his dates with them ; they had only dry bread, for dates were a Medinan product. The envoy took off his sword to be more comfortable, and on Abū-Baṣīr's praising it and asking if it were sharp unsheathed it and let him put his hand on the hilt. It was the work of a minute to kill the unwary captor. The freedman escaped to Muḥammad, but when Abū-Baṣīr also appeared and Muḥammad gave the freedman the chance of escorting him back to Mecca, he not surprisingly declined. As Abū-Baṣīr had been handed over to the Meccan clan, he was no longer technically a member of the Islamic community and Muḥammad had no responsibility technically for the bloodshed.

The Meccans, however, would now be more than ever incensed against Abū-Baṣīr, and could require him from Muḥammad if he remained in Medina ; so with some words of encouragement from Muḥammad he went to a spot near the coast which commanded the Meccan route to Syria. Here—again probably not without Muḥammad's encouragement—there gathered round him seventy would-be Muslims from Mecca, whom Muḥammad would have had to hand back had they gone to Medina. This band attacked small caravans of the Meccans and killed any man who came into their power. In this way, without breaking the letter of the treaty, Muḥammad partly restored the blockade. The men were not officially members of his community and he had no responsibility for their actions. The Meccans, on the other hand, though free to use violence on the men so far as Muḥammad was concerned, were now too weak to do so at such a distance from Mecca. In the end they appealed to Muḥammad to take the men into his community, presumably agreeing to waive their rights under the treaty. Abū-Baṣīr unfortunately died just as Muḥammad's letter to this effect reached him. In this whole affair, though to the Western critic Muḥammad seems to have encouraged and connived at a breach of the treaty, his conduct was formally correct by Arab standards and was not officially questioned by the Meccans.

In March 629 Muḥammad performed the lesser pilgrimage to Mecca along with about 2,000 men. This was in place of the pilgrimage he had been unable to make in the previous year, and in accordance with the treaty of al-Ḥudaybiyah the Meccans withdrew from their city for three days to avoid incidents. Many of the Meccans must have been impressed by this evidence of the growing strength of Islam, as well as of its essentially Arabian character. Doubtless it contributed to the conversion three months later of two men with great talents, Khālid ibn-al-Walīd of the clan of Makhzūm and ʻAmr ibn-al-ʻĀṣ of the clan of Sahm. The former by his superb generalship, especially in the years immediately following Muḥammad's death, must be reckoned as one of the creators of the Arab empire, while the latter was later prominent as a statesman and is remembered as the conqueror of Egypt. Muḥammad's estimate of their capabilities may be seen from the fact that a month or two after their arrival in Medina they were in charge of Muslim expeditions.

While in Mecca Muḥammad tried to effect a reconciliation with what remained there of his own clan of Hāshim. Abū-Lahab, the uncle about whom Muḥammad felt so bitterly because he had withdrawn clan protection from him, had died about 624, and the head of the clan now appears to have been another uncle, al-ʻAbbās. He is sometimes said to have been a secret Muslim from an early period, but this is an attempt by historians writing under the ʻAbbāsid caliphs (750–1258) to whitewash the ancestor of that dynasty. He may actually have fought against Muḥammad.[1] As a banker and financier, doubtless in a small way, and the

[1] Cf. A. Guillaume, *The Life of Muhammad: a translation of (Ibn) Isḥāq's Sīrat Rasūl Allāh*, London, 1955, xlvii, 338n.

purveyor of water for the pilgrims, he had little importance in the affairs of Mecca, and life there cannot have been very comfortable for him. He more than other Meccans had reason to regard hopefully his nephew's rise to power, that is, provided Muḥammad was prepared to overlook the past.

Muḥammad, in accordance with his principle of seeking reconciliation wherever possible, soon made it clear that al-'Abbās need have no qualms about his attitude. He made the handsome gesture of arranging to marry Maymūnah, the sister of the wife of al-'Abbās. This constituted a firm bond between the two men, for, unlike most of the rest of Mecca, the household of al-'Abbās was one where matrilineal kinship was dominant. The arrangements for the marriage were barely completed when Muḥammad had to leave Mecca, and it was celebrated and consummated on the way back to Medina. It is likely that al-'Abbās became a Muslim at this point, and remained in Mecca to work for Muḥammad.

The series of events which ended Muḥammad's truce with the Meccans began about November 629. It arose out of an old tribal quarrel that now flared up again, but in a setting in which the Meccans and the Muslims were involved. One of the tribes, Khuzā'ah, took advantage of the terms of the treaty of al-Ḥudaybiyah to declare themselves allies of Muḥammad. At some point they killed a man of the other tribe who had written verses hostile to Muḥammad. This other tribe, Bakr ibn-'Abd-Manāt, was an old ally of the Meccans. From the leaders of the Makhzūm group it secretly got a quantity of weapons. The plot was carefully laid and Khuzā'ah taken by surprise. After some losses they fled to the houses of two fellow-tribesmen in Mecca. A member of the tribe managed to take the news at once to Muḥammad.

The Meccans, after stopping the fighting and presumably sending the men of Bakr out of the city, realized that the situation was serious, and that it would be worse if Muḥammad discovered the extent to which some of them had aided and abetted the plotters. If they were not to submit to Muḥammad, they had the choice of three courses: they might disown the section of Bakr involved and let Muḥammad do what he liked with them; they might pay blood-money; they might declare war on Muḥammad. There were some in favour of each of the options, and it was difficult to reach agreement. To pay blood-money would mean a great loss of face; but a rupture of the treaty would lead to economic loss, and there was little hope of defeating Muḥammad.

In the end Abū-Sufyān, who now appears on the scene again, persuaded the Meccans to attempt a compromise, and he himself was sent to Medina to try to secure it. It was a sign of how the mighty had fallen that the Meccans had now to go to Muḥammad and ask him humbly for a favour. Exactly what was hoped for is not clear, but it was probably a solution which used against Muḥammad the principles which had been used against themselves in the case of Abū-Baṣīr. The Meccans would admit that a wrong had been done, but maintain that they were not responsible for it, possibly because the wrongdoers were not included in the treaty or because they had acted on their own; then they would renew the treaty from now on to include these people. Unfortunately Muḥammad was not prepared to play their game, and he was in a better position to use force against the tribe of Bakr than they had been against Abū-Baṣīr. After Abū-Sufyān's mission the Meccans were left with the same three or rather four choices as before; but Abū-Sufyān was now turning to the fourth—submission to Muḥammad.

Abū-Sufyān played a much more important part in the Muslim capture of Mecca than is generally realized. Muslim historians obscured this fact in order to avoid making his role appear more glorious than that of al-'Abbās. The accounts of his visit to Medina have been given a fanciful colouring. He is said to have gone first to his daughter, Umm-Ḥabībah, now Muḥammad's wife, but she refused even to let him sit on her bed, since he was an unbeliever and it was used by the prophet. Muḥammad is said to have refused to see him, and the other leading Emigrants to have been distinctly unhelpful, so that he had to leave with practically nothing accomplished.

In this account there are several inconsistencies, and the truth appears to be quite other. Abū-Sufyān had a more statesmanlike grasp of realities than his Meccan opponents, and after the failure of the great confederacy saw the hopelessness of continued resistance. He was probably reconciled to a decrease in dignity and importance and to a lower standard of living, and both before and after the siege he used his influence on the side of moderation and fostered internal unity. Muḥammad's marriage with his daughter doubtless encouraged him to hope for reconciliation without much loss of prestige. Such thoughts must have been in his mind before he went to Medina. Later events show that at some time, probably during his visit to Medina, he had come to an understanding with Muḥammad. Abū-Sufyān was to work for the surrender of Mecca without fighting ; he was to pronounce his formal protection (*jiwār*) of all who wanted it (that is, of all who accepted this policy), and Muḥammad would respect this protection. Such an agreement fitted in well with Muḥammad's aims.

The Submission of Mecca

The capture of Mecca was not an end in itself for Muḥammad, since, as has been maintained above, he was already thinking of an expansion beyond Arabia northwards. Yet Mecca and the Meccans were important for him.

Mecca had long since been chosen as the geographical focus of Islam, and so it was necessary for the Muslims to have freedom of access to it. Could Mecca be brought under his sway, his prestige and power would be greatly increased; without Mecca his position was comparatively weak. Moreover, as the affairs of the Islamic community grew in volume, Muḥammad had need of the military and administrative abilities of the Meccans, and he had been working for some time to gain their willing cooperation.

In the year and a half since the treaty of al-Ḥudaybiyah Muslim strength had increased rapidly. When Muḥammad's allies of Khuzā'ah appealed to him for help, he felt the time had come for action. Abū-Sufyān's visit showed him that few in Mecca would now resist, and that the 'diehard' leaders of the Makhzūm group would have little support. He therefore set about collecting a force sufficient to overawe the Meccans and ensure that none but the most inveterate opponents resisted actively.

During the preparations measures were taken to secure a large degree of secrecy. Nothing was said in Medina about the goal of the expedition, a small party was sent towards Syria to put men on a false scent, and the roads to Mecca were sealed off. By a strange lapse (which he alleged to be due to anxiety about wife and children in Mecca) one of the veterans of Badr tried to give information to the Meccans, but his letter was intercepted. Eventually on 1st January 630 Muḥammad was able to set out with an army which, including those who joined *en route*, numbered about 10,000 men.

The Meccans had received little exact information about this huge force and its destination. Even when it camped two short stages from Mecca it was possible that it might be going against tribes to the east of Mecca. To increase the dismay of the Meccans ten thousand fires were lit by Muḥammad's orders. Abū-Sufyān now came out to

Muḥammad along with some of the leading Meccans not of the Makhzūm group and formally submitted to him. In return Muḥammad promised a general amnesty; all who claimed the protection of Abū-Sufyān or who closed their houses and remained inside would be safe. With this declaration Abū-Sufyān returned to Mecca.

The following night Muḥammad pitched his camp nearer Mecca, and in the morning (probably 11th January 630) his forces, divided into four columns, advanced into Mecca from four directions. Only the column under Khālid ibn-al-Walīd met with resistance, and that was soon overcome. After twenty-four of the Meccans and four of their allies had been killed the rest fled. Two Muslims were killed when they mistook their way and ran into a body of the enemy. With such negligible bloodshed did Muḥammad achieve this great triumph.

A small number of persons specified by name was excluded from the general amnesty. Apart from 'Ikrimah, the son of Abū-Jahl, they were all guilty of particular faults of a criminal or treasonable character. Several were eventually pardoned, but some were executed. Because of the general amnesty the fleeing pagans were not energetically pursued. The leaders of the Makhzūm group, who had been organizing the resistance to Muḥammad, came out of hiding or returned to Mecca when they learnt that their safety was guaranteed. From some of the rich men Muḥammad indeed requested loans. He had treated them magnanimously, and, because he had forbidden pillage, his poorer followers were now in want; from these loans the latter received fifty dirhams apiece.

Muḥammad remained fifteen or twenty days in Mecca. Small expeditions were sent out to obtain the submission of the surrounding tribes and to destroy two important shrines dedicated to Manāt and al-'Uzzā respectively. In Mecca itself the Ka'bah and the private houses were cleansed of idols. A number of pressing administrative matters were dealt with, especially the defining of the boundaries of the sacred territory of Mecca. Most of the old offices and privileges of the Meccans were abolished, but the custody of the Ka'bah was continued in the same family, while al-'Abbās kept the right of supplying water to pilgrims.

Foremost among the reasons for this success of Muḥammad's was the attractiveness of Islam and its relevance as a religious and social system to the needs of the Arabs. The leading men might gain advantages from partial adherence to the old tribal standards and customs, but the ordinary people were chiefly aware of the disadvantages of the old system. As hardships multiplied through the Muslim blockade, the private interests of the leaders would come more and more into conflict with one another, and unity more and more difficult to preserve.

Muḥammad's own tact, diplomacy and administrative skill also contributed greatly. His marriages to Maymūnah and Umm-Ḥabībah helped to win over al-'Abbās and Abū-Sufyān, and he may have gained other advantages, of which we are not aware, from the discords among the Meccans. Above all, his consummate skill in handling the confederacy he now ruled, and in making all but an insignificant minority feel they were being fairly treated, heightened the contrast between the harmony, satisfaction and zest within the Islamic community and the malaise elsewhere. This must have been obvious to many and have influenced their choice.

In all this Muḥammad's faith in his cause, his vision and his far-seeing wisdom are most impressive. While his community was still small and devoting all its energies to avoiding destruction, he had conceived a united Arabia directed outwards, in which the Meccans would play a new role—a role no less important than their old role of merchants. He had harried them and provoked them ; then he had wooed them and frightened them in turn ; and now practically all of them, even the greatest, had submitted to him. Against considerable odds, often with narrow margins, but nearly always with sureness of touch, he had moved towards his goal. If we were not convinced of the historicity of these things, few would credit that the despised Meccan prophet could re-enter his city as a triumphant conqueror.

The Battle of Ḥunayn (31st January 630)

While Muḥammad was busy taking over responsibility for the affairs of Mecca, a military threat was looming up to the east. Two or three days' march away the group of tribes called Hawāzin was collecting an army twice the size of Muḥammad's. They were old enemies of the Meccans, and there had been fierce fighting on several occasions during Muḥammad's lifetime. With them were included Thaqīf, the tribe inhabiting the town of aṭ-Ṭā'if. The trade of this town had come under the control of the Meccan merchants, working through a pro-Meccan party among Thaqīf. The decline in the prestige of Mecca upset the balance of power in favour of the anti-Meccan party, and in January the whole of Thaqīf joined Hawāzin (though the pro-Meccan party fled almost as soon as the battle began).

While many of Thaqīf obviously hoped to assert their independence of Mecca, the precise expectations of the rest of Hawāzin (who were nomads) are obscure. They are said to have begun to concentrate as soon as they heard of Muḥammad's preparations at Medina. Perhaps they regarded the expansion of Muḥammad's power as a threat to themselves. Perhaps they only hoped to pay off old scores against the Meccans. Perhaps they expected an opportunity for booty after Muḥammad and the Meccans had exhausted themselves in the conflict which seemed inevitable.

The Meccans also realized something of the danger. There

is no suggestion that the leaders of the resistance to Muḥammad ever sought help from Hawāzin. Even when they fled none of them went in this direction. There must have been strong feeling between these tribes and the Meccans. Consequently Muḥammad, on becoming conqueror of Mecca, at once became also its champion against the threatening enemy. It was self-preservation more than hope of booty that made the pagan Meccans go out with him to Ḥunayn. Ṣafwān ibn-Umayyah thought submission to Muḥammad preferable to subjection to Thaqīf or Hawāzin; and he lent arms to Muḥammad as well as the money he had asked for. Altogether Muḥammad was able to add 2,000 men to his army, and judged himself strong enough to march out and give battle to an enemy reputed to have a force of 20,000.

Muḥammad left Mecca on 27th January, and on the evening of the 30th camped at Ḥunayn close to the enemy. The next morning the Muslims moved forward down the wādi in battle order; the vanguard, commanded by Khālid ibn-al-Walīd, included many men of the tribe of Sulaym. The Muslims, who had been over-confident, were somewhat dismayed at the huge mass of human beings and animals which they saw, for Hawāzin had brought all their women, children and livestock, staking everything on the issue of the battle. Suddenly the enemy cavalry, posted overnight in the side valleys, attacked the Muslim van. The men of Sulaym, though later they protested that they fought bravely, are said to have fled almost at once, and their consternation affected a large part of Muḥammad's army.

At this critical moment Muḥammad himself stood firm with a small body of Emigrants and Helpers. This turned the tide, and before long the enemy were in full flight. Some Thaqīf fought bravely for a time, then fled to the safety of their walls. The chief of the confederacy, Mālik ibn-'Awf, with his own tribe held a pass to gain time for those on foot;

and there seems to have been another stand in front of the enemy camp. In the end, however, all efforts proved unavailing. The fighting men were dispersed or taken prisoner or killed ; the women, children, animals and goods fell into the hands of the Muslims.

In the battle of Ḥunayn a larger number of men were involved than in any of Muḥammad's previous battles. It was not a stubbornly fought battle, however, and there seems to have been little hand-to-hand fighting. The Muslim losses were consequently small. The victory, none the less, was complete and decisive. Ḥunayn was the major encounter during Muḥammad's lifetime between the Muslims and the nomadic tribes. The collection and concentration of 20,000 men was a notable feat for a nomadic chief, and after Mālik ibn-'Awf's discomfiture none cared to repeat it against Muḥammad.

The Consolidation of Victory

From Ḥunayn Muḥammad went on at once to aṭ-Ṭā'if and set about besieging it. He had some siege-engines, probably adopted from the Byzantines, but even with these he made little headway. After some fifteen days he decided to abandon the siege. Thaqīf were resisting bravely, and there had been some casualties among the Muslims. If he allowed the siege to drag on, his men would become restive, blood would be shed, and a final reconciliation with Thaqīf would be rendered more difficult. A long siege would also dissipate some of the prestige gained at Ḥunayn. Besides he had Hawāzin and the booty of Ḥunayn to attend to. Thus, by abandoning the siege he lost nothing of importance, for he had other ways of influencing Thaqīf in his favour. Yet he may have been disappointed or annoyed ; this at least is a possible reason for his sharp treatment of a man who accidentally kicked him while they were riding back.

The booty had been left at a place called al-Ji'rānah, and there Muhammad spent from 24th February to 9th March. The prisoners were there also except that a few of the women had been given to some of Muḥammad's leading ' companions '. There was sufficient booty to give every man in the army four camels or the equivalent. The organization of the distribution must have been a formidable task, and it is not surprising that there was some trouble over it and complaints at the delay.

The clan chiefs and other leading men among the Meccans received a hundred or fifty camels each according to their rank. Abū-Sufyān and the man who accompanied him when he made his submission to Muḥammad may have received 300 camels each—perhaps a repayment for their contribution to the peaceful occupation of Mecca. These gifts to the leaders indicate that they were technically not members of Muḥammad's community but commanders of allied contingents.

Negotiations with Hawāzin had begun during the siege of aṭ-Ṭā'if, and while Muḥammad was at al-Ji'rānah Mālik ibn-'Awf and Hawāzin decided to accept Islam. At the same time they asked for their women and children back. This was granted, but as a favour, and they seem to have had to make a payment in return. No doubt their conversion was facilitated by the bleak prospect before them otherwise.

From al-Ji'rānah Muḥammad went to make the lesser pilgrimage at Mecca, then returned to Medina. In charge of his affairs in Mecca he left a young man of Abū-Sufyān's clan—probably an indication that, though he was on good terms with most people in Mecca, he tended to support Abū-Sufyān rather than his rivals.

It must rank as one of Muḥammad's greatest achievements that he effected a genuine reconciliation with the leading men of Mecca—the men who a few months before had been his implacable enemies. It is not surprising to find that Abū-Sufyān helped with the destruction of the idol of al-Lāt at aṭ-Ṭā'if and was governor of a district in South Arabia for a time ; later he is said to have been present at the battle of the Yarmūk in 636 and to have lived on till about 652. It is more surprising to learn that after Muḥammad's death when there was disaffection in some of the tribes Suhayl ibn-'Amr is credited with being chiefly responsible for keeping the Meccans loyal. Most interesting of all is the case of 'Ikrimah, son of Abū-Jahl. At first proscribed by Muḥammad, then pardoned, he became a keen Muslim and was given several important military and administrative posts. His zeal for Islam was such that remarks like the following are attributed to him : 'whatever money I spent fighting against you, I shall spend as much in the way of God '; ' I risked my life for al-Lāt and al-'Uzzā ; shall I hold back from risking it for God ? ' Appropriately he died as a ' martyr ' in one of the battles in Syria.

All the leading Meccans must have become at least nominally Muslims, even if they were not all genuine converts like 'Ikrimah. When this happened is not clear. It may well be that it happened after the distribution of booty at al-Ji'rānah, but the suggestion of later Muslim writers that they became Muslims *because* of the gifts they received there is almost certainly an anti-Umayyad slander. As noted above they were probably more influenced by the fact that Muḥammad had become their champion against their enemies of Hawāzin and Thaqīf.

VIII

RULER IN ARABIA

The Position after Ḥunayn

The conquest of Mecca and the victory of Ḥunayn did not make any technical difference to Muhammad's position in Medina itself. He was still the chief of the 'clan' of Emigrants, one among several clan-chiefs; and he was also the messenger of God, who from time to time received by way of revelation divine commands applicable to the whole community. It was presumably as messenger of God that he was commander-in-chief, since the Muslim expeditions were regarded as 'fighting in the way of God'. Although things were technically the same, however, subtle differences had been gradually making their appearance as Muḥammad's prestige grew. Most of the clan-chiefs in Medina now realized on which side their bread was buttered, and would be unlikely to go against Muḥammad. They had probably also sworn to obey him when they took the Pledge under the Tree at al-Ḥudaybiyah.

Another difference was that the 'clan' of Emigrants had greatly increased. Not merely had there been conversions of Meccans like Khālid ibn-al-Walīd. Individuals from nomadic tribes went to Medina to take part in the expeditions because they were more lucrative than other occupations like herding camels, and these individuals seem to have counted as Emigrants—perhaps because they were under the direct protection of Muḥammad himself. In one or two cases whole clans or tribes were allowed to call themselves 'Emigrants' as a title of honour. It is therefore quite credible that at the battle of Ḥunayn there were 700 Emigrants as against about 90 at Badr.

The most important change that was happening, however

was that whole tribes or clans, or important sections of them, began to send deputations to Medina to ask for alliance with Muḥammad. From the time of Muḥammad's return to Medina after Ḥunayn the trickle of such deputations became a stream. The strain on Muḥammad and his advisers must have been great. There were dozens of tribes and sub-tribes and smaller groups. Within a group of whatever size there were usually at least two factions or rival subdivisions. If a deputation came to Medina from a tribe, as often as not it was from one section of a tribe trying to steal a march on another section. To deal with such deputations tactfully Muḥammad must have had an extensive knowledge of the internal politics of the various groups. Not for nothing is Abū-Bakr, his chief lieutenant, said to have been an expert in genealogy, which included a knowledge of the relation to one another of the subdivisions of any group. That things went so smoothly says much for Muḥammad's wisdom in handling these affairs.

Along with this change there appears to go a new way of looking at the Islamic community. The word *ummah*, which has been translated ' community ', ceases to be used in the Qur'ān and the other documents of this period. The latter consist of texts of treaties and letters (which I hold to be mostly genuine), and speak instead of *jamā'ah* and *ḥizb Allāh*, meaning respectively ' collection, assembly, company or totality ' and ' the party of God '. In practice it was not necessary to have a special word for the Islamic community or state, since diplomatic and administrative business was carried on in the name of Muḥammad or in the name of God.

There is a considerable amount of material about the relation of the various tribes to Muḥammad, especially when references to members of the tribes are collected. Unfortunately much of this material is undated, and there are many gaps. Some of the treaties and letters, too, are difficult to interpret because they are written in very old, crabbed Arabic and there are corruptions in the text.

The general development would seem to have been as follows. In the early days—perhaps up to 627—he would be prepared to make pacts of friendship and non-aggression with non-Muslims. When he grew stronger, however, he was able to insist on further terms, such as the acknowledgement of himself as the messenger of God and the payment of 'contributions' or 'alms' to the 'treasury of God'. The terms varied from tribe to tribe. To the end he was probably willing to make alliances with strong tribes (especially those in a position to invade 'Irāq) without insisting on them becoming Muslims. The small tribes in the neighbourhood of Medina were the first to form alliances with Muḥammad. After the battle of Ḥunayn most of the tribes anywhere near Medina or Mecca had some agreement with him. Then the circle of alliances began to spread further, until it embraced the whole of Arabia.

Now that the Islamic community had become a vast confederacy expeditions of the razzia type were out of place. There are two or three small expeditions which might be classified thus in the summer of 630, but after that no more. Of these at least one led to the sub-tribe involved sending a deputation to Muḥammad to ask for an alliance. Another succeeded in destroying an important idol.

With the growth of his system of alliances Muḥammad's wealth grew. Until the capture of Khaybar the finances of the Islamic community were probably precarious, and the Emigrants lived partly off the charity or hospitality of the Helpers. The 'contributions' of his new allies must have eased Muḥammad's budget, even if his responsibilities were also increasing.

An interesting measure of Muḥammad's growing wealth is the number of horses on his expeditions. At Badr in 624 he had over 300 men and only 2 horses. When he returned there in 626 he had 1,500 men but still only 10 horses. Two years later at Khaybar there was about the same number of men, but 200 horses. At Ḥunayn after another two years 700 Emigrants had 300 horses and 4,000 Helpers another 500. Then came the great expansion. Later in the same year (630) on the expedition to Tabūk there are said to have been 30,000 men and 10,000 horses. The military significance of these figures can be seen from the fact that the Meccan cavalry, which played a decisive part at Uḥud, numbered 200 in a force of 2,000. After the battle of Ḥunayn Muḥammad was vastly stronger and richer than Mecca had ever been.

The Eclipse of Persia and its Consequences

At the time of the Hijrah the Persians had defeated the Byzantines and overrun Egypt, Syria and Asia Minor. They were even encouraging barbarians to ravage the European provinces of the Byzantine empire. About then, however, the tide turned. From 622 to 625 the Byzantine emperor Heraclius was campaigning in Asia Minor with some success. A short siege of Constantinople in 626 by the Persians proved a failure. In the following year Heraclius invaded the Persian empire and in December won an important victory near ancient Nineveh, though he had to retreat shortly afterwards. The Persian empire, however, was now cracking at the centre after the strain of the long series of wars. In February 628 the emperor was assassinated, and the son who succeeded was not secure on the throne and wanted peace. By about March 628 Heraclius could regard himself as victorious, but the negotiations for the evacuation of the Byzantine empire by the Persians were not completed until June 629. In September 629 Heraclius entered Constantinople as victor, and in March 630 restored the Holy Rood to Jerusalem.

Muḥammad would have some knowledge of these events. They must have influenced the attitude of the tribes on the way to Syria, making them less ready to come to terms with Muḥammad. The repercussion of which he became aware first, however, was probably that among the little communities which had been dependent on the Persians. Along the Persian Gulf and in South Arabia there were little states dominated by pro-Persian factions, usually minorities, unable to maintain themselves in power without Persian support in the background at least potentially. As it became clear that the Persian emperor was no longer in a position to do anything for them, these turned to the rising power in Arabia, Muḥammad, and begged his support. From al-Ji'rānah in March 630 Muḥammad sent an envoy to al-Baḥrayn (Bahrein) and about the same time another to 'Umān (Oman). In both places the pro-Muslim party was weak and only became firmly established when, after Muḥammad's death and the wars of apostasy, a strong Muslim army penetrated to the region.

In the Yemen or South Arabia the Persian governor Bādhām came to an agreement with Muhammad not later than 630. Whether he also became a Muslim is disputed. It seems possible that he did, since the Persians there had not been in the habit of receiving regular aid from the home country. On the death of Bādhām Muḥammad recognized his son as governor of Ṣan'ā', but also recognized several other men as his representatives in various parts of the region. With the troubles here are doubtless connected the expeditions to the south led by Khālid ibn-al-Walīd and 'Alī in June-July and December 631 respectively.

About March 632 one of the tribes there with its leader al-Aswad expelled two of Muḥammad's agents, killed the son of Bādhām, occupied Ṣan'ā' and brought much of the Yemen under their control. This is known as the first *riddah* or 'apostasy ' in the Yemen. It lasted only a month or two, for early in June al-Aswad was killed by one of his supporters, Qays ibn-al-Makshūḥ of the tribe of Murād. The latter was still anti-Muslim, for he was angered at Muhammad's recognition of another man as chief of Murād. The suppression of this second ' apostasy ' under Qays took place after Muḥammad's death and does not concern us here, except that throughout these troubles in the Yemen the Persian element (descendants of Persian fathers and Arab mothers) was one of the chief bulwarks of Muslim policy.

It was not only on the fringes of Arabia, however, that the Persian decline contributed to the growth of the Islamic state. Before his death Muḥammad must have become aware of the possibilities of raiding 'Irāq itself. Within raiding distance of 'Irāq were the grounds of the strong, largely Christian tribes of Bakr ibn-Wā'il and Taghlib. At a time which cannot be determined exactly—it may have been 611 or 624 or earlier or later—a battle had taken place at Dhū-Qār where regular Persian troops had been defeated by a force of Arabs, in which the chief contingent came from Shaybān, a large sub-tribe of Bakr. The importance of this battle was that it inspired the Arabs with new confidence in facing the Persians. As Persia rapidly weakened after 628 it is likely that some of these tribes began to think again of short raids into the settled lands.

About the same time the expansion of the Islamic state brought these tribes within the purview of Muḥammad. What happened is not clearly stated in the sources, but it is very probable that Muḥammad formed alliances with these tribes without asking them to become Muslims or to pay ' contributions '. The alliance would be directed towards the organization of extensive raids into 'Irāq, similar to those Muḥammad was thinking of into Syria. If this is approximately a correct account, then the invasion of 'Irāq was neither a tribal movement to which the Muslims tacked themselves on, nor an exclusively Muslim plan which the tribes were prevailed on to accept. Rather the propensity of the tribes to carry out razzias in 'Irāq was transmuted by Islamic ideas, and what might have petered out in a ruined countryside and diminishing quantities of booty became a war of permanent conquest.

Muḥammad in 630 could hardly have realized that the Persian empire would disappear within a decade. But he must have sensed its growing weakness, and shrewdly decided to be 'in on' any moves towards the heart of the empire. Because of this intuition of his the Islamic state became, among other things, the heir of the Persian empire.

The Drive to the North

Emphasis has already been laid on Muḥammad's interest in the road to Syria and the strategic importance of this for the whole development of the Islamic state. These points are further illustrated by the greatest of all Muḥammad's expeditions, that to Tabūk near the Gulf of Akaba (al-'Aqabah) from October to December 630. For this he is said to have collected an army of 30,000 men (as compared with 12,000 at Ḥunayn). It is the precursor of the wars of conquest rather than the conclusion of the series of Muḥammad's expeditions.

The tribes along the road to Syria were less open to conversion than most of the tribes with whom Muḥammad had to deal. They were largely or wholly Christian, and they had also a long tradition of association with the Byzantine empire. While that empire was in decline some of them may have toyed with the idea of throwing in their lot with Muḥammad; but by the time Muḥammad was sufficiently powerful for the proposition to be attractive, the prestige of the Byzantine empire stood higher than ever before, after its magnificent recovery and decisive victory over the Persians.

This is the background of the expedition to Tabūk. Muḥammad had doubtless heard of the triumphal restoration of the Holy Rood to Jerusalem by Heraclius in March. He would realize that he had no chance of winning the tribes here until he showed that he could bring greater force to bear on this region than could Heraclius. The mounting of this huge expedition in October was a counterblast to what Heraclius had done in March. It was also, of course, a reconnaissance of the route to Syria, and an assertion that the Muslim sphere of influence extended over much of the ground traversed. Treaties concluded with small Christian and Jewish communities on and near the Gulf of Akaba, guaranteeing them protection in return for a payment of tribute, imply that this assertion of a sphere of influence was intended to be permanent. A similar treaty with the ruler of the settled communities at Dūmat-al-Jandal was concluded by Khālid ibn-al-Walīd in command of a force detached from the main body. All this goes to show that, when Muḥammad set out in October 630 with his relatively enormous army, he was more or less aware that he was launching the Islamic state on a challenge to the Byzantine empire.

In the treaties just mentioned the outline was drawn of one part of the structure of the later Islamic empire. These settled communities of Jews and Christians were not asked to become Muslims, but only to submit to the Islamic state on certain conditions. The chief was the payment of an annual tribute in money or in kind. In return for this they would be allowed to manage their own internal affairs as they had done before, and in their relations with outsiders they would be under the protection of 'God and His Messenger', that is, of the Islamic state. Where a community surrendered without fighting, the tribute was much lighter than that demanded from Khaybar. Indeed, small communities were probably better off in most ways under the *pax Islamica.* The idea of such an arrangement is probably derived from the nomadic custom whereby a strong tribe would take a weaker one under its protection; it then became a matter of honour for the stronger to make its protection effective. The excellent record of Islam in the toleration of religious minorities is largely due to this fact—once it had said it would protect a group it was a matter of honour to do so effectively. Even on the political side the system of protected minorities was highly advantageous, and many of the troubles of the Arabic-speaking world today are due to the fact that it has broken down and that no other system has been found to replace it.

The significance of the expedition to Tabūk in the development of the Islamic state explains Muḥammad's insistence that all Muslims who were able to do so should take part in it. Now that Medina was basking in the sunshine of success some of its worthy farmers thought it was time to have a rest from their labours and enjoy their hard-won prosperity. The well-to-do ones objected both to the personal discomfort of taking part and to the contributions they were expected to make. Such men failed to realize that prosperity on the present basis would be short-lived and that for its continuing welfare the Islamic state must find an outlet northwards for the energies of the Arabs. Muḥammad, realizing all this and also that the outlet to Syria was only to be won by military force, could only get all his followers to take part by insisting that participation in the expedition was a religious duty.

Three incidents connected with the expedition to Tabūk throw some light on the nature and extent of the opposition to Muḥammad's new policy. There is said to have been a plot against Muḥammad on the journey; something was to happen to him on a dangerous bit of road on a dark night, and it would have looked like an accident. Then there was the ' mosque of dissension '. Just before the expedition set out Muḥammad was asked to honour by his presence a new mosque built by some Muslims in a remote corner of the Medinan oasis, but he postponed the matter till his return. On the way he somehow realized that an intrigue against himself was involved, and as soon as he returned to Medina he sent two men to destroy the mosque. The mosque-builders were apparently supporters of the intransigent ascetic, Abū-'Āmir ar-Rāhib, who may even himself have been in Medina at this time, and the new mosque was to give them a convenient meeting-place where they could hatch their plots without interruption.

About the same time the men who had stayed away from the expedition were being cross-examined and their excuses scrutinized. Three who were not involved in the intrigue of the mosque-builders were ' sent to Coventry ' for fifty days, and only restored to normal relations after a revelation had been received. The severity of the punishment shows how seriously Muḥammad regarded the matter. He saw that for the spiritual health of the community, it was essential that all able-bodied Muslims should share in the campaigns. It was also desirable, if most of the fighting men were to be away in distant lands for long periods, that no body of dissidents should be able to ensconce itself in a suburb of Medina.

Similar considerations underlie the strict measures taken about this period against Hypocrites. They are to be treated roughly, threatened with Hell as apostates, and practically excluded from the community. Those now branded as Hypocrites were not 'Abd-Allāh ibn-Ubayy and his party, but perhaps a group including those responsible for the ' mosque of dissension '. Strictness at this point doubtless prevented the growth of opposition of a kind that would have wrecked the little state after Muḥammad's death.

The analysis which has here been given of the reasons for Muḥammad's emphasis on expansion northwards, I would again insist, must not be taken to imply that he himself thought in what may be called an analytical way. His thinking would be better described as intuitive (if it be allowed that we have material which enables us to give any description). The religious aspect was almost certainly always uppermost in his thoughts, and the motive which drove him on was the desire to fulfil God's command to spread Islam. Yet it cannot be altogether by accident that the ideas he adopted (like the holy war), and the policies he inaugurated, were so thoroughly appropriate to the expansion in the twenty years after his death. Somehow or other, though he thought in terms of religious ideas, he must have been aware of the political realities. Somehow or other, even if he could not give an analytical account of the political realities, he must have been able to frame an adequate response to them. He had contrived, too, to share his awareness of political realities with at least Abū-Bakr and 'Umar among his followers. In the critical days following his death, when Medina itself might have been threatened by insurrectionaries, they went ahead with the expedition he was planning—one of 3,000 men to distant Mu'tah on the Syrian border.

The Extent of Muḥammad's Power

The traditional Muslim view is that in the last year of his life Muḥammad was the ruler of almost the whole of Arabia. The more sceptical European scholars, on the other hand, suggest that at his death he ruled only a small region round Medina and Mecca. The true state of affairs was somewhere between these two extremes, but it is difficult to determine precisely. The Islamic state in 632 was a conglomeration of tribes in alliance with Muḥammad on varying terms, having as its inner core the people of Medina and perhaps also of Mecca. After the Islamic state had become an empire, *every* Arab tribe naturally wanted to show that it had been in alliance with Muḥammad himself in his lifetime, and produced the best story it could of how it had sent a deputation and become Muslim. Even if these stories are accepted as roughly genuine, there are difficulties ; the deputation may have represented not the whole tribe but only themselves ; and the terms of alliance may not have given Muḥammad any say in the affairs of the tribe, and may not even have included profession of Islam.

An example of the weaker types of story produced is that of the deputation from Ghassān, the chief pro-Byzantine tribe on the Syrian marches. The deputation consisted of three unnamed members of the tribe, who went to Muḥammad in December 631. They were convinced of the truth of his claims, but went home and did nothing about it. Only one lived to make a public profession of Islam, and that was in 635 ! If this is the best story Ghassān could produce, the conclusion is inevitable that no members of the tribe became Muslims during Muḥammad's lifetime.

When due allowance has been made for all these points, we get a picture of the situation roughly as follows. The tribes in a broad region round Mecca and Medina were all firmly united to Muḥammad and had all professed Islam. In a similar position were those in the centre of Arabia and along the road to 'Irāq, but those nearest 'Irāq had not become Muslims. In the Yemen and the rest of the south-west many groups had professed Islam, but they generally constituted only a section of each tribe, and in all were probably less than half the population ; they were very dependent on support from Medina. The position in the south-east and along the Persian Gulf was similar, but the Muslims were probably much less than half the population. On the Syrian border beyond about the Gulf of Akaba there had been little success in detaching tribes from the Byzantine emperor.

If Muḥammad, then, had not made himself ruler of all Arabia, yet he had to a great extent unified the Arabs. Through his 'Arabic Qur'ān', and through the religious and political system he had created, he had developed the Arabs' hitherto only implicit awareness of themselves as an ethnological and cultural unit. It was to this unit that the 'Arabic Qur'ān' was addressed, and it marked them off from Abyssinians, Byzantines, Persians and Jews. The new religion was parallel to the religions of these peoples and could hold up its head in their company; and the political system associated with it avoided all dependence on foreigners or non-Arabs.

In view of these entanglements of religion with politics the reader may feel that the movement of the Arab tribes into the Islamic state was essentially political and not religious. This is not so, however. Since the exodus of the Israelites from Egypt religion and politics in the Middle East have always been closely linked with one another; and the fact that a movement had a prominent political aspect has never meant that it was not religious (as it often does in the modern West).

Islam provided an economic, social and political system, the *Pax Islamica.* Of this system religion was an integral part, since it gave the ideas on which the whole was based. The peace and security under the system were 'the security of God and of His messenger'. This system attracted men of the nomadic tribes in various ways. It offered an adequate livelihood, mainly by booty. It did not involve subjection to a distant potentate; all Muslims were equal, and Muḥammad treated his followers with the courtesy and respect shown by a nomadic chief to his fellow-tribesmen. When the Persian and Byzantine empires showed signs of disintegrating and men needed 'something to hold on to', the Islamic community promised to have the requisite stability.

The Arabs of that day almost certainly thought of the system as a whole, and were incapable of distinguishing in thought its economic, political and religious aspects. The supreme question for them was whether to enter the system or to remain outside. They could not have the economic and political benefits of membership without the religious profession of belief in God and His messenger; and a profession of belief of this kind made no sense unless a man was a member of Muḥammad's community, which was political as well as religious. There is thus nothing improbable in a mass movement into the Islamic community in 630 and 631 which was in some sense religious. In European analytical terms it may be primarily political (though this is perhaps only the expression of a European prejudice for the material), but in the integral reality of the events the religious and political factors were inseparable.

A system such as the *Pax Islamica* could not be built without creating opposition. About the beginning of 632 the opposition began to have a definite form. The movement of al-Aswad in the Yemen has already been mentioned. Even earlier a man called Musaylimah had set himself up as a prophet in the largely Christian tribe of Ḥanīfah in the centre of Arabia. He is said to have written to Muḥammad beginning 'From Musaylimah the messenger of God to Muḥammad the messenger of God', and suggesting a recognition of distinct spheres of influence. Muḥammad replied contemptuously 'From Muḥammad the messenger of God to Musaylimah the liar'...

These two movements, and two or three other local movements which appeared after Muḥammad's death, may be chiefly political in our sense. But it is interesting that they all found it necessary to attack the religious basis of the *Pax*

Islamica, and that they did so, not in the name of Christianity or any existing religion, but in the name of self-constituted Arab prophets. This is important corroborative evidence that part of the attraction of Islam for the Arabs was its freedom from foreign political entanglements. It is also clear from what has been said that, even when we allow that the opposition to the Islamic state was largely political, the Muslims were justified in regarding it as the ' war of apostasy ', since it included an attack on Islam as a religion.

The ultimate measure of Muḥammad's success in the political field, we conclude, was not that he ruled all Arabia, but that he created a structure which was able to suppress all opposition movements in the two years after his death and thereafter to become the basis of a vast empire.

The Last Months

In the midst of phenomenal outward success Muḥammad's domestic life had not been altogether happy. To his great joy his concubine Māriyah the Copt had borne him a son Ibrāhīm about April 630, but the little boy had died, perhaps in January 632. Two of his grown-up daughters seem to have died in 630. In that same year he had trouble because of the increasing jealousy of his wives, perhaps due to his rapidly increasing wealth. He withdrew from them all for a month and threatened to divorce them. Eventually, after he had received a revelation, he gave them a choice between divorce and a continuation of the marriage on his terms. Perhaps some women from recently allied tribes, whom he may have married for political reasons—the details are far from certain—chose divorce at this point. 'Ā'ishah and eight others preferred to continue as his wives. They were given a position of considerable honour in the community and called ' mothers of the believers ', but it came to be understood that they would not marry any Muslim after Muḥammad's death.

In March 632 Muḥammad led in person the greater pilgrimage to Mecca, the *ḥajj*. It was the first time he had done so, for Abū-Bakr had been the leader in the previous year. The pilgrimage was now a purely Muslim rite, since idolaters were forbidden to attend. This pilgrimage of 632, 'the pilgrimage of farewell', came to be regarded as establishing the course and form of the ceremonies in general outline, though later jurists disputed about the details of what Muḥammad had done. The pilgrimage now began and ended at Mecca, but included visits to various other places in the neighbourhood. It was comparatively easy for Islam to incorporate pagan practices and give them a new significance, and this is specially conspicuous in the case of the pilgrimage. The pagan meaning of ceremonies had often been forgotten; and the ethos of Islam enabled it to say that something had been appointed by God without any further reason being given. What Islam would never tolerate was a practice or idea that obviously contradicted the belief that 'there is no god but God'. Idols, for example, had to be rigorously destroyed. But an old ceremony like the lapidation of stone pillars during the pilgrimage was interpreted as the stoning of devils and so rendered innocuous.

As Muḥammad returned to Medina towards the end of March he was seen to be in poor health. Perhaps rumours about him encouraged the outbreaks of insurrection, while the serious news about the false prophets did not improve his condition. He continued to attend to business until about the beginning of June. Then, apparently suffering from fever and severe headache, he asked permission from his wives to leave off spending a night with each in turn and to remain all the time in 'Ā'ishah's apartment. Abū-Bakr replaced him as leader of the daily prayers. At length, on Monday, 8th June 632, he passed away with his head on 'Ā'ishah's lap.

He had made no arrangements for the continued administration of the affairs of the Islamic state except that he had appointed Abū-Bakr to lead the prayers. The end had come fairly suddenly, and for a time there was confusion in Medina, until it was agreed that Abū-Bakr should be his caliph or successor. The funeral took place on the night between Tuesday and Wednesday, not in the usual burial-ground but within 'Ā'ishah's apartment. Perhaps the most memorable remark is one attributed to Abū-Bakr as he addressed the assembled Muslims, men whose sunshine had suddenly been turned to deepest gloom, ' O ye people, if anyone worships Muḥammad, Muḥammad is dead, but if anyone worships God, He is alive and dies not '. This was the quality of the faith produced by companionship with Muḥammad.

IX

ASSESSMENT

Appearance and Manner

Muḥammad, according to some apparently authentic accounts, was of average height or a little above the average. His chest and shoulders were broad, and altogether he was of sturdy build. His arms were long, and his hands and feet rough. His forehead was large and prominent, and he had a hooked nose and large black eyes with a touch of brown. The hair of his head was long and thick, straight or slightly curled. His beard also was thick, and he had a thin line of fine hair on his neck and chest. His cheeks were spare, his mouth large, and he had a pleasant smile. In complexion he was fair. He always walked as if he was rushing downhill, and others had difficulty in keeping up with him. When he turned in any direction, he did so with his whole body.

He was given to sadness, and there were long periods of silence when he was deep in thought; yet he never rested but was always busy with something. He never spoke unnecessarily. What he said was always to the point and sufficient to make his meaning clear, but there was no padding. From the first to last he spoke rapidly. Over his feelings he had a firm control. When he was annoyed he would turn aside; when he was pleased, he lowered his eyes. His time was carefully apportioned according to the various demands on him. In his dealings with people he was above all tactful. He could be severe at times, though in the main he was not rough but gentle. His laugh was mostly a smile.

Of the many stories illustrating his gentleness and tenderness of feeling, some at least are worthy of credence. The widow of his cousin Ja‘far ibn-Abī-Ṭālib herself told her grand-daughter how he broke the news of Ja'far's death. She had been busy one morning with her household duties, which had included tanning forty hides and kneading dough, when Muḥammad called. She collected her children—she had three sons by Ja'far—washed their faces and anointed them. When Muḥammad entered, he asked for the sons of Ja'far. She brought them, and Muḥammad put his arms round them and smelt them, as a mother would a baby. Then his eyes filled with tears and he burst out weeping. 'Have you heard something about Ja'far?' she asked, and he told her he had been killed. Later he instructed some of his people to prepare food for Ja'far's household, 'for they are too busy today to think about themselves'.

He seems to have been specially fond of children and to have got on well with them. Perhaps it was the yearning of a man who saw all his sons die as infants. Much of his paternal affection went to his adopted son Zayd. He was also attached to his younger cousin 'Alī ibn-Abī-Ṭālib, who had been a member of his household for a time; but he doubtless realized that 'Alī had not the makings of a successful statesman. For a time a grand-daughter called Umāmah was a favourite. He would carry her on his shoulder during the public prayers, setting her down when he bowed or prostrated, then picking her up again. On one occasion he teased his wives by showing them a necklace and saying he would give it to the one who was dearest to him; when he thought their feelings were sufficiently agitated, he presented it not to any of them, but to Umāmah.

He was able to enter into the spirit of childish games and had many friends among children. He had fun with the children who came back from Abyssinia and spoke Abyssinian. In one house in Medina there was a small boy with whom he was accustomed to have jokes. One day he found the small boy looking very sad, and asked what was the matter. When he was told that his pet nightingale had died, he did what he could to comfort him. His kindness extended even to animals, which is remarkable for Muḥammad's century and part of the world. As his men marched towards Mecca just before the conquest they passed a bitch with puppies ; and Muḥammad not merely gave orders that they were not to be disturbed, but posted a man to see that the orders were carried out.

These are interesting sidelights on the personality of Muḥammad, and fill out the picture formed of him from his conduct of public affairs. He gained men's respect and confidence by the religious basis of his activity and by qualities such as courage, resoluteness, impartiality and firmness inclining to severity but tempered by generosity. In addition to these he had a charm of manner which won their affection and secured their devotion.

The Alleged Moral Failures

Of all the world's great men none has been so much maligned as Muḥammad. We saw above how this has come about. For centuries Islam was the great enemy of Christendom, since Christendom was in direct contact with no other organized states comparable in power to the Muslims. The Byzantine empire, after losing some of its best provinces to the Arabs, was being attacked in Asia Minor, while Western Europe was threatened through Spain and Sicily. Even before the Crusades focused attention on the expulsion of the Saracens from the Holy Land, medieval Europe was building up a conception of ' the great enemy '. At one point Muḥammad was transformed into Mahound, the prince of darkness. By the twelfth century the ideas about Islam and Muslims current in the crusading armies were such travesties that they had a bad effect on morale. Practical considerations thus combined with scholarly zeal to foster the study and dissemination of more accurate information about Muḥammad and his religion.

Since that time much has been achieved, especially during the last two centuries, but many of the old prejudices linger on. Yet in the modern world, where contacts between Christians and Muslims are closer than ever before, it is urgent that both should strive to reach an objective view of Muḥammad's character. The denigration of him by European writers has too often been followed by a romantic idealization of his figure by other Europeans and by Muslims. Neither denigration nor idealization is an adequate basis for the mutual relations of nearly half the human race. We are now back at the questions with which we began. We have an outline of the facts on which ultimate judgements must be based. What are our ultimate judgements to be ?

One of the common allegations against Muḥammad is that he was an impostor, who to satisfy his ambition and his lust propagated religious teachings which he himself knew to be false. Such insincerity, it was argued above (p. 17), makes the development of the Islamic religion incomprehensible. This point was first vigorously made over a hundred years ago by Thomas Carlyle in his lectures *On Heroes*, and it has since been increasingly accepted by scholars. Only a profound belief in himself and his mission explains Muḥammad's readiness to endure hardship and persecution during the Meccan period when from a secular point of view there was no prospect of success. Without sincerity how could he have won the allegiance and even devotion of men of strong and upright character like Abū-Bakr and 'Umar ? For the theist there is the further question how God could have allowed a great religion like Islam to develop on a basis of lies and deceit. There is thus a strong case for holding that Muḥammad was sincere. If in some respects he was mistaken, his mistakes were not due to deliberate lying or imposture.

The other main allegations of moral defect in Muḥammad are that he was treacherous and lustful. These are supported be reference to events like the violation of the sacred month on the expedition of Nakhlah (624) and his marriage to Zaynab bint-Jaḥsh, the divorced wife of his adopted son. About the bare facts there is no dispute, but it is not so clear that the facts justify the allegations. Was the violation of the sacred month an act of treachery or a justified breach with a piece of pagan religion ? Was the marriage with Zaynab a yielding to sexual desire or a mainly political act in which an undesirable practice of 'adoption' belonging to a lower moral level was ended ? Sufficient has been said above about the interpretation of these events to show that the case against Muḥammad is much weaker than is sometimes thought.

The discussions of these allegations, however, raises a fundamental question. How are we to judge Muḥammad ? By the standards of his own time and country ? Or by those of the most enlightened opinion in the West today ? When the sources are closely scrutinized, it is clear that those of Muḥammad's actions which are disapproved by the modern West were not the object of the *moral* criticism of his contemporaries. They criticized some of his acts, but their motives were superstitious prejudice or fear of the consequences. If they criticized the events at Nakhlah, it was because they feared some punishment from the offended pagan gods or the worldly vengeance of the Meccans. If they were amazed at the mass execution of the Jews of the clan of Qurayẓah, it was at the number and danger of the blood-feuds incurred. The marriage with Zaynab seemed incestuous, but this conception of incest was bound up with old practices belonging to a lower, communalistic level of familial institutions where a child's paternity was not definitely known ; and this lower level was in process of being eliminated by Islam.

From the standpoint of Muḥammad's time, then, the allegations of treachery and sensuality cannot be maintained. His contemporaries did not find him morally defective in any way. On the contrary, some of the acts criticized by the modern Westerner show that Muḥammad's standards were higher than those of his time. In his day and generation he was a social reformer, even a reformer in the sphere of morals. He created a new system of social security and a new family structure, both of which were a vast improvement on what went before. By taking what was best in the morality of the nomad and adapting it for settled communities, he established a religious and social framework for the life of many races of men. That is not the work of a traitor or 'an old lecher'.

It is sometimes asserted that Muḥammad's character declined after he went to Medina, but there are no solid grounds for this view. It is based on too facile a use of the principle that all power corrupts and absolute power corrupts absolutely. The allegations of moral defects are attached to incidents belonging to the Medinan and not the Meccan period ; but according to the interpretation of these incidents given in this book they marked no failure in Muḥammad to live up to his ideals and no lapse from his moral principles. The persecuted preacher of Mecca was no less a man of his time than the ruler of Medina. If nothing is recorded of the preacher to show us how different his attitude was from that of nineteenth-century Europe, it does not follow that his ideals were any loftier (by our standards) than those of the reforming ruler. The opposite is more likely to be the case, since the preacher was nearer to the pagan background. In both Meccan and Medinan periods Muḥammad's contemporaries looked on him as a good and upright man, and in the eyes of history he is a moral and social reformer.

So much must be said in fairness to Muḥammad when he is measured against the Arabs of his time. Muslims, however, claim that he is a model of conduct and character for all mankind. In so doing they present him for judgement according to the standards of enlightened world opinion. Though the world is increasingly becoming one world, it has so far paid scant attention to Muḥammad as a moral exemplar. Yet because Muslims are numerous, it will sooner or later have to consider seriously whether from the life and teaching of Muḥammad any principles are to be learnt which will contribute to the moral development of mankind.

To this question no final answer has yet been given. What has been said so far by Muslims in support of their claims for Muḥammad is but a preliminary statement and has convinced few non-Muslims.[1] It is still open to the Muslims of today, however, to give the rest of the world a fuller and better presentation of their case. Will they be able to sift the universal from the particular in the life of Muḥammad and so discover moral principles which make a creative contribution to the present world situation ? Or, if this is too much to expect, will they at least be able to show that Muḥammad's life is one possible exemplification of the ideal for all humanity ? If they make a good case, some Christians will be ready to listen to them and to learn whatever is to be learned.

In this enterprise the difficulties confronting Muslims are immense. A combination of sound scholarship and deep moral insight is needed, and this combination is rare. My personal view is that Muslims are unlikely to be successful in their attempt to influence world opinion, at least in the sphere of morals. In the wider sphere of religion they have

[1] Cf. Ameer Ali, *The Spirit of Islam*, London, 1922, etc. ; the first part is a life of Muḥammad. A fuller and less propagandist biography is *Le Prophète de l'Islam*, by M. Hamidullah, 2 vols. Paris 1959.

probably something to contribute to the world, for they have retained emphases—on the reality of God, for example—which have been neglected or forgotten in important sections of the other monotheistic religions; and I for one gladly acknowledge my indebtedness to the writings of men like al-Ghazālī. But towards convincing Christian Europe that Muḥammad is the ideal man little, indeed nothing, has so far been accomplished.

The Foundations of Greatness

Circumstances of time and place favoured Muḥammad. Various forces combined to set the stage for his life-work and for the subsequent expansion of Islam. There was the social unrest in Mecca and Medina, the movement towards monotheism, the reaction against Hellenism in Syria and Egypt, the decline of the Persian and Byzantine empires, and a growing realization by the nomadic Arabs of the opportunities for plunder in the settled lands round them. Yet these forces, and others like them which might be added, would not in themselves account for the rise of the empire known as the Umayyad caliphate nor for the development of Islam into a world religion. There was nothing inevitable or automatic about the spread of the Arabs and the growth of the Islamic community. Without a remarkable combination of qualities in Muḥammad it is improbable that the expansion would have taken place, and the military potential of the Arabs might easily have spent itself in raids on Syria and 'Irāq with no lasting consequences. These qualities fall into three groups.

First there is Muḥammad's gift as a seer. Through him—or, on the orthodox Muslim view, through the revelations made to him—the Arab world was given a framework of ideas within which the resolution of its social tensions became possible. The provision of such a framework involved both insight into the fundamental causes of the social malaise of the time, and the genius to express this insight in a form which would stir the hearer to the depths of his being. The European reader may be ' put off ' by the Qur'ān, but it was admirably suited to the needs and conditions of the day.

Secondly, there is Muḥammad's wisdom as a statesman. The conceptual structure found in the Qur'ān was merely a framework. The framework had to support a building of concrete policies and concrete institutions. In the course of this book much has been said about Muḥammad's far-sighted political strategy and his social reforms. His wisdom in these matters is shown by the rapid expansion of his small state to a world-empire after his death, and by the adaptation of his social institutions to many different environments and their continuance for thirteen centuries.

Thirdly, there is his skill and tact as an administrator and his wisdom in the choice of men to whom to delegate administrative details. Sound institutions and a sound policy will not go far if the execution of affairs is faulty and fumbling. When Muḥammad died, the state he had founded was a ' going concern ', able to withstand the shock of his removal and, once it had recovered from this shock, to expand at prodigious speed.

The more one reflects on the history of Muḥammad and of early Islam, the more one is amazed at the vastness of his achievement. Circumstances presented him with an opportunity such as few men have had, but the man was fully matched with the hour. Had it not been for his gifts as seer, statesman, and administrator and, behind these, his trust in God and firm belief that God had sent him, a notable chapter in the history of mankind would have remained unwritten.

Was Muḥammad a Prophet ?

So far Muḥammad has been described from the point of view of the historian. Yet as the founder of a world-religion he also demands a theological judgement. Emil Brunner, for example, considers his claim to be a prophet, holds that it ' does not seem to be in any way justified by the actual content of the revelations ', but admits that, ' had Mohammed been a pre-Christian prophet of Arabia, it would not be easy to exclude him from the ranks of the messengers who prepared the way for the revelation '.[1] Without presuming to enter into the theological complexities behind Brunner's view, I shall try, at the level of the educated man who has no special knowledge of either Christian or Islamic theology, to put forward some general considerations relevant to the question.

I would begin by asserting that there is found, at least in some men, what may be called ' creative imagination '. Notable instances are artists, poets and imaginative writers. All these put into sensuous form (pictures, poems, dramas, novels) what many are feeling but are unable to express fully. Great works of the creative imagination have thus a certain universality, in that they give expression to the feelings and attitudes of a whole generation. They are, of course, not imaginary, for they deal with real things ; but they employ images, visual or conjured up by words, to express what is beyond the range of man's intellectual conceptions.

Prophets and prophetic religious leaders, I should maintain, share in this creative imagination. They proclaim ideas connected with what is deepest and most central in human experience, with special reference to the particular needs of their day and generation. The mark of the great prophet is the profound attraction of his ideas for those to whom they are addressed.

Where do such ideas come from ? Some would say ' from the unconscious '. Religious people say ' from God ', at least with regard to the prophets of their own tradition,

[1] *Revelation and Reason*, translated by Olive Wyon, London, 1947, p. 230.

though a few would go so far as to claim with Baron Friedrich von Hügel, 'that everywhere there is *some* truth; that this truth comes originally from God'..[1] Perhaps it could be maintained that these ideas of the creative imagination come from that life in a man which is greater than himself and is largely below the threshold of consciousness. For the Christian this still implies some connexion with God, for, according to Saint John, in the Word was life, and Jesus said 'I am the Life'.

The adoption of one of these views does not settle all the questions at issue. What about those ideas of the creative imagination which are false or unsound? Baron von Hügel is careful to say only that truth comes from God. Religious tradition has also held that ideas might come from the devil. Even if the creative imagination is an instrument which *may* be used by God or Life, that does not necessarily imply that all its ideas are true or sound. In Adolf Hitler the creative imagination was well developed, and his ideas had a wide appeal, but it is usually held that he was neurotic and that those Germans who followed him most devotedly became infected by his neurosis.

In Muḥammad, I should hold, there was a welling up of the creative imagination, and the ideas thus produced are to a great extent true and sound. It does not follow, however, that all the Qur'ānic ideas are true and sound. In particular there is at least one point at which they seem to be unsound—the idea that 'revelation' or the product of the creative imagination is superior to normal human traditions as a source of bare historical fact. There are several verses in the Qur'ān (11. 51; 3. 39; 12. 103) to the effect that 'this is one of the reports of the unseen which We reveal to

[1] *Essays and Addresses*, First Series, London, 1928, 253; also Index s. v. Lugo. Cf. G. Basetti-Sani, *Mohammed et Saint François*, Ottawa, 1959, 211, etc.

thee ; thou didst not know it, thou nor thy people, before this '. One could admit a claim that the creative imagination was able to give a new and truer interpretation of a historical event, but to make it a source of bare fact is an exaggeration and false.

This point is of special concern to Christians, since the Qur'ān denies the bare fact of the death of Jesus on the cross, and Muslims still consider that this denial outweighs the contrary testimony of historical tradition. The primary intention of the Qur'ān was to deny the Jews' interpretation of the crucifixion as a victory for themselves, but as normally explained it goes much farther. The same exaggeration of the role of ' revelation ' has also had other consequences. The Arab contribution to Islamic culture has been unduly magnified, and that of the civilized peoples of Egypt, Syria, 'Irāq and Persia, later converted to Islam, has been sadly belittled.

Too much must not be made of this slight flaw. Which of us, conscious of being called by God to perform a special task, would not have been more than a little proud ? On the whole Muḥammad was remarkably free from pride. Yet this slight exaggeration of his own function has had grave consequences and cannot be ignored.

Finally, what of our question ? Was Muḥammad a prophet ? He was a man in whom creative imagination worked at deep levels and produced ideas relevant to the central questions of human existence, so that his religion has had a widespread appeal, not only in his own age but in succeeding centuries. Not all the ideas he proclaimed are true and sound, but by God's grace he has been enabled to provide millions of men with a better religion than they had before they testified that there is no god but God and that Muḥammad is the messenger of God.

NOTE ON THE SOURCES

In a sense the primary source for the life of Muḥammad is the Qur'ān. It is contemporary and authentic. Unfortunately it is fragmentary as a historical record, and often difficult to interpret. For the most part the 'revelations' came to Muḥammad in comparatively short passages. Subsequently these were joined together into chapters of varying length called *sūrahs*. There may also have been some revision.[1] Traditional accounts have been preserved of the occasions on which certain passages were revealed. While sometimes these accounts are clearly sound, in other cases they contradict one another, or for good reasons seem improbable. The use of the Qur'ān as a historical source thus presupposes a knowledge of the general outline of Muḥammad's life.

This general outline is found in the early biographies, notably the *Sīrah* or *Life* by Ibn-Is'ḥāq (d. 768) as edited by Ibn-Hishām (d. 833) and the *Maghāzī* or *Expeditions* of al-Wāqidī (d. 822). These contain, besides the general outline, many stories about Muhammad himself and his associates. There are also large collections of 'Traditions', that is, anecdotes about sayings or doings of Muḥammad. The chief interest in the latter is usually legal or theological and not biographical. Western scholars have criticized all this material on the point of reliability. Some have taken the unduly sceptical view that nothing is to be trusted except the Qur'ān (though they have then tacitly assumed the truth of the general outline). This should lead to the conclusion that no life of Muḥammad is possible. The present study is based on the opposing view that at least the material in the early biographies is to be accepted as true, except where there are particular reasons for thinking that an anecdote has been distorted (or invented) through legal, theological or

[1] Cf. p. 17 f. above.

political motives. It is also assumed that most of the background material, culled from a large number of varied works, is sound. This standpoint, I would claim, leads to a coherent view of Muḥammad's life and achievement.

The present work is essentially an abridgement of my books *Muhammad at Mecca* and *Muhammad at Medina* (Oxford, 1953, 1956). The chief difference is that in the present volume the chronological order has been more strictly adhered to. Here and there this may have produced a slight change of emphasis, but there is no fundamental change in the views presented. I have, however, made a fresh translation of the passages of the Qur'ān here quoted. References to the Qur'ān have been included in the text according to the older European numeration of Gustav Flügel; scholars are now tending to adopt the modern Egyptian numeration of the verses, but most popular books in English still adhere to the older system. Since the two books mentioned are fully documented, no references are given here except some half-dozen which are additional to those in the earlier books.

NOTE ON BIBLIOGRAPHY

There are several English translations of the Qur'ān. That of George Sale, first published in 1734 and often reprinted (so that second-hand copies are easily obtainable), is still valuable as a clear presentation of the classical Muslim interpretation. In contrast to it stands the translation of Richard Bell[1] which applies the methods of 'higher criticism' to the Qur'ān and tries to give the meaning it had when first recited; this translation thus aims primarily at scholarly exactitude. The translation of greatest literary distinction is

[1] *The Qur'ān, translated, with a critical re-arrangement of the surahs*, Edinburgh, 1937–39.

that of A. J. Arberry, professor of Arabic at Cambridge.[2] Of translations by Muslims that of Marmaduke Pickthall [3] has considerable merit, but the more recent one of N. J. Dawood [4] has greater simplicity and always gives an intelligible meaning. The Qur'ān is never an easy book to read, and those who only want an idea of its contents will find A. J. Arberry's selections useful.[5] The contents of the Qur'ān are summarized in a systematic order and provided with an index in H. U. W. Stanton's *The Teaching of the Qur'ān*.[6] A slightly fuller summary is to be found in D. S. Margoliouth's *Mohammed* in a series entitled 'What did they teach?' [7] Richard Bell's posthumous *Introduction to the Qur'ān* contains important discussions of many questions concerning the form, composition, chronology and textual history of the Qur'ān.[8]

Of the other primary sources, we are now fortunate in having an English translation of Ibn-Hishām by Alfred Guillaume.[9] Despite occasional slips and blemishes which have been noted in various reviews, it may be warmly recommended. For the Arabian background we have in English DeLacy O'Leary's *Arabia before Muhammad* [10], the earlier part of R. A. Nicholson's *Literary History of the Arabs* [11], and Richard Bell's Gunning Lectures entitled, *The Origin of*

[2] *The Koran Interpreted*, London, 1955.

[3] *The Meaning of the Glorious Koran, an explanatory translation*, London, 1930

[4] *The Koran, a new translation*, Harmondsworth, 1956.

[5] *The Holy Koran: an introduction with Selections*, London, 1953.

[6] London, 1919.

[7] London, 1939.

[8] Edinburgh, 1953; cf. my article 'The Dating of the Qur'ān; a Review of Richard Bell's Theories', *Journal of the Royal Asiatic Society*, London, 1957, 46-56.

[9] *The Life of Muhammad; a Translation of (Ibn) Isḥāq's 'Sīrat Rasūl Allāh'*, London, 1955.

[10] London, 1927.

[11] London, 1907; second edition, Cambridge, 1930.

Islam in its Christian Environment.[12] The latter is also in part a study of Muḥammad.

Of the lives of Muḥammad in English that by Sir William Muir [13] follows in detail the standard Muslim accounts, though not uncritically. The slighter work of Tor Andrae, *Mohammed, the Man and his Faith* [14] is a sympathetic presentation of the more purely religious aspects, perhaps unduly eschatological. *Mystical Elements in Mohammed* by J. C. Archer is a short monograph.[15] The long article on Muḥammad in the *Encyclopaedia of Islam* [16] is by Frants Buhl who also wrote a balanced full-length study.[17] In lighter vein, though a work of careful scholarship, is *Aishah, the Beloved of Mohammed* by Nabia Abbott.[18] General works on Islam with an interesting section on Muḥammad are Sir Hamilton Gibb's *Mohammedanism* and Kenneth Cragg's *Call of the Minaret.* [19]

The critical discussion of the sources for the life of Muḥammad raises vast problems. The later editions of Sir William Muir's *Life* contain a useful statement of the position generally accepted by Western scholars towards the end of the nineteenth century. The important study of the Traditions of Muḥammad's sayings and doings by Ignaz Goldziher [20] led to increased scepticism with regard to this

[12] London, 1926.

[13] London, 1858-61 ; latest edition, revised by T. H. Weir, Edinburgh, 1923.

[14] London, 1936, translated from Swedish.

[15] New Haven, 1924.

[16] First edition, Leyden, 1913, etc.; also in *The Shorter Encyclopaedia of Islam.*

[17] Originally in Danish, 1903 ; expanded and revised German translation, Leipzig, 1930.

[18] Chicago, 1942.

[19] London, 1949, etc.; New York and London, 1956.

[20] *Muhammedanische Studien,* vol. 2, Halle, 1890 (soon to be available in English). A similar position was taken up by A. Guillaume, *The Traditions of Islam,* Oxford, 1924.

material. Joseph Schacht's *Origins of Muhammadan Jurisprudence* [21] marks an even further degree of scepticism. While this was chiefly in the legal field, the Belgian Jesuit Henri Lammens in the early years of this century published a number of works expressive of a sceptical attitude in the purely historical field. The influence of Lammens has continued among French orientalists, and a moderate scepticism is the basis of *Le Problème de Mahomet* by Régis Blachère.[22] The less sceptical position on which the present study is founded is defended in my previous works *Muhammad at Mecca* (pp. xi–xvi) and *Muhammad at Medina* (pp. 336–38), and in articles entitled 'The Condemnation of the Jews of Banū Qurayẓah' and 'The Materials used by Ibn Isḥāq'.[23] Interesting questions of another kind are discussed by Maxime Rodinson in 'The Life of Muhammad and the Sociological Problem of the Beginnings of Islam'.[24] The theoretical basis of important aspects of my interpretation of Muḥammad is more fully treated in my forthcoming book, *Islam and the Integration of Society*.[25]

[21] Oxford, 1950.
[22] Paris, 1952.
[23] *Muslim World*, xlii, 1952, 164–71; Report of the Conference on Historical Writing on the Near and Middle East in 1958.
[24] *Diogenes*, no. 20, winter 1957; English edition, 28–51; French edition, 37–64.
[25] London, 1961, esp. chs. 2, 3.

INDEX

(The article *al-*, etc., is neglected in alphabetical arrangement.)